T0288290

THE BRIDGE STREET HISTORY CENTER
OF GRANBURY, TEXAS,
presents

Civil War
CAMPAIGNS
in the
WEST

STEVEN E. WOODWORTH
AND CHARLES D. GREAR
SERIES EDITORS

Civil War Campaigns
in the West

Ohio

Indiana

Illinois

Cincinnati

West
Virginia

Louisville

Lexington

Frankfort

Missouri

Cairo

Kentucky

Perryville

*Cumberland
River*

Virginia

Nashville

Knoxville

North
Carolina

Forts Henry
and Donelson

Tennessee

Stones River

Franklin-
Spring Hill

Arkansas

Shiloh

Chattanooga

South
Carolina

Memphis

Corinth

Iuya

Iuka

*Tennessee
River*

Chickamauga

Resaca-Adairsville

Dallas-Pickett's Mill

Kennesaw Mountain-Peachtree Creek

Atlanta

Ezra Church

Jonesboro

*Mississippi
River*

*Tallahatchie
River*

Fort Pemberton

Alabama

*Yazoo
River*

Chickasaw
Bayou

Meridian

Montgomery

Savannah

Georgia

Vicksburg

Grand
Gulf

Jackson

Champion
Hill

Port Gibson

Mississippi

Mobile

Florida

Louisiana

New Orleans

Gulf of Mexico

Charles D. Grear

VICKSBURG
Besieged

Edited by Steven E. Woodworth
and Charles D. Grear

Southern Illinois University Press
Carbondale

Southern Illinois University Press
www.siupress.com

23 22 21 20   4 3 2 1

Publication of this book has been financially supported by the Bridge
Street History Center of Granbury, Texas.

Library of Congress Cataloging-in-Publication Data
Names: Woodworth, Steven E., editor. | Grear, Charles D., [date]
editor.
Title: Vicksburg besieged / edited by Steven E. Woodworth and
Charles D. Grear.
Other titles: Civil War campaigns in the west.
Description: Carbondale : Southern Illinois University Press, [2020] |
Series: The Bridge Street History Center of Granbury, Texas, presents
Civil War campaigns in the West | Includes bibliographical references
and index. | Summary: "Ranging in scope from military to social
history, this book examines formal siege operations, sharpshooting,
night raids in no-man's-land, the experience of Vicksburg civilians,
and other military operations connected with the final phase of the
long struggle for control of the great Confederate stronghold on the
Mississippi River" — Provided by publisher.
Identifiers: LCCN 2019041120 (print) | LCCN 2019041121 (ebook) |
ISBN 9780809337835 (cloth) | ISBN 9780809337842 (ebook)
Subjects: LCSH: Vicksburg (Miss.)—History—Siege, 1863. | United
States—History—Civil War, 1861–1865—Campaigns.
Classification: LCC E475.27 .V6145 2020 (print) | LCC E475.27 (ebook)
| DDC 973.7/344—dc23
LC record available at https://lccn.loc.gov/2019041120
LC ebook record available at https://lccn.loc.gov/2019041121

To my in-laws, Lucy and Armando Garza

Again, for Leah

CONTENTS

ILLUSTRATIONS

Maps

Figures (following page 110)

ACKNOWLEDGMENTS

Books cannot be developed without the help of many people. We, the editors, serve only a small role in creating this volume. The staff of Southern Illinois University Press has invested countless hours throughout every step of the publishing process, from designing the book to printing and marketing. Thank you. We owe our deepest gratitude to all the contributors. Their cooperation and dedication to this book made it a joy to work on—more important, it would not exist without them. Thank you all. As always, Southern Illinois University Press editor Sylvia Frank Rodrigue deserves distinct recognition for all her efforts. Sylvia campaigns for our books and goes above and beyond what is expected of any editor. Lastly, we would like to express our deepest appreciation to our families for their constant support. They inspire us in all our endeavors.

Vicksburg Besieged

INTRODUCTION

Charles D. Grear

From March 29 to May 22, 1863, General Ulysses S. Grant had successfully invaded the interior of Mississippi, defeated a Confederate force at Jackson, pushed Confederates from their positions at Champion Hill and Big Black River Bridge, and forced General John C. Pemberton to entrench his Rebel army around Vicksburg. With his prize in sight and morale high throughout the ranks, Grant ordered an assault to break Confederate defenses on May 19. The assault failed to breach the Confederate works around Vicksburg. A second assault on May 22 failed to exploit a tenuous hold Union soldiers had on the Railroad Redoubt. With little ground gained and Union casualties totaling 4,131 men, Grant decided to besiege the Confederate "City on a Hill." Within days Grant quickly finished surrounding Vicksburg and brought more men to reinforce his lines to keep Pemberton's army in place. Determined to capture the Confederate army, control the length of the Mississippi River, and divide the South in half, Grant completed the Vicksburg Campaign that began in mid-November in less than six weeks from May 25 to July 4. Though the guns fell silent there were still threats to Grant's army, and the impact of the siege influenced many people for months to come. This volume is not limited strictly to the days of the siege but the lasting impact in the months that followed as the Vicksburg Campaign came to its conclusion.

Both Union and Confederate leaders understood the importance of Vicksburg. President Abraham Lincoln famously wrote, "Let us get Vicksburg and all that country is ours. The war can never be brought to a close until that key is in our pocket."[1] Jefferson Davis, a native Mississippian, owned a plantation just south of Vicksburg, so its defense meant more to him than the loss of the Mississippi River. It was personal. Davis met with his cabinet and trusted general, Robert E. Lee, to discuss options for relieving Pemberton and his army at Vicksburg. Davis wanted a detachment from Lee's Army of Northern Virginia to reinforce Joseph E. Johnston's army that remained intact even after Grant forced it to evacuate Jackson, Mississippi, on May

14. Now dubbed the "Army of Relief," it was the weapon with which Davis and Johnston hoped to attack Grant's rear and force him to lift the siege. Lee, on the other hand, offered to invade Pennsylvania with the hopes that a threat on Northern soil would encourage the Union army to transfer men from the Western Theater and lift the siege. That was a longshot. Lee simply wanted to keep his men in the Eastern Theater where he felt the Confederacy needed them most.

With the lull in active fighting and influx of more men to his army, Grant began reorganizing his forces. This also gave him the opportunity to resolve his personal feud with General John A. McClernand by removing him from command and replacing him with General E. O. C. Ord. Though McClernand protested his removal to Secretary of War Edwin M. Stanton and President Lincoln, it was to no avail. Unbeknownst to McClernand, it was these leaders who gave Grant full authority over his lieutenants during the campaign. Grant's willingness to tolerate McClernand, until the proper moment, reflects his style of command. Andrew Bledsoe's chapter further explores these themes by examining Grant and his command staff during the siege of Vicksburg. Rumors surrounded Grant throughout the Civil War and even extended to the men he trusted to run the day-to-day and mundane operations of his army. Contemporary assessment of Grant's command staff by military and political officials varied from excellence to drunkenness and incompetence. Bledsoe's thorough examination of Grant's staff gives insight into his hands-on approach to commanding an army.

Influenced by his earlier setback at Holly Springs where Earl Van Dorn spoiled his attack at Chickasaw Bayou by raiding his supplies staged there, Grant wanted to protect his logistical lines that fed his soldiers and guns firing on Vicksburg. United States Colored Troops defended the vital Union supply lines in two of the three critical positions on the Louisiana side of the Mississippi River at Milliken's Bend and Lake Providence. In chapter 2, Scott L. Stabler and Martin J. Hershock examine the contributions of African American soldiers to the siege of Vicksburg. These soldiers' defense of these critical positions allowed Grant to continue the siege of Vicksburg and focus attention on the potential attack from Confederate General Johnston in the east. The valor of African American troops influenced public opinion of freedmen and reinforced Lincoln's policy of arming black men in the war for emancipation.

Grant ordered engineers to the front lines to develop a siege system for the Union army by establishing gun emplacements, designing trenches, and teaching soldiers the processes of laying siege. The Army of the Tennessee developed thirteen approaches to advance on the Confederate city. Engineers used proven methods for building these approaches, such as building sap rollers to protect the men digging the trench from Confederate sharpshooters and artillery fire. Soldiers on both sides, particularly sharpshooters, endured the constant danger of being killed or wounded while manning the lines. Though not a new concept, a sharpshooter's war emerged during the siege of Vicksburg. Confederate marksmen shot at Union sappers to delay their advance on the defensive lines, and Union sharpshooters responded to silence them and keep Confederate artillery crews from firing their cannons. Jonathan Steplyk's chapter explores not only the role that Union and Confederate sharpshooters performed during the siege, but soldiers' opinions and reactions to their exploits. Additionally, Steven E. Woodworth examines the nocturnal activities between the Union siege lines and Confederate defensive positions. Nights were some of the most active and interesting times along the Vicksburg lines.

Confederates made life miserable in other ways for Union sappers and Southern freedmen digging the trenches. They sent fireballs, charges wrapped in wet hay, toward the sap rollers and fired rounds with cloth soaked in turpentine to set them ablaze. Union sappers would rebuild the protective barriers and keep digging. As Union soldiers neared Confederate redoubts and redans, they began mining tunnels under the defensive structures. They would pack the tunnels with explosives, detonate them to compromise the foundation, and collapse the structure, in hopes of exploiting the hole they created in the Confederate defenses. The combination of West Point siege theory and the ingenuity of Midwestern soldiers such as Andrew A. Hickenlooper led to the successful detonation of two mines. These exploits are detailed in Justin Solonick's chapter. Though the two mines did not culminate in breaching the Confederate lines, they encouraged Grant to plan another full-scale frontal assault on July 6. The assault never launched since Pemberton surrendered his army in the early hours of July 4.

The forty-seven-day siege took its toll on men from both sides. The siege began in late spring and continued into the hot and humid summer of Mississippi. Men not only endured the heat but the insects, such as lice, mosquitoes, ants, and ticks, along with snakes that plagued the trenches. Soldiers also suffered from illness, boredom from static warfare, the stress from constant shelling, and exposure to enemy fire. Union soldiers endured the strain of hard labor, while Confederate soldiers bore the anticipation of an approaching enemy. Soldiers relieved these stresses through the usual methods—playing cards, writing letters, reading, and other games. They also took chances that exposed them unnecessarily to enemy fire, such as running across the top of the fortifications. The static nature of the fighting also led to increased fraternization between the enemies. Soldiers on picket duty would meet after dark when the sharpshooters and artillery ceased firing to swap goods, coffee and tobacco being most common, and socialize. Sometimes they would share their plans to spare the men on the other side from harm, since both sides endured the same hardships. At daylight the men would return to their opposing trenches and commence shooting.

Despite the shared misery, Union soldiers had advantages over their Confederate counterparts. Reinforcements allowed men to rotate out of the front lines to more comfortable camps in the rear. Additionally, the Union established supply lines to deliver a constant supply of food, other comforts, and consistent mail service. Forty-seven days cut off from the outside world under constant bombardment took a toll on Confederate soldiers. They began to desert more frequently as they reconsidered their roles in the siege. Without supplies coming into Vicksburg, Confederates and civilians began to ration their food to a fraction of their usual diets. Civilians experienced other hardships, such as the need to care for wounded soldiers, the loss of property to Union shells, and the necessity of living in caves, dugouts, and trenches to avoid artillery fire. Civilians proved just as resourceful as their military counterparts during this extended time of deprivation and stress. John J. Gaines's chapter provides insight into the impact and experiences of civilians trapped in Vicksburg.

By July 1, Pemberton grew more desperate and his patience exhausted. He polled his generals whether they should fight their way out of Vicksburg to the south or surrender. His lieutenants responded that the weak and malnourished men could not successfully escape. With their opinion expressed, Pemberton arranged to discuss the surrender of Vicksburg on July 3. As usual Grant demanded unconditional surrender, but the two leaders' associates worked out the terms of surrender late into the night. Thus the formal surrender did not take place until July 4. With the end of the siege and the Union capture of Vicksburg, the Confederacy lost 29, 491 men surrendered, 9,091 killed or wounded, 172 cannons, 38,000 artillery shells, 58,000 pounds of black powder, 50,000 rifles, 600,000 rounds of ammunition, and 350,000 percussion caps. Grant's army lost 10,142 killed, wounded, and missing.[2]

With the responsibility of laying siege to Vicksburg behind him, Grant could focus on the siege of Port Hudson, the last holdout in the campaign for the Mississippi River. With the July 9 surrender, Grant ordered General William T. Sherman to run off Johnston and his "Army of Relief." At the time of Pemberton's surrender, Johnston's forces were marching toward Big Black River. On hearing the surrender of Vicksburg, Johnston retreated to Jackson, arriving on July 8. The Confederates entrenched themselves for a

Union frontal assault that never materialized. Instead Sherman decided to lay siege to Johnston's army, hoping to pressure him into withdrawing. Richard H. Holloway's chapter reveals the unique music and actions that Louisiana soldiers performed during the siege of Jackson. By July 16, Johnston evacuated the city without Sherman following. Too little water and too much summer heat deterred Union pursuit. With the capitulation of the Confederates at Port Hudson on July 9 and the retreat of Johnston, the Vicksburg Campaign concluded, forever transforming the course of the American Civil War.

Though the single greatest turning point of the Civil War is debated among historians, all agree that the surrender of Vicksburg had a significant impact on the war. Northerners reacted to the news with jubilation because the Union gained complete control of the Mississippi River and isolated the Trans-Mississippi Department from the rest of the Confederacy. Southerners mourned the loss of Vicksburg. A pall settled over the South with the loss of an army and control of Vicksburg. Adding to their despair was the news of Robert E. Lee's defeat at Gettysburg and his retreat south to Virginia on the same day as Pemberton's surrender. Charles D. Grear's chapter analyzes the response of Trans-Mississippian Confederates to the fall of Vicksburg and the impact it had on their morale and desire to continue the war.

Grant's persistence, ingenuity, and guile led to an achievement eclipsed only by his later bagging of Lee at Appomattox Courthouse. His star shone brightly after Vicksburg, and for the first time in the war a conclusion seemed possible. Months later Lincoln promoted Grant to major general in the Regular Army and granted him command of the newly organized Military Division of the Mississippi.

After the surrender, the captured Confederate soldiers were paroled, many went to parole camps to wait for their exchange, others such as the Louisianans went home, and others deserted the ranks. Pemberton was paroled in October 1863, but never commanded an army again. After resigning his commission as a general officer, he received a commission as a lieutenant colonel and commanded the artillery during the defense of Richmond late in the war. The Vicksburg Campaign is usually eclipsed by Gettysburg, but its overall importance to the American Civil War cannot be denied as a greater milestone on the road to final Union victory.

Notes

1. David Dixon Porter, *Incidents and Anecdotes of the Civil War* (New York: D. Appleton and Co., 1866), 96.

2. Michael B. Ballard, *Vicksburg: The Campaign That Opened the Mississippi* (Chapel Hill: University of North Carolina Press, 2004), 398.

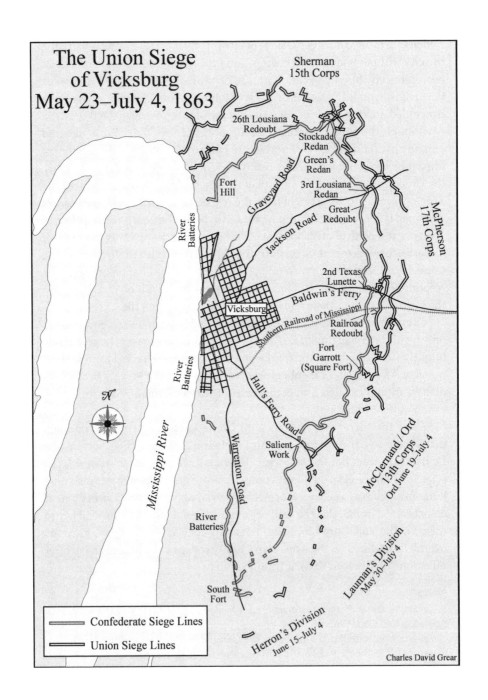

The Union Siege
of Vicksburg
May 23–July 4, 1863

Sherman
15th Corps

26th Lousiana
Redoubt

Stockade
Redan

Green's
Redan

3rd Lousiana
Redan

Great
Redoubt

Fort
Hill

Graveyard Road

Jackson Road

McPherson
17th Corps

River
Batteries

2nd Texas
Lunette

Baldwin's Ferry

Vicksburg

Southern Railroad of Mississippi

Railroad
Redoubt

Fort
Garrott
(Square Fort)

River
Batteries

Hall's Ferry Road

McClernand / Ord
13th Corps
Ord June 19–July 4

Mississippi River

Warrenton Road

Salient
Work

River
Batteries

Lauman's Division
May 30–July 4

South
Fort

Herron's Division
June 15–July 4

Confederate Siege Lines

Union Siege Lines

Charles David Grear

1
—

"BY HAZARD AND BY SPASMS": GRANT AND
HIS STAFF AT THE SIEGE OF VICKSBURG

Andrew S. Bledsoe

"I f General Grant had about him a staff of thoroughly competent men, disciplinarians and workers," wrote Assistant Secretary of War Charles A. Dana on July 13, 1863, "the efficiency and fighting quality of his army would soon be much increased. As it is, things go too much by hazard and by spasms; or, when the pinch comes, Grant forces through, by his own energy and main strength, what proper organization and proper staff officers would have done already."[1] Dana, a former *New York Tribune* journalist, had been dispatched to Major General Ulysses S. Grant's Army of the Tennessee in the spring of 1863 as a special commissioner of the War Department, ostensibly to investigate the pay service of the republic's Western armies. Dana's true mission, however, was something more sensitive; Secretary of War Edwin M. Stanton instructed him, "Your real duty will be to report to me every day what you see."[2] Stanton wanted details on Grant's Vicksburg Campaign, and he expected Dana to look into ugly rumors about the general's drinking that were swirling among "the temperance men" in Washington and elsewhere.[3] Dana, equipped with this commission, joined Grant at Milliken's Bend, Louisiana, on April 6, 1863, was received "cordially" at army headquarters. According to Dana, "Grant was always glad to have me with his army. He did not like letter writing, and my daily dispatches to Mr. Stanton relieved him from the necessity of describing every day what was going on in the army. From the first neither he nor any of his staff or corps commanders evinced any unwillingness to show me the inside of things."[4]

Swayed by the general's candor and pleased with this insider's perspective, Dana satisfied himself that the wild stories about Grant's drunken binges during the campaign and siege of Vicksburg were baseless. Grant's staff officers, however, raised additional concerns for Dana, and thus for Stanton and the War Department. In addition to the drinking rumors, stories of headquarters incompetence had dogged Grant almost from the beginning of his Civil War career. On November 20, 1862, Major William R. Rowley, one of Grant's aides, made things worse when he wrote to Illinois Congressman Lyman A. Trumbull, a major Grant patron, complaining that "Gen Grant has four Col[onel]s on his staff 3 appointments . . . and I doubt whether either of them have gone to bed sober for a week[.]" Rowley also believed a fourth officer, Colonel George P. Ihrie, had been assigned to Grant's staff entirely by accident, simply because Ihrie's previous service had been praised in dispatches. Ihrie owed his position, "as I understand without any solicitation on the part of Gen Grant," Rowley explained to Illinois Congressman Elihu B. Washburne, another Grant patron. "And [Ihrie] is not much better than the rest although possessing more military talent he is a . . . sneaking Loco Foco of the N Y Herald stripe" and thought to be a political henchman of Illinois Senator Lyman A. Trumbull.[5]

An alarmed Washburne asked Grant about the situation at army headquarters. Though Washburne's letter to Grant is lost, Rowley apparently had a chance to read it and respond to Washburne soon after. Rowley declared, "I hope [your letter] will draw out an answer from [Grant] of the right kind but I fear he will hardly have the heart to cut loose from the four Colonels. It is *very* important that it should be done. You perhaps can realize the necessity of it. Rawlins rote me last night that he would write you immediately upon the subject and state some facts. I hope that when I am called back from Columbus, Ohio, to find fewer loafers about head Quarters."[6]

This, then, was the peculiar command culture Dana stepped into at Grant's headquarters in the spring of 1863, and the Assistant Secretary of War was determined to get to the bottom of things. After lengthy observations, Dana reported to Stanton that he found Grant's staff to be "a curious mixture of good, bad, and indifferent." Judging the general as "neither an organizer nor a disciplinarian himself," Dana surmised it was only natural that Grant's military family consisted of "a mosaic of accidental elements and family friends." But of the dozen or so officers serving as Grant's personal staff during the siege of Vicksburg, Dana believed only four were actual "working men," while two others were "able to accomplish their duties without much work," and the rest consisted of "several who either don't think of work, or who accomplish nothing no matter what they undertake."[7]

Historians' assessments of Grant's military staff and their performance during the siege of Vicksburg range from effusive, to critical, to everything in between. Historian Bruce Catton, for instance, praises Grant's assistant adjutant general Lieutenant Colonel John A. Rawlins as "the keeper of Grant's conscience" while simultaneously criticizing him for "build[ing] up his own reputation," concluding that "[w]ith a defender like Rawlins, Grant had no need of any enemies."[8] Historian R. Steven Jones believes Grant "accidentally brought aboard good men" to his staff in 1862–63, "but in general, the staff was inefficient" and consisted of an "abundance of drinkers" who "created tension and impeded work" during the campaign and siege.[9] Historian E. B. Long believes that Rawlins, while essential to many of Grant's successes, greatly exaggerated his own importance but shared his chief's views that the rest of the staff during the Vicksburg siege were more or less dispensable.[10] Grant's staff officers reflected the nature and character of Civil War armies as a whole. Mostly volunteers, unschooled in the art and science of nineteenth-century warfare and owing their positions to a combination of patronage, politics, favoritism, and merit, the men who held commissions on Grant's personal staff served at the pleasure of their general. Both personal and special staffers could be called upon to fulfill specialized roles, demanding technical ability and advanced training in ordnance, logistics, topography, engineering, and combat command. Typical of the American experience in the Civil War, few of Grant's Vicksburg staffers possessed even a modicum of experience or training in these areas.[11]

Dating back to at least the seventeenth century, European practice of employing personal military staffs had, by the 1860s, greatly developed in both utility and sophistication. By the Napoleonic era, French and Prussian military planners revolutionized the function of headquarters staffs to encompass virtually every necessary enterprise a commanding officer might require. Napoleon's chief of staff Louis Alexandre Berthier hoped that his *Document sur le Service de l'État-Major Général à l'Armée des Alpes*, written in 1796, would serve as a model for staff operations. Dividing an army's staff into four broad subgroups, each overseen by an adjutant general, Berthier unified staff operations under a single *chef d'état major* (chief of staff) who would serve as a conduit for a commander's orders and, in his words, be "the central pivot of all operations" in an army. "Nobody can send out anything in his own name; everything must come from the chief of staff. . . . All correspondence is addressed to him; he signs everything; in case he is absent he will issue special orders."[12] The Prussian staff model, like the French example, placed even more emphasis on the centrality of chiefs of staff to army operations. Prussian planners like Gerhard von Scharnhorst and August Wilhelm von Gneisnau elevated chiefs of staff to a decisive command role and implemented strict staff officer qualification standards.[13] Unlike the French and Prussian approaches, the Duke of Wellington was largely indifferent to these trends on the continent and eschewed vesting authority in a chief of staff or training dedicated staffers for the British army. By the Crimean War

(1853–56), Great Britain had yet to engage in a systematic effort to produce an effective body of staff officers along European lines.[14]

Although the American military establishment created a general staff in 1862, the United States Army's usage of military staffs prior to and during the Civil War reflected the British model more than any other. American staff officers received practically no specialized instruction on how to carry out European-style staff functions, and the United States Military Academy at West Point provided its graduates with no guidance as to staff duties. Only in 1862 did Lieutenant William P. Craighill, an engineering instructor at West Point, publish his *Army Officer's Pocket Companion* on Civil War–era staff duties.[15] Contemporary military literature on the French and Prussian staff models was widely available prior to the war, and works by thinkers such as Scharnhorst, Antoine-Henri de Jomini, and Paul Thiebault were available to American officers fluent in German or French.[16] Many of these ideas were distilled by West Point instructors such as Dennis Hart Mahan and, in varying degrees, incorporated in the academy's pre–Civil War intellectual culture.[17] Nevertheless, Civil War personal staff officers were neither formally trained nor specifically expected to assist field generals with matters of operational or tactical planning, and staffers intervened in command decisions only to the extent that their generals called upon them to do so.[18]

As the Vicksburg siege got underway, Grant commanded approximately 44,000 effective troops, organized into five different corps of ten divisions. The Army of the Tennessee's corps system, originating with the Napoleonic concept of *corps d'armee*, each consisted of two to four divisions or other elements, and army corps were, theoretically, capable of independent actions and operational flexibility. Dedicated division and corps staffs helped commanders manage their respective commands, and these generals in turn reported to Grant through his own personal staff. While simplifying the difficulties inherent in coordinating and directing multiple elements within the army as a whole, the Army of the Tennessee's organizational effectiveness still depended in great measure on the abilities of its division, corps, and army staffs.[19]

Grant recognized how difficult it would be to manage a complex siege operation with a volunteer army and an inexperienced, untrained personal staff. As early as December 14, 1862, Grant informed the General in Chief, Major General Henry W. Halleck, that "[m]y individual labors have been harder probably than that of any other Gen. officer in the Army except probably yours and [George B.] McClellen [sic], with the exception of the time you was present with the Army in the Field. Much of this was due to having an entire Staff of inexperienced men in Military matters." Grant believed that "[o]f my individual

Staff there are but two men who I regard as absolutely indispensable. One of them is Lt. Col. [John Aaron] Rawlins, A[ssistant]. A[djutant]. Gen. and Capt [Theodore S.] Bowers A[ide]. D[e]. C[amp]." As to Rawlins, Grant believed him "the ablest and most reliable man in his Dept. of the Volunteer service, and with but few equals in the regular Army." Major Theodore S. Bowers, a printer before the war, served as Rawlins's primary assistant and was, Grant asserted, "capable, attentive and indispensable to me."[20] The rest of the lot, presumably, Grant could do without.

Undoubtedly, Lieutenant Colonel John Aaron Rawlins was the cornerstone of Grant's personal staff. Born February 13, 1831, Rawlins was the son of an Illinois farmer and charcoal burner whose early life was marked by a meager existence on the family farm. Rawlins's father, succumbing to the twin temptations of the California gold fields and overindulgence in whiskey, left his wife and children in precarious financial straits for much of Rawlins's childhood; thus, young Rawlins had to supplement the family income by selling charcoal in Galena, Illinois. As soon as he could, the bright Rawlins left the farm and enrolled in a local seminary. When his money ran out, he resumed charcoal burning and scraped together enough savings to move to town and attach himself to a Galena attorney, Isaac P. Stevens. In October 1854, Rawlins was admitted to the bar and became Stevens's partner. A year later, Stevens retired and handed the firm over to Rawlins; by the time he was 29, Rawlins had a thriving law practice and had established himself as a leader in his town. A firm Democrat and Stephen A. Douglas elector with no great love for slavery, Rawlins delivered a stem-winding political speech for Union and the flag after Fort Sumter that caught Grant's attention. Despite Rawlins's lack of military training or experience, Grant saw something in him; Rawlins was, as he put it, "no ordinary man." Grant's instincts about Rawlins served him well, and Rawlins proved "an able man, possessed of great firmness, and could say 'no' so emphatically to a request which he thought should not be granted that the person he was addressing would understand at once that there was no use of pressing the matter."[21] Grant tapped Rawlins as his aide and, eventually, assistant adjutant general and chief of staff. Their fruitful partnership endured for the remainder of the war and beyond.

Dana believed Rawlins was a "very industrious, conscientious man, who never loses a moment, and never gives himself any indulgence except swearing and scolding," and seems to have admired Rawlins's "great influence over [Grant], especially because he watches him day and night" for signs of intoxication.[22] Sylvanus Cadwallader, a *Chicago Times* correspondent attached to Grant during the siege of Vicksburg, thought Rawlins especially important in keeping the general on the straight and narrow regarding his drinking. In

Cadwallader's view, Rawlins "quietly but relentlessly exercised his personal and official influence and authority" in Grant's headquarters and made it clear that "any staff officer who furnished Gen. Grant a single drink . . . or in any way whatever connived at, or concealed, the general's drinking, would be summarily ordered to his proper command, or be disgraced, broken in rank, or run out of the service, if in his power to accomplish it." Rawlins's authority on these matters, claimed Cadwallader, "was fully recognized" and "[m]ore than one staff officer was barely given the option of resigning, or of being crushed by the iron hand of the great Chief of Staff."[23] Though Rawlins lacked formal military training, he was a natural organizer and administrator, and his legal education and experience served him well in a role historian Catton characterized as "headquarters bureaucrat" and custodian of the Army of the Tennessee's administrative and command apparatus.[24]

Rawlins's experiences with his alcoholic father also informed his relationship with Grant.[25] So concerned was Rawlins with Grant's reputation for hard drinking that he extracted an abstinence pledge from the general; an extraordinary concession and a testament to the peculiarly intimate relationship between them. Grant did not always live up to his promises. On June 6, 1863, during the Vicksburg siege, Rawlins wrote an indignant and rather overdramatic letter to Grant, pleading with the general to guard himself against intemperance. "You have the full control of your appetite and can let drinking alone. Had you not pledged me the sincerity of your honor early last March that you would drink no more during the war, and kept that pledge during your recent campaign, you would not to-day have stood first in the world's history as a successful military leader," Rawlins implored. "Your only salvation depends upon your strict adherence to that pledge." Left unspoken in Rawlins's plea was the fact that his future career and professional reputation also depended upon Grant's success and sobriety. "You cannot succeed in any other way," Rawlins continued. "If my suspicions are unfounded, let my friendship for you and my zeal for my country be my excuse for this letter."[26] Rawlins could not entirely prevent Grant from drinking, but he was determined to do his best.

Dana believed that Rawlins was not a particularly outstanding staff officer, and though he certainly had other qualities to recommend him, the Illinois lawyer was certainly no wordsmith. "Grant thinks Rawlins a first-rate adjutant, but I think this is a mistake," Dana told Stanton. "He is too slow, and can't write the English language correctly without a great deal of careful consideration. Indeed, illiterateness is a general characteristic of Grant's staff, and in fact of Grant's generals and regimental officers of all ranks."[27] Lieutenant Colonel James Harrison Wilson, another Grant staffer and Rawlins intimate, did much to shape the long-held belief that Rawlins, and not Grant himself, was primarily responsible for the clarity and excellence of many of Grant's written reports and orders during the Vicksburg siege and Campaign. Wilson's laudatory postwar biography of Rawlins heaped praise on his official writings, claiming that "[e]very order, whether verbal or written, passed through his hands and was delivered on time. Not one went astray, was badly expressed, or was in any degree uncertain in tenor or obscure in meaning."[28] Wilson insisted that Grant "was looked upon by the War Department as a poor correspondent and at best but an indifferent reporter of his own deeds," but with Rawlins as his primary scribe, "this was to be changed, and the complete story was to be told." In Wilson's version, Grant's custom was to write out "with his own hand an outline of what had taken place from first to last as far as he could recall it, and then turned that over to Rawlins as a basis for the final and complete report, in which every date and figure should be verified and every essential detail should be fully given. Henceforth this was the rule and practice, and the duty of carrying them into effect fell upon Rawlins and . . . Bowers." In other words, Rawlins, not Grant himself, deserved the lion's share of credit for the supposed clarity of his orders and reports. This was because, Wilson explained, Rawlins was "a methodical lawyer," and Bowers "an experienced newspaper man and ready writer," and "as a consequence Grant's reports from that day forth are justly regarded as models of clearness and completeness."[29]

Major General William Tecumseh Sherman's perspective on Rawlins's abilities is entirely different. Sherman maintained that "[t]he campaign of Vicksburg, in its conception and execution, belonged exclusively to General Grant, not only in the great whole, but in the thousands of its details." Further, Sherman declared, "I still retain many of his letters and notes, all in his own handwriting, prescribing the routes of march for divisions and detachments, specifying even the amount of food and tools to be carried along." Sherman believed that "[m]any persons gave his adjutant-general, Rawlins, the credit for these things, but they were in error; for no commanding general of an army ever gave more of his personal attention to details, or wrote so many of his own orders, reports, and letters, as General Grant." Sherman's account, while at odds with Wilson's, is much more consistent with Dana's version. Complicating affairs even further were Rawlins's premature death in 1869, and postwar quarrels between Grant and Wilson, as well as between Rawlins and Sherman. No matter which version of Rawlins's role in orders-writing and the generation of official reports is true, Grant consistently maintained that Rawlins was "indispensable" to him, both personally and as his adjutant, and would continue to do so for the remainder of the war.[30]

Fortunately for Rawlins, he had an important ally in his efforts to protect and promote his general in James Harrison Wilson. Assigned to Grant's special staff in November 1862, Wilson was a coveted commodity early in the war, and his training filled many gaps in knowledge and experience on Grant's staff that Rawlins could not hope to on his own. An 1860 graduate of West Point with a brilliant academic record and staff and topographical engineering experience, Wilson was only a junior officer at the time, but both Major General John A. McClernand and Major General James B. McPherson sang his praises, loudly and often. McClernand had great plans for Wilson's role in the Vicksburg Campaign and helped facilitate Wilson's assignment to the West from his former position on Major General George B. McClellan's staff.[31] McPherson, attempting to wrangle any competent engineers for himself, initially managed to convince Rawlins to have Wilson assigned to his staff. When Rawlins relented, McPherson was elated. "You are a trump," McPherson told Rawlins in October 1862. "I would rather have Wilson for my engineer than any officer I know. We are old friends; came home from California together last year."[32]

Soon after Wilson's arrival at La Grange, Tennessee, in the fall of 1862, Rawlins, who had thoroughly researched the young engineer prior to his new assignment, decided to claim Wilson for Grant's staff. As Wilson described it, Rawlins met him "with a dark and serious face" and informed him that "he knew all about me and my people, that I was from Illinois, as he was, that regular engineer officers were much needed in that army, and that I should be fully employed" in the coming operations against Vicksburg. Grant's adjutant also quickly brought Wilson into his confidence, making him an informal member of the general's military family in the process. Rawlins, said Wilson, spoke about Grant with "startling frankness, disguising nothing and extenuating nothing," even sharing his concerns about the general's struggles with alcohol. Calling Grant's alcoholism "the sword of Damocles" and showing Wilson the "written pledge in Grant's own hand writing," Rawlins methodically explained the culture of Grant's staff, the shortcomings and foibles of the officers in Grant's military family, and his expectations for Wilson at headquarters. Grant was the man to lead the republic's armies to victory, Rawlins assured Wilson, provided "his friends could 'stay him from falling'" into drunkenness. As Grant's self-appointed and sometimes sanctimonious moral guardian, Rawlins intended to do precisely that.[33]

Rawlins's concerns were not just limited to Grant's battle with the bottle. There were, Rawlins explained to Wilson, "some good officers on the staff, but more bad ones, and that he wanted me [Wilson] to help clean them out." Together, Wilson and Rawlins would "form an alliance, offensive and defensive," and begin the work of "weeding out worthless officers, guarding the general against temptation and sustaining [Grant] in the performance of the great duties which he would be called on to perform."[34] The process of refining Grant's staff into an effective body would take time. "Rawlins was not long in picking [bad staff officers] out," wrote Wilson, "though it took him more than a year, with all the help he could get, to overcome the General's partiality for some and to get rid of others." Grant's loyalty to his friends, while an admirable personal quality, ultimately resulted in mediocre staff officers overstaying their utility during the Vicksburg siege. "During their connection with the staff several gave much trouble and were the source of constant anxiety," Wilson sniffed. "They were roystering, goodhearted, good-natured, hard-drinking fellows, with none of the accomplishments and few of the personal qualities of good soldiers, and did not hesitate, when opportunity offered, to put temptation in the way of those they thought would meet it halfway." Rawlins, Wilson declared, "had no patience with them, but from the start kept close watch upon them, and as they became more and more indiscreet or reckless, and he better and better informed as to their real qualities, he induced the general to send them away one after the other, till all the objectionable ones were gone."[35]

Wilson was self-assured and highly opinionated, even a bit of a prig. Even so, both Rawlins and Grant listened attentively to Wilson's advice because of his extensive formal training in engineering and, if Wilson is to be believed, applied many of these suggestions to the siege of Vicksburg. Wilson shared his opinions liberally, suggesting to Grant that the Army of the Tennessee desperately need a unified command structure as well as an overhauled engineering component. After a lengthy conversation with Grant in the early morning hours of January 20, 1863, Wilson was "happy to say General Grant approved of my system of army organization and adopted without qualification my view of the necessity of a united command in the Mississippi Valley, and what's more as soon as we returned here, he wrote an earnest letter to Halleck earnestly urging a united command west, under some competent general—and the necessity of making everything tend towards the grand object."[36] And, like Rawlins, Grant trusted Wilson, charging the latter with the responsibility of delivering the critical order to relieve McClernand of command in June.[37] Despite Wilson's tendencies toward self-aggrandizement, he proved important to Grant's efforts to improvise and adapt during the siege of Vicksburg, to bring an air of professionalism and rigor to Grant's staff, and to serve as a loyal and trustworthy ally in a political and command environment full of rivals, critics, and ill-wishers.[38]

Wilson also brought invaluable technical engineering knowledge to Grant's staff at exactly the time it was most needed. As historian Justin S.

Solonick points out, Grant "dispersed various aides-de-camp with some knowledge of engineering among Sherman's corps and the divisions of [Major General Francis] Herron and [Brigadier General Jacob] Lauman," including Wilson, who "provided informal supervision of some of the engineering activities on the Thirteenth Corps front, probably due to want of experienced engineers and Grant's distrust of McClernand" after the failed assault attempt of May 22.[39] Wilson was soon promoted to lieutenant colonel and made Inspector General of the Army of the Tennessee, and boasted that Grant and Rawlins "would necessarily and frequently have to lean upon my book knowledge . . . [and] my observation and experience."[40] Dana regarded Wilson's engineering abilities almost as highly as the cocky lieutenant colonel did himself. "He is a captain of engineers in the regular army, and has rendered valuable services in that capacity," Dana told Stanton of Wilson on July 13, 1863. "The fortifications of Haynes's Bluff were designed by him and executed under his direction. His leading idea is the idea of duty, and he applies it vigorously and often impatiently to others." To Dana, Wilson's regular army professionalism and rigorous military training were precisely the antidote that Grant's amateurish staff needed. Unfortunately, some of the volunteer officers on Grant's staff felt differently, and Wilson rubbed them the wrong way. "In consequence," Dana explained, "[Wilson] is unpopular among all who like to live with little work. But he has remarkable talents and uncommon executive power, and will be heard from hereafter."[41] Truthfully, Wilson's expertise was sorely needed at Grant's headquarters. Captain Adam Badeau, a Grant disciple and staff officer from 1864 until the end of the war, acknowledged that Grant's army, along with his personal and special staff, were woefully underprepared for the technical demands of siege warfare at Vicksburg. "The lack of engineer officers gave the siege one of its peculiar characteristics: at many times, and at different places, the work to be done depended on officers and men without either theoretical or practical knowledge of siege operations, and who had, therefore, to rely, almost exclusively, on their native good sense and ingenuity." Further, Badeau admitted, "[m]uch valuable time was in this way lost, and many a shovelful of earth was thrown that brought the siege no nearer to an end."[42]

When his staff fell short or failed to learn on the job, Grant had to make do in managing the siege on his own. Badeau believed that the Army of the Tennessee's dearth of engineers and staff specialists at Vicksburg resulted in Grant giving "more personal attention to the supervision of the siege than he would otherwise have done." Badeau, attempting to put the best possible gloss on the situation, believed Grant's "military education fitted him for the duty, and he rode daily around the lines, directing the scientific operations, infusing his spirit into all his subordinates, pressing them on with energy to the completion of their task, and, with unflagging persistency devising and employing every means to bring about the great end to which all labor, and skill, and acquirement was made to tend."[43] Because of these informal, ad hoc assignments to oversee aspects of the Vicksburg siege operations, Rawlins, Wilson, and other Grant staffers provided an essential, if difficult to quantify, asset for the management of the overall enterprise. Above all else, Grant's staff had to adapt to difficult and demanding conditions, with little or no expertise or experience to guide them. "This fertility of resource and power of adaptation to circumstances, possessed in so high a degree by the volunteers," Badeau believed, required these officers "to learn to be engineers while the siege was going on." With their help, the Army of the Tennessee was able to initiate and carry out the massive siege operations. Without them, the outcome might have been quite different.[44]

Wilson was not the only Grant staffer prone to self-promotion; Rawlins was a natural politician and instinctively ambitious. Both officers found an important use for their political skills in Charles A. Dana. Dana, as the War Department's eyes and ears on the ground, was an immensely important figure for their chief's future, and thus their own. After some consultation, the two staffers went to work on Dana, executing an all-out "charm offensive" during the Vicksburg siege to persuade him, and Secretary of War Stanton, that their man Grant was the key to Union victory.[45] Per Wilson, "[Rawlins] fully concurred in my suggestion that we should take Dana into our confidence, not only in reference to the plan of operations which must now be carried into effect, but in regard to the real state of affairs at headquarters and to the basis of our own unshaken faith in Grant's capacity to lead the army to victory." Rawlins and Wilson "made Dana our messmate, took him into our offices and tents, or had his own tent pitched adjacent to ours. We invited Dana to ride with us on every occasion, and long before the campaign ended he became our constant companion."[46]

The stratagem worked. After their efforts, Dana believed that Wilson "was a brilliant man intellectually, highly educated, and thoroughly companionable. We became warm friends at once, and were together a great deal throughout the war. Rarely did Wilson go out on a specially interesting tour of inspection that he did not invite me to accompany him, and I never failed, if I were at liberty, to accept his invitations." Dana was certain that "[m]uch of the exact information about the condition of the works which I was able to send to Mr. Stanton Wilson put in my way."[47] As Wilson explained of his and Rawlins's deliberate hospitality to Dana, "We confided in him without reservation, and [Dana] in turn confided fully in us. At that time he was suffering from weak or overworked eyes and found it difficult to write by the light of the usual camp candle, or lantern. Hence, it soon became customary for me to act at night as his amanuensis, a service which for obvious reasons I was always glad to render."[48] According to historian Steven E. Woodworth, after Wilson and Rawlins were finished with him, "Dana's dispatches read like communiqués from Grant's own staff—as indeed they sometimes were."[49]

Dana was particularly impressed by Rawlins's gruff, no-nonsense management style. "Rawlins was one of the most valuable men in the army, in my judgment. He had but a limited education . . . but he had a very able mind, clear, strong, and not subject to hysterics." He found Rawlins's streams of profanity and occasional abrasive treatment of Grant astonishing. "[Rawlins] bossed everything at Grant's headquarters," Dana remembered. "He had very little respect for persons, and a rough style of conversation. I have heard him curse at Grant when, according to his judgment, the general was doing something that he thought he had better not do. But he was entirely devoted to his duty, with the clearest judgment, and perfectly fearless. Without him Grant would not have been the same man." Even years after the war, Dana apparently did not understand that both Rawlins and Wilson were managing not only Grant's staff and army, but also Dana himself. In his memoirs of the war, Dana rhapsodized about how "Rawlins was essentially a good man, though he was one of the most profane men I ever knew; there was no guile in him—he was as upright and as genuine a character as I ever came across."[50] Had Dana understood how Rawlins and Wilson were manipulating him, he might have revised his opinions about the staffers' supposed guilelessness.

While Dana admired both Rawlins and Wilson, he had little regard for Grant's other staff officers at Vicksburg. Neither did Rawlins and Wilson. Grant's two senior aides-de-camp, Colonel Clark B. Lagow and Colonel John Riggin Jr., drew most of the complaints. "How they had got on Grant's staff he never explained," Wilson complained, "but [Rawlins] made it clear that they were rounders with but little character and less military knowledge or useful experience. He intimated not only that their services were useless, but that their example and influence were thoroughly bad, and that he wanted my help to get rid of them." Rawlins told Wilson he worried about "lots of men in this army, some on Grant's staff, who not only drink themselves but like to see others drink, and whenever they get a chance they tempt their chief, and I want you to help me clean them out."[51] It is unclear whether or how Wilson, an outsider among the Galena crowd, could edge out two colonels who owed their positions to prewar friendships with Grant. In any case, Lagow and Riggin had, by May and June of 1863, established their reputations as mediocre staff officers. The pair of colonels were, according to Dana in

July of that year, "both personal friends of Grant's. [Lagow] is a worthless, whisky-drinking, useless fellow. [Riggin] is decent and gentlemanly, but neither of them is worth his salt so far as service to the Government goes." Dana found no evidence that any of Grant's aides did anything of value during the Vicksburg Campaign. "Indeed, in all my observation, I have never discovered the use of Grant's aides-de-camp at all," he fumed to Stanton. "On the battlefield [Grant] sometimes sends orders by them, but everywhere else they are idle loafers. I suppose the army would be better off if they were all suppressed, especially the colonels."[52]

Colonel John Riggin, one of Dana's "idle loafers," served as a liaison between Grant and Major General Nathaniel P. Banks in New Orleans but seems to have done little else during the Vicksburg siege. When Riggin eventually resigned in October, Rawlins declared, "I have no regret [about Riggin] . . . and shall express none."[53] Dana also griped about Grant's junior aides-de-camp and their apparent worthlessness. "Grant has three aides with the rank of captain. Captain [Orlando H. Ross] is a relative of Mrs. Grant. He has been a stage driver, and violates English grammar at every phrase. He is of some use, for he attends to the mails."[54] In reality, Ross was a cousin of General Grant's, whose duties included relaying messages and official documents.[55] "Captain [Joseph C. Audenried] is an elegant young officer of the regular cavalry," continued Dana. "He rides after the general when he rides out; the rest of the time he does nothing at all."[56] Audenried, like Ross, served as an aide and courier as needed.[57] "Captain Badeau, wounded at Port Hudson since he was attached to Grant's staff, has not yet reported," Dana added. "The chief engineer, Captain [Cyrus B.] Comstock, is an officer of great merit," allowed Dana. "He has, too, what his predecessor, Captain [William F.] Prime, lacked, a talent for organization. [Comstock's] accession to the army will be the source of much improvement."[58] Also on Grant's personal and special staffs at various times, serving in both formal and informal roles, were Colonel George P. Ihrie,[59] Lieutenant Horatio N. Towner,[60] Colonel George M. Pride,[61] and others who scarcely appear in correspondence or orders during the siege.

The first of Grant's staff to fall from grace was Colonel William S. Hillyer, an officer Grant initially held in high esteem. Hillyer left the staff during the Vicksburg siege and before making Dana's acquaintance, and contemplated leaving the army for some time before the summer of 1863, for he tendered his resignation on April 27, 1863, pleading the need to attend to his law practice and financial affairs. Grant accepted the resignation, and his endorsement of Hillyer's decision was effusive, perhaps overly so. The general proclaimed that Hillyer had "served faithfully and intelligently" since the beginning of the war, and that "[i]n every position [Hillyer] has given entire satisfaction and I am lothe to loose him."[62] Despite his resignation, Hillyer remained on staff as a personal favor to Grant and, on May 31, even served as Grant's emissary to Stephen A. Hurlbut in Memphis, delivering orders and advice for moving troops and supplies to support the siege at Vicksburg. The prickly Hurlbut deemed Hillyer "very agreeable" but was "not aware of any assistance rendered by him" during the assignment and felt Hillyer's "forte is not Quarter Master's duty."[63] Hillyer may have displayed personal charm, but his heart seems not to have been in his duties at that point, as he was well overdue for discharge from the army.

Grant may have agreed with Hurlbut's assessment of Hillyer, but neither he nor Rawlins took overt steps to force Hillyer out of the general's military family. Fortunately, Hillyer took care of the issue himself by leaving the army for St. Louis and civilian life sometime in June 1863, without telling Grant or Rawlins beforehand. Although his resignation had been accepted, Hillyer quickly realized how bad his departure must have looked to outsiders, and perhaps to Grant himself. From St. Louis, Hillyer wrote a lengthy letter to Grant on June 30, apologizing for his sudden exit and attributing the lapse in courtesy to health problems. Hillyer described a severe case of "rheumatism" that left him paralyzed on his right side, "and even now I am unable to raise my right hand to my head and can neither dress or wash myself or cut my food. I can use my hand now but no other portion of my right arm," he explained. "You may have thought strange of my somewhat abrupt leaving. But bodily pain is apt to make a man forgetful of the courtesies and propri[e]ties of life and I was suffering very much." Worried that Grant's critics might use the episode to cast aspersions on the general, Hillyer added,

> I found out here and in Memphis that your enemies and mine were disposed to attribute my leaving the army to misunderstandings and dissatisfactions between us—and I have taken every occasion to make known the fact that there never had been an unkind word thought or expression between us, (so far as I know), during the whole of our official intercourse. . . . I have never had a truer, firmer, friend than you, and that there was no man living for whom I have a higher respect or as warm an affection—that the only regret I had in leaving the army was in leaving you. . . ."[64]

Wilson believed Grant "regarded Hillyer as an able man who had been a friend . . . in the days of his poverty," and was thus willing to overlook his deficiencies as an officer. Personal loyalty and friendships mattered to Grant, as evidenced by his acceptance of inferior staffers like Hillyer and Lagow.

Later, claimed Wilson, Grant admitted that he "doubted [Hillyer's] disinterestedness as well as his honesty."[65]

Colonel Clark B. Lagow's troubles, unlike Hillyer's, began months before Vicksburg. Grant wished to reward the two officers for their "courage and good conduct" serving on his staff at Belmont, Fort Donelson, and Shiloh, and had both Lagow and Hillyer promoted to colonel on April 16, 1862. These promotions temporarily jumped them both ahead of Rawlins, a major at the time, though Grant believed Rawlins "ought to be a Brigadier General" because of his excellent service. Grant also named Lagow his inspector general and made Hillyer the new provost marshal, giving them formal roles on his personal staff beyond that of aides-de-camp.[66] Lagow quickly ran into trouble. In October 1862, Grant sent Lagow and cavalry chief Colonel Theophilus Lyle Dickey to explain his complicated operational plans for the Iuka-Corinth campaign to Major General William S. Rosecrans, though without much apparent success. Rosecrans left Grant's command later that month amid a cloud of bitterness, possibly made worse by Lagow or other staffers. In an October 22, 1862, letter of explanation to Halleck, Rosecrans grumbled about "the spirit of mischief among the mousing politicians on Grant's staff" who intended to "get up in his mind a spirit of jealousy." Rosecrans was certain that these "politicians" hoped to "manage matters with the sole view of preventing Grant from being in the background of military operations" and such an outcome would make Grant "sour and reticent."[67] It is unclear if Rosecrans was referring specifically to Lagow, but Lagow could not have been far from Rosecrans's mind when he penned the letter to Halleck.

From November 1862 to March 1863, Lagow was absent from the campaign due to illness, but upon his return in April 1863, Grant assigned him the important responsibility of overseeing a second running of Vicksburg's batteries with a flotilla of supply vessels. Lagow executed this assignment in the early morning hours of April 22–23, experiencing a ferocious Confederate bombardment and losing the steamer USS *Tigress* with a couple of mortally wounded men. Despite the cost, Grant regarded the operation as a "great success," but curiously declined to mention Lagow's role other than a brief note of explanation to Halleck on April 25. Only Lagow's gathered reports of the incident give any clue to his role in the mission, and Grant refrained from praising the colonel in any way, either in dispatches or in later memoirs or other writings.[68] On May 24, Grant detached Lagow on another special assignment, with instructions to escort about 1,000 Confederate prisoners to Island No. 10 near Memphis. Lagow bungled this assignment badly. On May 29, 1863, Major General Stephen A. Hurlbut, commanding the garrison in Memphis, wrote to Grant excoriating Lagow for neglecting his prisoners, depriving officers and men of provisions, overloading the Confederates onto a single river vessel, and not knowing how many Federal guards were actually under his authority. There is no record of Grant's or Rawlins's reaction to Hurlbut's complaints, nor of Lagow's response to these criticisms. Despite his early friendship with Grant, Lagow's days on the staff were numbered.[69]

By July 1863, Dana believed that Grant "wishe[d] to get rid of" Lagow at the earliest opportunity, a point reinforced by Lagow's lackluster performance during and after Vicksburg.[70] The final straw for Lagow would come after a November 14–15, 1863, incident at Chattanooga. William W. Smith, Julia Dent Grant's cousin, was visiting Grant's Chattanooga headquarters when he witnessed "[q]uite a disgracefull party—friends of Col Lagow, stay up nearly all night playing &c. The Gen breaks up the party himself about 4 oclock in the morning." Lagow and his friends were drinking, carousing, and possibly gambling; this behavior is particularly shocking given Rawlins's iron-clad rules against such activity, particularly around Grant. Smith reported that the next morning Lagow "don't come to table to-day," and the colonel was "greatly mortified at his conduct last night. Grant is much offended at him and I am fearful it will result in his removal."[71] Smith was correct. As predicted, Lagow resigned his commission "on account of disability" just four days later, effective December 1, 1863. Lagow was permitted to resign because, in Dana's words to Stanton, "Grant would prefer that he should not be dismissed," presumably out of a sense of decency and their prewar friendship.[72] As Smith recorded, "Rawlins wanted [Lagow] off the staff, and after the unfortunate spree that the General himself broke up, [Rawlins] saw that he was treeted coldly by him." Lagow, "with . . . sore, depressed spirits," left Chattanooga and his career as a staff officer a day earlier than scheduled. From then on, claimed Wilson, Grant "denounced Lagow and Riggin as triflers out of their depth, whose services were worth nothing and whose influence was wholly bad." Wilson's account seems rather overblown, but Grant's irritation at Lagow was no doubt quite real and apparently shared by much of the rest of his staff, especially Rawlins.[73]

That Grant tolerated Lagow, Riggin, Hillyer, and other unsatisfactory staffers so long reflects his approach to managing his staff in the summer of 1863. Grant made deliberate choices in overseeing his staff, and in his overall style of command; his method was not, as Dana claimed, merely accidental. Since Grant valued trustworthiness and harmony within his military family, he clung to old loyalties, occasionally to the detriment of military effectiveness. Grant relied on a hands-on method of command, particularly in the siege operations at Vicksburg, and whether by choice or by necessity personally assumed many of the duties and responsibilities that a more effective staff might otherwise have handled. Grant chose this approach, in part, because he had to work with the material most readily at hand. Wilson, Prime, and Comstock, the only Grant staffers with significant engineering training, played important roles during the Vicksburg siege, as did other West Pointers and engineers scattered throughout the Army of the Tennessee. Rawlins, of course, anchored Grant's staff and turned in valuable service throughout the siege. Without these efforts, Grant's task would have been even more difficult, and as it was, his command burden was immense; as he so succinctly put it, my "individual labors have been harder probably than that of any other Gen. officer in the Army."[74] These contributions aside, however, the majority of Grant's staff at the siege of Vicksburg turned in tepid performances that had no great impact on the campaign's operational objectives.

While certainly untidy, often inefficient, and hampered by amateurishness, Grant's staff nevertheless demonstrated flashes of proficiency. Like Grant, these officers attempted to improvise and adapt under difficult circumstances, often with little guidance or experience. This was the essence, as Dana put it, of waging war "by hazard and by spasms" or, failing that, by Grant's "own energy and main strength," a method quite common in the volunteer armies of the Civil War.[75] That Grant's siege could succeed so brilliantly in spite of these problems is a testament to the capable officers among Grant's military family as well as the general's skill, adaptability, and determination to win.

Notes

1. Dana to Edwin M. Stanton, July 13, 1863, in Charles A. Dana, *Recollections of the Civil War* (New York: D. Appleton and Company, 1898), 72.

2. Dana, *Recollections*, 21.

3. James Harrison Wilson, *The Life of John A. Rawlins* (New York: The Neale Publishing Company, 1916), 120–21.

4. Dana, *Recollections*, 30.

5. William R. Rowley to Elihu B. Washburne, November 20, 1862, John Y. Simon, ed., *The Papers of Ulysses S. Grant*, 31 vols. (Carbondale: Southern Illinois University Press, 1967–2009), 7:32. (Hereafter cited as PUSG.) The Locofoco Party was a faction of the Democratic Party, originating in New York City in the 1830s. Locofocos generally supported Jacksonian policies of free trade and opposed federal government involvement in the banking system.

6. Rowley to Washburne, December 16, 1862, PUSG, 7:32.

7. Dana to Edwin M. Stanton, July 13, 1863, in Dana, *Recollections*, 72; J. F. C. Fuller, *Grant and Lee* (New York: Scribner and Sons, 1933), 73.

8. Bruce Catton, "Introduction," in John Y. Simon, ed., *The Personal Memoirs of Julia Dent Grant* (Carbondale: Southern Illinois University Press, 1988), 5.

9. R. Steven Jones, *The Right Hand of Command: Use & Disuse of Personal Staffs in the Civil War* (Mechanicsburg, PA: Stackpole Books, 2000), 122.

10. E. B. Long, "John A. Rawlins: Staff Officer Par Excellence." *Civil War Times Illustrated* 12 (January 1974): 4–9, 43–46, 8–11; Elmer Gertz, "Three Galena Generals." *Journal of the Illinois State Historical Society* 50 (Spring 1957): 24–35.

11. Jones, *Right Hand of Command*, 9–11; Andrew S. Bledsoe, *Citizen-Officers: The Union and Confederate Volunteer Junior Officer Corps in the American Civil War* (Baton Rouge: Louisiana State University Press, 2015), 50.

12. Raymond-Marie-Alphonse de Philip, *Etude sur le Service d'Etat Major pendant les Guerres du Premier Empire* (Paris: R. Chapelot, 1900), 24; Gunther E. Rothenberg, *The Art of Warfare in the Age of Napoleon* (Bloomington: Indiana University Press, 1978), 209; Martin Van Creveld, *Command in War* (Cambridge and London: Harvard University Press, 1985), 69–71.

13. Walter Goerlitz, *History of the German General Staff, 1657–1945* (New York: Frederick A. Praeger, 1953), 21–22.

14. James D. Hittle, *The Military Staff: Its History and Development* (Harrisburg, PA: Military Service, 1944; reprint, Harrisburg, PA: Stackpole, 1961), 140–51.

15. William P. Craighill, *The Army Officer's Pocket Companion: Principally Designed for Staff Officers in the Field* (New York: D. Van Nostrand, 1862).

16. Antoine-Henri, Baron de Jomini, *The Art of War*, trans. O. F. Winship and E. E. McLean (1854; reprint, Radford, VA: Wilder Publications, 2008); Gerhard von Scharnhorst, *Handbuch für Offiziere in den Angewandten Theilen der Krieges Wissenschaften* (Hannover: Helwing, 1815); Paul Thiebault, *Manuel Général du Service des États-Majors Généraux et Divisionnaires Dans les Armées* (Paris: Magimel, 1813).

17. Henry Wager Halleck, *Elements of Military Art and Science; or, Course of Instruction in Strategy, Fortification, Tactics of Battles, &c.*, (New York: D. Appleton and Company, 1846), 235–55; Edward Hagerman, "From Jomini to Dennis Hart Mahan: The Evolution of Trench Warfare and the American Civil War," *Civil War History* 13:3 (Sept. 1967), 197–220; Carol Reardon, *With a Sword in One Hand and Jomini in the Other: The Problem of Military Thought in the Civil War North* (Chapel Hill: The University of North Carolina Press, 2012), 8; Ian C. Hope, *A Scientific Way of War: Antebellum Military Science, West Point, and the Origins of American Military Thought* (Lincoln: The University of Nebraska Press, 2015), 10.

18. T. Harry Williams, *Lincoln and His Generals* (New York: Random House, 1952), 5; Gary B. Griffin, *Strategic-Operational Command and Control in the American Civil War* (Fort Leavenworth, KS: United States Army Command and General Staff College, 1993), 10, 44; Edward Hagerman, *The American Civil War and the Origin of Modern Warfare: Ideas, Organization, and Field Command* (Bloomington: Indiana University Press, 1990), 22.

19. Mark Mayo Boatner III, *The Civil War Dictionary* (New York: Vintage Books, 1987), 177, 611; François Victor Adolphe de Chanal, *The American Army in the War of Secession* (Leavenworth, KS: G. A. Spooner, 1894), 219; Fred Albert Shannon, *The Organization and Administration of the Union Army, 1861–65*, 2 vols. (Cleveland: A. H. Clark, 1928), 2:271.

20. Grant to Henry W. Halleck, December 14, 1862, PUSG, 7:28–32.

21. Ulysses S. Grant, *Personal Memoirs of U. S. Grant*, 2 vols. (New York: Charles L. Webster and Company, 1885), 1:256.

22. Dana to Stanton, July 13, 1863, in Dana, *Recollections*, 72–73.

23. Sylvanus Cadwallader, Benjamin P. Thomas, ed., *Three Years with Grant as Recalled by War Correspondent Sylvanus Cadwallader* (Lincoln: University of Nebraska Press, 1996), 118.

24. Simpson, "Introduction," in Catton, ed., *Memoirs of Julia Dent Grant*, 4.

25. Steven E. Woodworth, "John A. Rawlins," in David T. Zabecki, ed., *Chief of Staff: The Principal Officers Behind History's Great Commanders*, 2 vols. (Annapolis, MD: Naval Institute Press, 2008), 1:74–86, 77–78.

26. It is unclear if Rawlins's letter (dated June 6, 1863, at 1:00 A.M.) was ever delivered to Grant, or if the original incarnation of the document survived. Certainly several people claimed to have seen copies of the letter. PUSG, 8:322–25. Rumors that Grant engaged in a drunken spree at Satartia, Mississippi, were fodder for speculation for years, but there is no definite evidence that Grant's so-called "Satartia bender" actually took place as critics intimated. See Brooks D. Simpson, "Introduction to the Bison Books Edition," in Cadwallader, *Three Years with Grant*, v–xix; Michael B. Ballard, *Grant at Vicksburg: The General and the Siege* (Carbondale: Southern Illinois University Press, 2013), 43–64.

27. Dana to Stanton, July 13, 1863, in Dana, *Recollections*, 73.

28. Wilson, *Life of Rawlins*, 127.

29. Ibid., 147.

30. William Tecumseh Sherman, *The Memoirs of General William T. Sherman* (Bloomington: Indiana University Press, 1957), 334; See supra note 18.

31. Wilson, *Under the Old Flag*, 2 vols. (New York and London: D. Appleton and Company, 1912), 1:131–38; Wilson to John A. McClernand, November 24, 1862, PUSG, 6:295–96.

32. U.S. War Department, *The War of the Rebellion: Official Records of the Union and Confederate Armies*, 128 vols. (Washington, DC: Government Printing Office, 1881–1901), series 1, vol. 17, pt. 1, 300. Hereafter cited as *OR*. All references are to series 1 unless otherwise indicated.

33. Wilson, *Life of Rawlins*, 100.

34. Ibid., 99–100.

35. Ibid., 60–61.

36. Wilson to Adam Badeau, January 20, 1863, PUSG, 7:235.

37. Wilson, *Life of Rawlins*, 132–35.

38. Edward G. Longacre, *From Union Stars to Top Hat: A Biography of the Extraordinary General James Harrison Wilson* (Harrisburg, PA: Stackpole Books, 1972).

39. Justin S. Solonick, *Engineering Victory: The Union Siege of Vicksburg* (Carbondale: Southern Illinois University Press, 2015), 51.

40. Wilson, *Under the Old Flag*, 1:135.

41. Dana to Stanton, July 13, 1863, in Dana, *Recollections*, 73.

42. Adam Badeau, *Military History of U. S. Grant*, 3 vols. (New York: D. Appleton and Company, 1885), 1:337–38.

43. Badeau, *Military History of U. S. Grant*, 1:338.

44. Ibid.

45. Woodworth, "John A. Rawlins," 81.

46. Wilson, *Life of Rawlins*, 121.

47. Dana, *Recollections*, 61–62.

48. Wilson, *Life of Rawlins*, 121.

49. Woodworth, "John A. Rawlins," 81.

50. Dana, *Recollections*, 62–63.

51. Wilson, *Under the Old Flag*, 1:136.

52. Dana to Stanton, July 13, 1863, in Dana, *Recollections*, 74.

53. Rawlins to Mary Emma Hurlbut, October 12, 1863, John A. Rawlins Papers, Chicago Historical Society.

54. Dana to Stanton, July 13, 1863, in Dana, *Recollections*, 74.

55. PUSG, 8:169, 491.

56. Dana to Stanton, July 13, 1863, in Dana, *Recollections*, 74. Dana redacted Ross's and Audenreid's names from the reprinted letter included in his memoirs, but he included them in his "Reminiscences of Men and Events of the Civil War," *McClure's Magazine* 10 (November 1897–April 1898): 253–66, 254.

57. PUSG, 9:43–44, 46.

58. Dana to Stanton, July 13, 1863, in Dana, *Recollections*, 74.

59. PUSG, 8:25.

60. PUSG, 7:500.

61. PUSG, 7:125–26.

62. Grant's April 27, 1863, endorsement of William S. Hillyer to Lorenzo Thomas, April 27, 1863, PUSG, 8:219.

63. Hurlbut to Rawlins, June 10, 1863, PUSG, 8:306.

64. Hillyer to Grant, June 30, 1863, PUSG, 8:219.

65. Wilson, *Under the Old Flag*, 1:138.

66. PUSG, 3:292; 5:52–53, 73.

67. *OR*, series 1, vol. 17, pt. 2, 286–287.

68. *OR*, series 1, vol. 24, pt. 1, 31, 564–573.

69. Stephen A. Hurlbut to Rawlins, May 29, 1863, PUSG, 8:243.

70. Dana to Stanton, November 1, 1863, PUSG, 9:328.

71. William W. Smith Diary, November 14–15, 1863, PUSG, 9:475.

72. *OR*, series 1, vol. 31, pt. 2, 60.

73. Wilson, *Under the Old Flag*, 1:138.

74. See supra note 20.

75. See supra note 1.

2
——

"STANDING ON THE BANKS": AFRICAN AMERICAN
TROOPS IN THE VICKSBURG CAMPAIGN

Scott L. Stabler and Martin J. Hershock

In March of 1863, Abraham Lincoln wrote to Andrew Johnson (then serving as the military governor of Tennessee), "The bare sight of fifty thousand armed, and drilled black soldiers on the banks of the Mississippi, would end the rebellion."[1] Black troops did not just "stand" on the banks of the Mississippi River in 1863. On the contrary, as spring gave way to summer, they fought bravely and won battles not only to aid liberty for their own race, but to preserve the country that they too called home.

Until the late twentieth century, most Americans would not know that African Americans fought for their own freedom during the Civil War. Historians, most of them white, held a predilection for white generals or for the white soldiers who filled the rank and file of the Union army. Indeed, many would likely have agreed with historian W. E. Woodward's 1928 claim: "The American negroes are the only people in the history of the world, so far as I know, that ever became free without any effort of their own."[2] This void is certainly in evidence when reviewing the standard works on the Vicksburg Campaign; there remains shockingly little in the pervasive narrative about African Americans. Partly this is a function of the fact that African American troops did not play a direct role in the attacks on Vicksburg proper. More troubling, however, is the lingering racially charged spell that thinking such as Woodward's has cast over this narrative. Fortunately, contemporary scholars recognize the contributions and salience black troops gave in facilitating their own freedom. As James McPherson wrote in his seminal work, *The Negro's Civil War*, "Perhaps most importantly of all, the contribution of Negro soldiers helped the North win the war and convinced many white Northerners that the Negro deserved to be treated as a man and an equal."[3] This is particularly true when one examines the 1863 Vicksburg Campaign with a wider lens and focuses on the broader campaign that led to the fall of

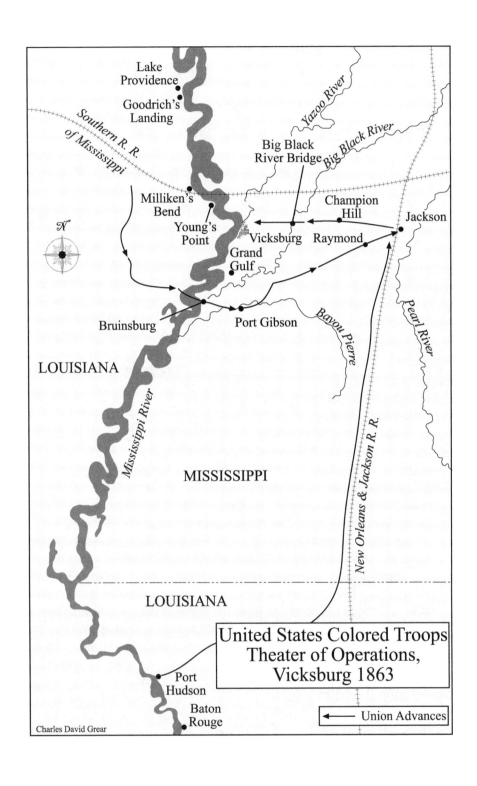

Lake
Providence

Goodrich's
Landing

Southern R. R. of Mississippi

Yazoo River

Big Black River

Big Black
River Bridge

Champion
Hill

Jackson

Milliken's
Bend

Young's
Point

Vicksburg

Raymond

Grand
Gulf

Bruinsburg

Port Gibson

Bayou Pierre

Pearl River

LOUISIANA

Mississippi River

MISSISSIPPI

New Orleans & Jackson R. R.

LOUISIANA

Port
Hudson

Baton
Rouge

Charles David Grear

**United States Colored Troops
Theater of Operations,
Vicksburg 1863**

⟵ Union Advances

this Confederate stronghold. African American troops, only recently organized into the Union army, played a pivotal role in this campaign and in so
doing, affirmed their own claim to equality and swayed Northern popular
opinion about their abilities.

African American troops, or the United States Colored Troops (USCT),
undeniably aided the Union victory at Vicksburg. By mid-June of 1863, with
General Ulysses S. Grant's grip tightening on Vicksburg, his fears lessened
about an attack from the east by Confederate General Joseph Johnston. Increasingly then, Grant focused his attention on protecting his perimeter on
the Louisiana side of the Mississippi River. The Union held three key positions
there that, if lost, would allow General John C. Pemberton, the Confederate
commander at Vicksburg, to resupply, thus breaking Grant's siege of the city.
The USCT manned, in significant numbers, two of these positions, Milliken's
Bend and Lake Providence. On June 7, Confederate General Richard Taylor
tried to dislodge the Yankees from the aforementioned locations along with
nearby Young's Point. Due largely to the efforts of Union gunboats and black
troops, the Confederates failed at all three endeavors. At both Milliken's
Bend and Lake Providence, the USCT performed bravely and in so doing
further shifted Northern public opinion relative to the efficacy and wisdom
of arming African Americans.[4]

In his exhaustive three-volume history of the Vicksburg Campaign,
historian Edwin Bearss argues that "many historians . . . ignore the efforts
of the trans-Mississippi Confederates to support their comrades east of
the Mississippi River." "Perhaps," he speculates, "this is because the trans-
Mississippi Confederates failed."[5] While true, it may also be the case that
these operations, because they were contested by significant numbers of
African American soldiers, have also fallen victim (as has the overall story
of black military contributions during the war) to a blatant disregard. The
fact that these Confederate efforts failed, in part, because of the stout defense
of black soldiers (combatants most white Americans at the time assumed
would not and/or could not fight) likely further contributed to the pervasive
trend of historians to ignore this theater of operation.

Resisting and Advocating Black Enlistment

African Americans during the Civil War faced many obstacles on the path
to enlistment. Though President Abraham Lincoln privately endorsed mus-
tering black troops early in the war, he feared the backlash of public opinion,
especially in the often tenuously loyal border states of Maryland, Delaware,
Kentucky, and Missouri, if he did so. "To arm the negroes," he wrote in August
1862, "would turn 50,000 bayonets from the loyal Border States against us

that were for us."[6] Lincoln likewise had to contend with widespread Northern public hostility to the idea of arming blacks, a population that most white Northerners viewed as inherently inferior, cowardly, and simple-minded. Frederick Douglass and his fellow African Americans, on the other hand, immediately recognized the significance of black troops to the Union cause. In a May 1861 newspaper column, "How to End the War," Douglass wrote, "Let the slaves and free colored people be called into service, and formed into a liberating army, to march into the South and raise the banner of emancipation among the slaves."[7] It did not take long for the exigencies of war and/or personal belief to goad Union commanders in this latter direction.

Lincoln's reticence to use black soldiers proved insufficient in thwarting those determined to tap into this ready source of military manpower. Faced with the reality of occupying and administering a hostile population deep within the Confederacy, geographically separated from the Union heartland, and confronted with a flood of fugitive slaves flocking to their lines, Union commanders throughout the South challenged this policy for most of 1862 in the hopes of tapping into this accessible and underutilized source of military manpower. Still, it would not be until January 1863 and the issuance of the Emancipation Proclamation that black troops officially gained acceptance, on an unrestricted basis, into the service of the United States Army.

To deal with this new reality, the War Department, in May 1863, created a distinct Bureau of Colored Troops. In addition to much of the white conservative Northern population's general disdain of this new policy, white soldier backlash followed quickly. The Democratic standard-bearing *Detroit Free Press* published an article from an unnamed soldier the next month that portrayed a common theme—fear. "If they make negroes soldiers and place them on an equality with the white soldier, they <u>must</u> give him all the rights and privileges of a white soldier. Equal political privileges must soon lead to equal social privileges, and then the intelligent, well-educated negro, though black as night, will come to these people and demand their fair daughters, and take them too."[8] Many also worried black troops would not fight. Captain Henry Romeyn of the 14th USCT recalled that the arming of blacks elicited remarks of intense dislike and distrust such as "The nigger won't fight" and "No white private will ever take orders from a nigger Sergeant!"[9] In a caustic April 1863 editorial titled, "The Enrollment of the Negro Soldier—Utter Futility of the Idea," the *New York Herald*, a Democratic newspaper, dismissed the idea of employing black soldiers as "an absolute waste of time and money." Continuing, the paper railed, "[I]t is worse than ridiculous to talk of arming ignorant negro slaves, who have neither inclination nor intelligence for so important a work."[10]

Racial prejudice continued to stymie efforts to place black soldiers on an equal footing with whites after enlistment.[11] The *New York Herald* argued that "these people can be serviceably employed in a variety of ways—on the trenches, in creating fortifications, in ploughing up the fields for cultivation, and in ministering to the many wants of the advancing army. Let their services be employed in any way; but to enroll them as soldiers is to demoralize the regular army and to increase the difficulties we would avoid."[12] General Nathaniel P. Banks, Union commander over the Department of the Gulf, framed it even more bluntly. The enlistment of black troops, he declared in a General Order dated May 1, 1863, "is not established upon any dogma of equality or other theory, but as a practical and sensible matter of business. The Government makes use of mules, horses, uneducated and educated white men, in the defense of its institutions. Why should not the negro contribute whatever is in his power for the cause in which he is as deeply interested as other men? We may properly demand from him whatever service he can render."[13]

Transformation in attitudes toward blacks in the army, however, came as some white soldiers reached the conclusion that a black body could stop a bullet as well as a white one. As a columnist for the *Milwaukee Daily Sentinel* put it in April 1863, "As soon as it becomes a matter of life and death, as indeed it has, men will not hesitate long between the question of black or white, and saving their bodies from being pierced with the bullet of a rebel. . . ."[14] An even more compelling example of transformation came from an Illinois private. In a March 1863 letter to his wife, Charles Willis of the 8th Illinois initially compared USCT troops to eight-year-olds. Only one month later though, he made an "honest confession." At that time, he wished to "put muskets in the hands of the latter." By June, he had come 180 degrees, writing home that he was considering "applying for a position [officer] in a [black] regiment myself." Similar changes in Union soldiers' attitudes continued throughout the war as black troops proved their mettle in battle.[15]

Beyond the formal contributions of African American troops to the Vicksburg Campaign, Grant's efforts to capture the Mississippi River stronghold were also aided by thousands of former slaves (both male and female) who toiled on behalf of his army. From the war's beginning, slaves ran to Union lines for freedom and protection, especially in the aftermath of Lincoln's preliminary announcement of emancipation after the Battle of Antietam.[16] Runaways (or contraband) did more than cripple the South's economic war-making efforts. Using their feet, contrabands took an extremely active role in altering Union soldiers' viewpoints surrounding slavery and of the abilities/competence of the nation's black population.[17] Under the Confiscation Acts of 1861 and 1862, escaped slaves remained in Union army lines, residing in so-called contraband camps. One of the largest and most interesting of these "camps" was the one established in the strip of territory between Young's Point, Milliken's Bend, and Lake Providence on the Louisiana side of the Mississippi River just north of Vicksburg. Here, in the aftermath of Grant's November 1862 southward advance from Tennessee, historian Noah Trudeau writes, "suddenly and in unprecedented numbers, whole black communities began to tramp into the Union lines seeking freedom, presenting Grant with the prospect of thousands of extra mouths to feed."[18] Almost immediately, Grant began to utilize African Americans around Vicksburg. General-in-Chief Henry Halleck wanted Grant to recruit additional black labor to "cheerfully and faithfully carry out that policy" and pressed the general to use his "official and personal influence to remove prejudices on this subject."[19] Legally allowed to only provide provisions for former male slaves conducting work for the Union army and yet unwilling to stand by while thousands of black women and children went hungry, Grant determined to employ nearly all the former slaves to harvest the crops standing on the now-abandoned plantations populating the region. It was also argued that establishing a loyal population along the banks of the Mississippi River would protect Union navigation on the river and lay the groundwork for future USCT soldiers.[20]

Initially tasked to John Eaton, a chaplain with an Ohio unit, Grant's ideas for African Americans assumed fuller form after the arrival of Brigadier General Lorenzo Thomas from Washington in early 1863. Among Thomas's first actions was the appointment of three commissioners to oversee the leasing of these plantations to entrepreneurs (including fifteen African Americans) entering into one-year contracts with the U.S. Treasury Department. Included in these lease agreements were contracts for contraband laborers (both male and female) who were to receive wages, room and board, and the assurance of good treatment for their work on behalf of the lessee. Reporting on this effort in October 1863, Thomas noted, "Those employed have thus been of no expense to the Government, but have supported themselves and their families. They are perfectly contented, and look forward with hope to future elevation of character. The experiments, adopted hastily and from necessity with many misgivings, I now regard a complete success."[21]

In early July of 1863, the large concentration of former slaves working on Treasury Department–administered plantations, marked the area as an obvious target for Confederate raids. In recognition of this, and at the encouragement of General Grant who, when considering the burgeoning contraband population, noted, "It would be very easy to put a musket in his hand and make a soldier of him and if he fought well eventually to put the ballot in his hand and make him a citizen," Thomas busily engaged in planning the region's defense.[22] Initially this involved elements of Grant's army, but shortly after his arrival in the area, Thomas also busied himself raising troops from the local contraband population with the intention of turning over the responsibility for protecting the area and its inhabitants to these newly formed black regiments.[23]

On April 8, 1863, Thomas spoke to General James McPherson's assembled corps at Lake Providence, Louisiana, just fifty miles north of Vicksburg at the Northern fringe of the recently created plantation lease district. There he called on white soldiers to support the president's decision to enlist blacks and to welcome the freedmen into the army.[24]

> You know full well, for you have been over this country . . . that the rebels have sent into the field all their available fighting men,—every man capable of bearing arms against us, and have kept their slaves at home to raise the means of subsistence for this army. In this way he can bring to bear against us all of the strength of the so-called Southern Confederacy, whilst we at the North can only send into the field a portion of our whites, being compelled to leave at home another portion to cultivate our fields and raise supplies. . . . The administration has determined to take from these rebels that source of supply; to take their negroes and compel them to send back a portion of their whites. . . . I am here this day, to say that I am authorized to raise as many regiments of blacks as can possibly be collected. . . . I shall take the women and children, and the men who cannot go into our army organization, and put them on these plantations, then take these regiments and put them in the rear. . . . Knowing the country well, they will be able to track out these accursed guerillas and drive them from the land. When I get regiments raised in this way, you may sweep out into the interior as far as you please.[25]

That Thomas's appeal met with approval among the assembled troops and the former slaves now residing in the area is undeniable. "Within twenty-four hours," the *Milwaukee Daily Sentinel* reported, "there was over a hundred and fifty applications for commissions in the negro units." Additionally, the paper went on to report, "four negro regiments were organized, under the supervision of General Thomas, and . . . others will speedily be organized."[26] Three of Thomas's early regiments served at Milliken's Bend. By the end of the war, Thomas had helped enroll 76,000 black troops, nearly half of the 180,000 total that joined the USCT.[27]

Battle of Port Hudson

As Thomas busily recruited and trained his newly formed black regiments near Vicksburg, African American soldiers, under the command of General Banks, engaged in direct military action further south along the Mississippi River at Port Hudson, the last Confederate stronghold on the Mississippi River south of Vicksburg. The twenty siege guns and thirty-one field guns posted in parapets on its bluffs kept Union ships from freely moving along the Mississippi in support of Grant's operations to the north, and thus Banks ordered it attacked.

After first moving inland to cut off the port's supply line, Banks then turned his 13,000 troops, including the 1st and 3rd Louisiana USCT, toward Port Hudson. By May 22, Banks had Port Hudson surrounded. Combat came to the USCT four days later. With verve, the USCT made seven separate assaults on Confederate positions, but each stalled at an 8x30-foot ditch entrenchment fifty yards in front of the enemy guns. By 4 P.M. the troops withdrew for the day. In the course of a few short hours, the 1,080 USCT on the field incurred 308 casualties in their failed assault; the highest of any unit in the battle. The unsuccessful attack marked the first engagement of any significance between black and white troops. The African American troops performed very well.[28] It was this assault that furthered the reputation of the United States Colored Troops.[29]

The bravery of the USCT soldiers drew plaudits from across the country. Captain Robert F. Wilkinson wrote, "One thing I am glad to say, is that the black troops at Port Hudson fought and acted superbly. The theory of negro inefficiency is, I am very thankful at last thoroughly exploded by facts. We shall shortly have a splendid army of thousands of them." The *New York Times* stated, "They were comparatively raw troops, and were yet subjected to the most awful ordeal. . . . The men, white or black, who will not flinch from that, will flinch from nothing. It is no longer possible to doubt the bravery and steadiness of the colored race, when rightly led."[30] The *New York Tribune* poignantly wrote, "That heap of six hundred corpses, lying there dark and grim and silent before and within the rebel works, is a better proclamation of freedom than even President Lincoln's."[31] Banks's official report noted their bravery, "The severe test to which they were subjected, and the determined manner in which they encountered the enemy, leaves upon my mind no doubt of their ultimate success."[32]

Milliken's Bend

Grant's army pressed in on Vicksburg (Grant's men had already laid siege to the city after failed Union frontal assaults on May 19 and May 22), and Banks's intentions on Port Hudson were becoming evident. Given this, Lieutenant

General Edmund Kirby Smith, Commander of the Confederacy's Trans-Mississippi Department, in a surprising reorientation of strategic focus, proposed to Major General Richard Taylor that he proceed up the Tensas River and establish a base on the Mississippi to harass Union shipping and disrupt Grant's supply line. Smith had previously doggedly advocated for a campaign to rid southern Louisiana of Federal forces rather than committing to the relief of Pemberton's forces at Vicksburg. Reinforced by Major General John G. Walker's Texas division, Taylor would attack Grant's communication/supply line (the Young's Point, Milliken's Bend, Lake Providence line) west of the Mississippi River. Hesitantly Taylor demurred—he had hoped to move against New Orleans and thus lift Banks's siege of Port Hudson. He left his small Confederate army and personally moved north to meet up with Confederate forces marching from Arkansas to begin the assault on the Union bases to the north and west of Vicksburg.[33]

Milliken's Bend, about twenty miles upstream from Vicksburg, served as a key depot for the Union army. The battle fought there on Sunday, June 7, 1863, was designed to take place in tandem with a simultaneous attack on the nearby post of Young's Point. The combat involved 1,500 Texans and just over 1,000 Union soldiers, mostly United States Colored Troops affiliated with the 9th, 11th, and 13th regiments of Louisiana Infantry, African Descent, and the 1st Mississippi Infantry, African Descent, who had only been issued their muskets sixteen days prior. "Soldiers in a more raw and crude shape, could hardly be imagined than these negroes but recently gathered from the plantations, where they had been familiar only with the hoe and the plow. They had to be taught everything that goes to make up a soldier, from standing erect to the manual of arms," a contributor to the *National Tribune* wrote in a 1905 article recounting the battle.[34] The conflict began in the early hours as Confederates under the command of General Henry E. McCulloch, after marching through the night from Richmond, Louisiana, pressed forward against Union forces.[35] McCulloch's men faced pesky resistance from the black pickets but managed to push the pickets aside and press forward toward the landing. Finding themselves facing the main body of the Union force positioned behind an old levee topped with felled trees and cotton bales, McCulloch's men prepared for their final push. When launching their attack, Confederate soldiers (in some accounts carrying a black flag with a death's head insignia), pledged no quarter for the white officers leading these black regiments and shouted, "No quarter for the officers, kill the damned abolitionists, spare the niggers."[36]

As the Rebel forces bore down on the Federal position, they were met with a frightful volley from the Union line, which led the Confederates to momentarily "waver [sic] and recoil, a number running in confusion to the rear," wrote General Elias S. Dennis in his official report.[37] McCulloch's men, however, quickly regained their composure and rushed forward, cresting the defensive walls. As the Union center, held by the 160 men of the white 23rd Iowa (who were just arriving on the battlefield from their river transport) gave way, many of the 1st Mississippi's white officers fled to boats docked along the shore.[38] Braver officers managed to rally the retreating Iowans, however, and they were immediately joined by their black compatriots who, according to the *New York Herald*, "came up with volley after volley delivered with good effect and rapidity," driving the Rebels back with much loss of life.[39] Confederate brigade commander McCulloch reported, "[Our] charge was resisted by the negro portion of the enemy's force with considerable obstinacy, while the white or true Yankee portion ran like whipped curs almost as soon as the charge was ordered."[40] Echoing the charges of white officer cowardice, the Washington, D.C., *Evening Star* asserted that "the negroes fought better than their white officers, many of whom, it is said, skulked."[41] McCulloch also recorded that "terrible hand-to-hand combat" took place. Reporting to his superiors after the battle, General Dennis confirmed this fact, noting that

> the African regiments being inexperienced in the use of arms, some of them having been drilled but a few days, and the guns being very inferior, the enemy succeeded in getting upon our works before more than one or two volleys were fired at them. Here ensued a most terrible hand to hand conflict of several minutes' duration, our men using the bayonet freely and clubbing their guns With fierce obstinacy, contesting every inch of ground, until the enemy succeeded in flanking them, and poured a murderous enfilading fire along our lines, directing their fire chiefly to the officers, who fell in numbers. Not till they were overpowered and forced by superior numbers did our men fall back behind the bank of the river, at the same time pouring volley after volley into the ranks of the advancing enemy.[42]

In his brief report on the battle, Union Rear Admiral David Dixon Porter, though not an immediate witness, contended that "the enemy attacked Milliken's Bend, commenced driving the negro regiments, and killed all they captured. This infuriated the negros, who turned on the rebels and slaughtered them like sheep, and captured 200 prisoners."[43] "Upon both sides," William Lloyd Garrison's *Liberator* reported, "men were killed with the butts of muskets. White and black men were lying side by side, pierced by bayonets, and in some instances, transfixed to the earth. In one instance, two men—one white and one black—were found dead, side by side, each having the other's bayonet through his body." The intensity of the fighting, the *Liberator* continued, proved that the struggle "was a contest between enraged men; on the one side from hatred of race, and on the other, desire for self preservation, revenge for past grievances, and the inhuman murder of their comrades."[44]

The fighting became quite sanguinary. In this desperate struggle six black soldiers in one company had their bayonets broken.[45] Historian Richard Lowe described the fighting as "skull smashing." A letter writer to the *New York Herald* described the African American troops as "the black bosom of destruction . . . a small, dark colored mighty hurricane."[46] One member of the 9th Louisiana, "Big Jack" Johnson, only recently recruited from a nearby plantation, bravely battled the swarming Rebel surge using his rifle butt as a cudgel, shattering the gun's wooden stock in his hands. As Lieutenant David Cornwell, one of the 9th's white officers, recalled, "Jackson passed me like a rocket. With the fury of a tiger he sprang into that gang and smashed everything before him" all the while drawing shouts of "shoot that big nigger" from his Rebel foes. Bayoneted multiple times, Johnson fought on until finally killed by a Rebel shot to the head.[47] Emotionally attesting to the nobility of the black troops who fought alongside him, a Union veteran of the battle shared an incident told to him shortly after the battle: "A black Sergeant on the line of defense saw his former master—a rebel Major—coming right at his front . . . when he saw his 'old Massa' he sprang to the top of the embankment and shouted, 'Hi Massa!' and as soon as he was recognized shot the Major; then, clubbing his gun, sprang to the enemy's line and fell fighting madly, selling his life for the best price he could get."[48] Whether true or not the story conveys the widespread awareness of the deeply personal intensity of armed service for the African American soldiers at Milliken's Bend, an intensity manifest in their heroic defense of their position. Indeed, the *Chicago Tribune* reported in its June 18, 1863, edition, "It is said that the colored men paid off the enemy man for man, and perhaps, a little more, for their inhumanity."[49] "While it is painful to record this butchery," Union Captain Abraham E. Strickle wrote to General Grant, "it is a pleasure to know that they stood firm . . ."[50]

For their part, as historian Linda Barnickel notes, McCulloch's Texans unleashed their full invective on their black opponents "bayoneting them by the hundreds," as one Texas soldier recalled. Another later wrote, "We clubbed guns, bayoneted, cut with the sword, until the enemy fled helter skelter." Many years later another Texas veteran of the fight shared that most of the white officers, "as the boys used to say 'Sidadlled' [*sic*]" leaving "their poor negro comrades to their own fate. We killed 750 Negroes in the trenches and the blood ran in some places several inches deep." A Union officer, serving with the 9th Louisiana, after witnessing the brutality, railed "I never more wish to hear the expression, 'The Niggers won't fight.'"[51] Indeed, another correspondent to General Grant wrote shortly after the battle, "The capacity of the negro to defend his liberty, and his susceptibility to appreciate the power and motives in the place of the last, have been put to such a test under our observation as to be beyond further doubt."[52]

Despite the USCT's best efforts and heavy loses, the Union line melted. Only the arrival of the Federal gunboat *Choctaw* to the scene and its quick firing on the advancing Rebel troops, forced them into retreat. The Confederates suffered 185 casualties while inflicting 652 upon the Union (63 killed and 130 wounded in the 9th Louisiana alone, making for a 60 percent casualty rate) with 266 of these missing, including many of the fleeing white officers.[53]

What happened to the missing black soldiers and their officers at Milliken's Bend varied and remains a point of some controversy. Under an April 1863 Confederate law, white Union officers of black troops faced execution for inciting "servile insurrection." Black soldiers fell under state law, mostly to be returned to slavery. It stunned General Kirby Smith to find out that Taylor had taken prisoners at Milliken's Bend. Smith opined that quarter would encourage more slaves to flee and take up arms. General Grant, however, had heard rumors of hangings from a Confederate deserter who went so far as to claim that "General Taylor and command were drawn up to witness the executions." In response, he sent a letter to Taylor stating that Confederates captured at Milliken's Bend received treatment as prisoners of war. He emphasized that all soldiers wearing a Union uniform must receive care as POWs despite their race. Grant wrote, "The act of hanging has no official sanction, and that all parties guilty of it will be duly punished." Taylor denied any hangings or unfair treatment. Several weeks after the battle, however, two captured white officers, Captain Corydon Heath and 2nd Lieutenant George L. Conn were executed by a "military mob" in the middle of the night. Another of their white officer peers spent the rest of the war in a POW camp in Texas. Determining exactly what happened to the black captives remains muddled. From various testimonies, it seems most went back to their plantations, some moved west, and still others served the Confederate army in some capacity. It remains unlikely, though, that executions were common.[54]

The USCT's efforts at Milliken's Bend drew much praise. Thomas Sedgwick of the 10th Illinois Cavalry recalled how he and his compatriots, being pursued by Rebel troopers, "came in sight of men in bright new blue uniforms, who soon opened fire on 'our friends the enemy.' They supposing it a large force for our support, ceased their all-too-friendly advance on us. When we had time to look well at our men in blue, we discovered they had black faces. I had been raised an Abolitionist, yet was opposed to the plan of arming negroes before that day, but I can tell you of one who became a sudden convert right then and there, perfectly willing that negroes should have as good a right to be shot as myself."[55] A soldier from the 23rd Iowa likewise noted that the "negroes . . . stood much better than I supposed they would, being so green in the business."[56] Another Illinois soldier, Captain M. M. Miller, a white officer for one of the black Louisiana regiments, wrote to his hometown Galena, Illinois, newspaper that, "I never felt more grieved and sick at heart then when I saw how my brave soldiers had been slaughtered. It was a horrible fight, the worst I was ever engaged in—not even excepting Shiloh," yet "I can say for them that I never saw a braver company of men in my life . . . they fought and died, defending the cause that we serve."[57] The noted journalist Charles Dana wrote that "the bravery of the blacks in the battle at Milliken's Bend completely revolutionized the sentiment of the army. . . . I heard prominent officers who formerly in private had sneered at the idea of negroes fighting express themselves after as heartily in favor of it."[58] Reporting to his superiors on the fighting at Milliken's Bend, Grant said, "In this battle most of the troops engaged were Africans, who had but little experience in the use of fire-arms. Their conduct is said, however, to have been most gallant, and I doubt not but with good officers they will make good troops." In its July 11 edition, Indiana's *Weekly Vincennes Gazette* reported the receipt of an anonymous commentary on the recent battle's import by their counterparts at the *Evansville Journal.* "Why was the battle at Milliken's Bend like a total eclipse of the sun?" the paper asked its readers. "Because, " it went on to answer, "*darkness* prevailed."[59] In November 1863, Halleck told Secretary of War Edwin Stanton, "It is represented that the colored troops in these desperate engagements fought with great bravery."[60] Lorenzo Thomas used the USCT performance at Milliken's Bend to push for their pay raise. For Milliken's Bend, the Official Records noted, "The negroes met the enemy on the ramparts, and both sides freely used the bayonet, a most rare occurrence in warfare. The rebels were defeated with heavy loss."[61]

The Confederates threatened two other positions along the river in addition to Milliken's Bend. At Young's Point, Louisiana, Confederate forces formed and then withdrew without attacking the white Union forces positioned there. The location formed the starting point for Grant's earlier failed plan of making canals to circumvent Vicksburg. Some 4,000 blacks helped build these canals.[62] A third Confederate attack came at Lake Providence, fifty miles north of Vicksburg on the Mississippi River. Two days after the Young's Point confrontation, about 600 Confederates attacked 800 Union forces. Among those 800 were 300 soldiers of the 8th Louisiana Volunteers of African Descent. After parrying two Rebel assaults, the 8th moved out, firing four volleys that devastated the retiring foe.[63]

USCT performance at both conflagrations stunned white Southerners. Writing in her journal shortly after the battle, a dumbfounded Kate Stone lamented, "[I]t is hard to believe that Southern soldiers—and Texans at that—have been whipped by such a mongrel crew of white and black Yankees. There must be some mistake." Likewise, Louisianan Sarah Wadley noted in disbelief, "[I]t is terrible to think of such a battle as this, white men and freemen fighting with their slaves, and to be killed by such a hand, the very soul revolts from it."[64] Writing many years after the battle, Confederate commander, John Walker affirmed, "[T]his was the first instance during the war in which negroes in the service of the Federal government came into collision with the troops of the Confederacy, and the obstinacy with which they fought, and the loss of one-hundred and twenty killed and wounded of McCulloch's men, opened the eyes of the Confederates to the consequences to be apprehended by the Federal employment of these auxiliaries."[65]

Despite the valor of the black Union troops at Milliken's Bend, not everyone was necessarily convinced that they had proven their worth and ability. On the contrary, deeply entrenched prejudice continued to hold sway with many. On August 28, 1863, for instance, the *Cincinnati Daily Enquirer* reprinted a letter (written by "A") to the editor of the *Chicago Times*. A's critique of the black troops, mired as it was in the pervasive racism of the day, was withering. "From Helena[, Arkansas,] to Vicksburg," A begins, "we have a worthless, pauper negro population, that the Government is feeding and caring for, amounting to at least 40,000, and out of that we have five skeleton regiments, and no one of them, except Colonel [William] Wood's First Arkansas [Volunteer Infantry] Regiment [of African Descent], over half full." Given the laziness creating this situation, A continued, "[T]he Government will find that, the fewer we get the better off we will be as the fight at Milliken's Bend will prove." While admitting that he had not actually witnessed the battle, A goes on to say that he arrived on the battlefield shortly after the struggle, "The Abolitionist papers heralded it to the world how the negroes fought, and that they died in in the intrenchments, etc. And so they did but they were killed before they could get out of the ditches. The number of Rebels killed," A railed, "exhibits their worthlessness as soldiers." Commending the soldiers of the white 23rd Iowa Infantry, A goes on to say that, "the Iowa soldiers fought desperately, as they have always done heretofore . . . and their general expression was that, 'the negroes were not worth a damn in a fight.'" Now in a frenzy, A concluded by asserting that "this rebellion will have to be put down by white men, and that every negro that we put into the service is but that much of an incumbrance.

But the Abolitionists must have Sambo prominent in every thing. It may be fun to them, but it is death to the country."[66]

Increasingly, however, in the main, opinions such as A's subsided within the white Northern population. In a late July editorial titled, "A Question Settled," the editor of the *New Haven Daily Palladium* addressed the pervasive question of "Will the African race fight?" "Milliken's Bend and Port Hudson . . . and other memorable places where the blacks have fought," the paper unabashedly asserted, "attest the courage and military capacity of the freedmen." Indeed, the paper presciently noted, "[T]he question would have remained undecided forever if it had been left to white men to settle. Philanthropy and Prejudice would have continued to battle in the future as they have in the past. But fortunately a new disputant has now entered the arena, and his arguments are likely to settle the question forever. This new disputant is the negro himself. His arguments are heroic deeds upon the field of battle."[67] The following day the *Chicago Tribune* echoed this sentiment, writing, "Since the assault on Port Hudson and the defense of Milliken's Bend, the Copperheads can no longer deny that the negroes will fight. The question is settled, even to their satisfaction. And the feeling of hostility to the employment of blacks as soldiers has ceased among all classes."[68] While perhaps overstating the extent to which hostility toward black troops had subsided, the *Tribune's* broader point about the sea change evident in American society writ large was not. Many, the African American run *Christian Recorder* asserted in a February 1865 piece,

> believe us born for slavery, but we have a higher destiny, and that destiny is to be co-extensive with America. Wherever her flag is to float, honored, respected—the emblem of freedom and progress—the ensign of hope to the struggling millions of Europe—the champion of right on the land, on the rolling seas—foremost in commerce and agriculture, in the arts of peace and war, there we negroes will have full and undisputed representation; and when the historian shall pen the greatness of this struggle in counting the heroic deeds of our armies at Fort Darling, Milliken's Bend, Port Hudson, and [Fort] Wagner, [Fort] Fisher, Petersburg, will stand in order, and coming generations will recognize the negroes nobly defended human freedom, and maintained the government.[69]

Subsequent Operations in Northeastern Louisiana

Though thwarted at Milliken's Bend and environs, General Kirby Smith remained wedded to his plan for military operations in the Government Plantation district in northeastern Louisiana. Attacks here, he knew, would not be threatening enough to draw Grant out of his entrenchments around Vicksburg. At the same time, however, if successful, these attacks could lead to Confederate control over the western bank of the Mississippi River opposite the beleaguered city, interrupting Union supplies and reinforcements and providing Pemberton's army with a means of escape. Smith also ordered his forces operating in the area, under the command of Major General John G. Walker, to torch the plantations growing cotton for the government and to run off or capture the blacks working on the plantations.[70] To assist Walker in undertaking operations in the Goodrich's Landing/Lake Providence region, Smith ordered Lieutenant General Theophilus Holmes, Commander of the Army of Arkansas, to dispatch troops south to Lake Providence. Concerned about a possible Federal push into Arkansas from Memphis, Holmes determined not to send any of his regular troops and instead ordered the formation of a provisional cavalry brigade under the command of Colonel William H. Parsons, with orders to rendezvous near Gaines Landing, Arkansas, on the west bank of the Mississippi.[71] On the morning of June 29, 1863, patrols from Parson's brigade swept through the area near Goodrich's Landing burning everything connected to the government-run plantations. Here over 2,000 black men, women, and children were rounded up and marched westward to be restored to their owners. Those who sought to escape, if found under arms, or who were the property of disloyal Confederate citizens faced execution.[72] The Confederates, the *Daily Cleveland Herald* later reported, "destroyed everything on the plantations that could be destroyed, and on the plantations abandoned by their owners, now being worked by loyal men, killed quite a number of the negroes employed in cultivating the fields, and drove several hundred into the interior as captives."[73]

Simultaneously, five miles north of the Landing, at a place known locally as Mound Plantation (due to the presence of a large Indian mound), Parsons's provisional troopers encountered two companies (E and G) of the 1st Arkansas Volunteers of African Descent. These units, part of the force just recently recruited and organized by Thomas, had only arrived on the plantation two weeks prior and likely trooped off to their new assignment singing the marching song (sung to the tune of "John Brown's Body") penned for the unit by their New York–born abolitionist commander:

> *We have done with hoeing cotton, we have done with hoeing corn,*
> *We are colored Yankee soldiers, now, as sure as you are born;*
> *When the masters hear us yelling, they'll think it's Gabriel's horn,*
> *As we go marching on.*[74]

Though entrenched in a strong position atop the Indian mound (the troops had constructed a crude fort supported by rifle pits, had loosened the soil along the mound's slope, and had hauled a number of large logs to the top of the mound that could be rolled down on attacking forces), Walker reported that the position "was of great strength, and would have cost us many lives and much precious time to have captured by assault."[75] The black troops were badly outnumbered. In a lurch, their white officers winnowed. They proposed surrender to the advancing Confederates on condition that the white officers be treated as prisoners of war while the black soldiers were to be treated unconditionally.[76] Writing shortly after the engagement, Walker lamented, "I consider it an unfortunate circumstance that any armed negroes were captured."[77]

Not surprisingly then, upon surrender the 113 black soldiers and 3 white officers of the 1st Arkansas endured brutal treatment by their captors, especially when they were handed off to the 22nd Texas, one of the units that had fought at Milliken's Bend. As one private in the unit recounted, "12 or 15" of the African American soldiers were murdered before the POWs even reached the holding area designated for them.[78] A survivor of the ordeal (Lewis Bogan) recalled being allowed to stop "to get something to eat and the alarm was given 'the Yankees are coming' & they started us along again and was I very tired & fell & Jim helped me up; when one of the rebel guards, a soldier, told Jim to let go of me & another . . . gave out just then & they shot him." Another private, Charles Bogan, also vividly remembered, "I know we were threatened with hanging & killing every minute & we were pretty badly scared." Burdened as well by the hundreds of captured plantation workers, their Confederate captors had little patience for those unable to keep pace. "They made us carry the children," Charles Bogan noted, "and if we gave out they would hit us with their muskets or anything they had in their hands."[79]

The same day, upon receipt of the news of the Confederate depredations in the plantation district, Admiral Porter and Brigadier General Hugh Reid quickly moved to counter the threat. From his headquarters at Lake Providence, Reid ordered the white 1st Kansas Mounted Infantry to ride south toward Goodrich's Landing while Porter, from his base at Young's Point, dispatched a marine brigade to hasten to the same location.[80] Early on the morning of June 30, the Confederate force began its march north toward Lake Providence with the intent of wreaking havoc on the government plantations there. Five miles south of the lake, the Confederates encountered the men of the 1st Kansas protected by dense woods. The Confederates launched an immediate attack and drove the Kansans back to within three miles of Lake

Providence. Here, the Confederates were able to make out in the distance a number of Union transport vessels accompanied by gunboats, and so the attack was called off and a withdrawal back across the Tensas River ordered. Shortly after breaking off their attack and heading southwest, the Confederate rear guard went into action near the Mound Plantation against Porter's marines and two black regiments (the remainder of the 1st Arkansas and the 10th Louisiana) from Goodrich's Landing. After a sharp firefight in which three Union soldiers and a similar number of Confederates died, the Rebels succeeded in crossing the Tensas and burning the bridge behind them. The skirmishes at Goodrich's landing and Lake Providence were over, and, as historian Edwin Bearss notes, "Efforts by the trans-Mississippi Confederates to either relieve the Vicksburg army or make a successful diversion in support of General Pemberton had ended in frustration and failure."[81]

Conclusion

Shortly after the successful capture of Vicksburg by Union forces, William Whiting, the solicitor to the War Department, drafted a letter in response to an invitation extended to him to address a convention of colored citizens at Poughkeepsie, New York. Reflecting upon recent events and the critical role played by African American troops in turning the tide on the western front, Whiting effusively praised their recent efforts:

> What has the Africo-American to fight for? He fights for the land which, now about to be freed from the curse of slavery, will be to him "his country." In rallying around the flag of the Union, he adds strength and support to the noble armies of the West and of the East, who on the fields of Vicksburg and Gettysburg, have added fresh laurels to their imperishable fame. Not alone for his country's honor, not for empire, not for conquest, not alone for the crushing of rebellion is the African's blade unsheathed. He fights for the honor and manhood of his race, for justice, humanity, and freedom. When love of country, and of fame, when thirst for justice and a sense of *wrongs yet unavenged*, shall nerve the arm and fire the blood already kindled by the flames of freedom, how is it possible that the soldier can be otherwise than brave and terrible in battle, when slavery and death are behind him, and life and liberty lie only in the path of victory? . . . They [black volunteers] are now springing up, like dragon's teeth, from the soil into which they have been crushed. Masters of the ground they tread upon, they are sweeping forward in steady, solid legions. . . . A man once made free by law cannot be again made a slave.[82]

For the many Americans who may have harbored doubts about African Americans' willingness to fight, the Vicksburg Campaign provided ready proof that they were more than up to the task. The black soldiers under arms, as Whiting so eloquently noted, had gone well beyond simply demonstrating their ability and bravery—they had shown themselves, in fact, to be true republican sons of the nation, forged in the crucible of battle and wedded, like their white counterparts, to the founding ideals of the nation. Without any doubt, Union veteran James McElroy recalled in a 1905 contribution to the *National Tribune*, "The way that they [black troops] fought at Milliken's Bend, therefore, brought about a remarkable change in the public's attitude. There was no doubt that if properly officered and led they would do most effective fighting, and from that very day every one began to look more favorably upon the colored man in the uniform of the Union Army."[83] Though the war would stretch for almost another two years, the achievements of African American soldiers at Vicksburg assured that questions of civil rights and equity would remain at the forefront of the national debate. "They will have to pay us wages, the wages of their sin," soldiers of the 1st Arkansas USCT reminded those they encountered as they caroled the regiment's "marching song" heading from Southern town to Southern town, "They will have to bow their foreheads to their colored kith and kin. They will have to give us house-room, or the roof shall tumble in! As we go marching on."[84]

Notes

1. Lincoln to Andrew Johnson, 26 March 1863, in Roy P. Basler, ed., *The Collected Works of Abraham Lincoln*, 9 vols. (New Brunswick, NJ: Rutgers University Press, 1953), 6:150–51.

2. W. E. Woodward, *Meet General Grant* (New York: Literary Guild of America, 1928), 372.

3. James M. McPherson, *The Negro's Civil War: How American Negroes Felt and Acted during the War for the Union*, 3rd ed. (1965; New York: Vintage Books, 2003 [1965]), xi.

4. Michael B. Ballard, *Vicksburg: The Campaign That Opened Up the Mississippi* (Chapel Hill: University of North Carolina Press, 2004), 391.

5. Edwin Cole Bearss, *The Campaign for Vicksburg*, vol. 3, *Unvexed to the Sea* (Dayton: Morningside Press, 1986), 1153.

6. James A. Rawley, *Abraham Lincoln and a Nation Worth Fighting For* (Lincoln: University of Nebraska Press, 2003), 227.

7. Frederick Douglass, *Frederick Douglass on Slavery and the Civil War: Selections from His Writings* (Mineola, NY: Dover Publications, 2003), 43.

8. *Detroit Free Press*, June 10, 1863.

9. Henry Romeyn, "The Colored Troops," *National Tribune* (Washington, DC), July 14, 1887, 1. Reader's note: Due to a spelling error, Henry Romeyn's last name is sometimes spelled "Romyen" in early military records.

10. *New York Herald*, April 24, 1863.

11. Henry Romeyn, "With Colored Troops in the Army of the Cumberland," *War Papers, Being Papers Read before the Commandery of the District of Columbia* (Wilmington, NC: Broadfoot Publishing Company, 1993), 49.

12. *New York Herald*, April 24, 1863.

13. *Daily Cleveland Herald*, May 20, 1863.

14. *Milwaukee Daily Sentinel*, April 23, 1863.

15. Randall M. Miller and Jon W. Zophy, "Unwelcome Allies: Billy Yank and the Black Soldier," 39, no. 3 *Phylon* (3rd Quarter, 1978), 236–38.

16. Ira Berlin, Barbara J. Fields, Steven F. Miller, Joseph P. Reidy, Leslie S. Rowland, *Slaves No More: Three Essays on Emancipation and the Civil War* (New York: Cambridge University Press, 1992), 23.

17. Chandra Manning, *What This Cruel War Was Over: Soldiers, Slavery and the Civil War* (New York: Vintage Books, 2008), 13; Ira Berlin, "Who Freed the Slaves? Emancipation and Its Meaning," in *Major Problems in the Civil War and Reconstruction*, ed. Michael Perman and Thomas Paterson (Stamford, CT: Cengage Learning, 1998), 291. For a look at African American agency see Walter Johnson, "On Agency," *Journal of Social History*, 37, no. 1 (Autumn 2003), 113–24. For more information about self-emancipation see David Williams, *I Freed Myself: African American Self-Emancipation in the Civil War* (New York: Cambridge University Press, 2014).

18. Noah Andre Trudeau, *Like Men of War: Black Troops in the Civil War, 1862–1865* (Boston: Little, Brown, 1998), 98.

19. U.S. War Department, *The War of the Rebellion: A Compilation of Official Records of the Union and Confederate Armies*, 128 vols. (Washington DC: Government Printing Office, 1880–1901), series 1, vol. 23, pt. 3:157. Hereafter cited as *OR*. All references are to series 1 unless otherwise indicated.

20. *Boston Daily Advertiser*, April 23, 1863.

21. Ibid., November 13, 1863.

22. John Eaton, *Grant, Lincoln, and the Freedmen: Reminiscences of the Civil War with Special Reference to the Work for the Contrabands and Freedmen of the Mississippi Valley* (New York: Longmans, Green, and Co., 1907), 15.

23. James R. Arnold, *Grant Wins the War: Decision at Vicksburg* (New York: John Wiley and Sons, 1997), 70–71.

24. William Wells Brown, *The Negro in the American Rebellion: His Heroism and His Fidelity* (Boston: Lee and Shepard, 1867), 125–27.

25. *North American and United States Gazette*, April 20, 1863.

26. *Milwaukee Daily Sentinel*, April 23, 1863.

27. Richard Lowe, "Battle on the Levee: The Fight at Milliken's Bend," in *Black Soldiers in Blue*, ed. John David Smith (Chapel Hill: University of North Carolina Press, 2002), 108.

28. Benjamin Quarles, *The Negro in the Civil War* (Boston: Little, Brown, 1953), 214–20; Hondon B. Hargrove, *Black Union Soldiers in the Civil War* (Jefferson, NC: McFarland, 1988), 128–34.

29. Hargrove, *Black Union Soldiers*, 138–39.

30. Quoted in Lawrence Lee Hewitt, *Port Hudson, Confederate Bastion on the Mississippi* (Baton Rouge: Louisiana State University Press, 1987), 177–78.

31. Quoted in Brown, *Negro in the American Rebellion*, 175–76.

32. Ibid., 172.

33. Warren E. Grabau, *Ninety-Eight Days: A Geographer's View of the Vicksburg Campaign* (Knoxville: University of Tennessee Press, 2000), 385–87. Also see T. Michael Parrish, *Richard Taylor: Soldier Prince of Dixie* (Chapel Hill: University of North Carolina Press, 1992), 287–88.

34. "Opening the Mississippi," *National Tribune*, November 16, 1905.

35. Brown, *The Negro in the American Rebellion*, 220–22.

36. Bearss, *The Campaign for Vicksburg*, 3:1180. Though green, the African American troops, led by Colonel Hermann Lieb, were in a strong defensive position. See Richard Lowe, *Walker's Texas Division C.S.A.: Greyhounds of the Trans-Mississippi* (Baton Rouge: Louisiana State University Press, 2004), 87. Lowe also questions the validity of the claim of the black flag account and/or the degree to which Walker's men engaged in the wanton slaughter of black troops. Lowe, *Walker's Texas Division*, 97–98.

37. *OR*, vol. 24, pt. 2, 453-54.

38. Bearss, *The Campaign for Vicksburg*, 3:1180. Though it lacks detail regarding the Milliken's Bend battle, a personal account of life in the 23rd Iowa can be found in Harold D. Brinkman, ed., *Dear Companion: The Civil War Letters of Silas I. Shearer* (Ames, IA: Sigler Printing and Publishing, 1995). Other useful accounts of the battle can be found in William L. Shea and Terrence J. Winschel, *Vicksburg Is the Key: The Struggle for the Mississippi River* (Lincoln: University of Nebraska Press, 2003), 165; Ballard, *Vicksburg*, 391.

39. *New York Herald*, June 19, 1863.

40. Henry E. McCulloch quoted in Bearss, *Campaign for Vicksburg*, 3:1181.

41. *Evening Star*, June 13, 1863.

42. *OR*, vol. 24, pt. 2, 448.

43. *OR*, vol. 24, pt. 2, 451.

44. *Liberator*, June 26, 1863.

45. Brown, *Negro in the American Rebellion*, 222.

46. Lowe, *"Battle on the Levee,"* 122; T. H. Whipple letter of June 15, 1863, printed in the *New York Herald*, June 19, 1863.

47. Lowe, *Walker's Texas Division*, 92; Linda Barnickel, *Milliken's Bend: A Civil War Battle in History and Memory* (Baton Rouge: Louisiana State University Press, 2013), 91.

48. "The Milliken's Bend Scrap," *National Tribune*, December 7, 1905.

49. *Chicago Tribune*, 18 June 1863.

50. *OR*, vol. 24, pt. 2, 454.

51. Barnickel, *Milliken's Bend*, 93–94.

52. *OR*, vol. 24, pt. 2, 456.

53. Arnold, *Grant Wins the War*, 283–84.

54. Barnickel, *Milliken's Bend*, 119–34; Parrish, *Richard Taylor*, 293. Accounts of hangings did appear in the Northern press. See, for example, *Chicago Tribune*, December 22, 1863.

55. "The Milliken's Bend Scrap," *National Tribune*, December 7, 1905.

56. Trudeau, *Like Men of War*, 55.

57. *Chicago Tribune*, July 3, 1863.

58. Quoted in Arnold, *Grant Wins the War*, 284.

59. *OR*, vol. 24, pt. 2: 446; *Weekly Vincennes Gazette*, July 11, 1863.

60. *OR*, vol. 24, pt. 2, 7.

61. Ibid., vol. 24, pt. 2, 453.

62. Eaton, *Grant, Lincoln, and the Freedmen*, 44.

63. Hargrove, *Black Union Soldiers*, 144–45.

64. Quoted in Trudeau, *Like Men of War*, 59.

65. Walker quoted in Lowe, *Walker's Texas Division*, 99.

66. *Cincinnati Enquirer*, August 28, 1863.

67. *New Haven Daily Palladium*, July 28, 1863.

68. *Chicago Tribune*, June 29, 1863. Copperheads were Northern Democrats that did not support the war effort.

69. *Christian Recorder*, February 25, 1865.

70. Bearss, *Campaign for Vicksburg*, 3:1216.

71. Grabau, *Ninety-Eight Days*, 388.

72. Bearss, *Campaign for Vicksburg*, 3:1199.

73. *Daily Cleveland Herald*, July 6, 1863.

74. Quoted in Trudeau, *Like Men of War*, 99.

75. *OR*, vol. 24, pt. 2, 465.

76. Trudeau, *Like Men of War*, 100. A correspondent for the *Indianapolis Journal* described the men of the 1st Arkansas as being, "perfect in equipment, and, considering that they had been armed less than a month, admirable in discipline." *Milwaukee Daily Sentinel*, June 18, 1863.

77. *OR*, vol. 24, pt. 2, 465.

78. Trudeau, *Like Men of War*, 101.

79. Ibid., 102.

80. Bearss, *Campaign for Vicksburg*, 3:1200.

81. Ibid., 1200–1201, quote on p. 1202.

82. *The Liberator*, July 31, 1863.

83. "Opening of the Mississippi," *National Tribune*, November 16, 1905.

84. Quoted in Trudeau, *Like Men of War*, 102.

3

PLYING THE DEADLY TRADE: THE SHARPSHOOTERS' WAR AT THE SIEGE OF VICKSBURG

Jonathan M. Steplyk

In the 47 days of the Vicksburg siege, besiegers and besieged faced a host of hazards, from artillery salvos to nagging mosquitoes to the sweltering Mississippi sun. Among the most dangerous of these threats were the eagle-eyed men, fingers on triggers, scanning the enemy's positions for human targets. Writing in 1903, Iowa veteran Samuel Pryce remembered them as "the snipers—the body snatchers," but most Union and Confederate soldiers in summer 1863 knew them as sharpshooters, and they had their own deadly and critical roles to play in the siege of Vicksburg.[1]

Civil War histories offer up accounts from a number of combatants who spoke contemptuously of sharpshooters, men such as Frank Wilkeson, an artilleryman in the Army of the Potomac, who professed that during his service he had hated Yankee and Rebel sharpshooters alike:

> [A]s a campaign cannot be decided by killing a few hundred enlisted men—killing them most unfairly and when they were of necessity exposed,—it did seem as though the sharpshooting pests should have been suppressed. Our sharpshooters were as bad as the Confederates, and neither of them were of any account as far as decisive results were obtained. They could sneak around trees or lurk behind stumps, or cower in wells or in cellars, and from the safety of their lairs murder a few men. Put the sharpshooters in battle-line and they were no better, no more effective, than the infantry of the line, and they were not half as decent.[2]

Historians have cited Wilkeson and several other likeminded veterans numerous times, but as noteworthy as such sentiments are, such accounts offer an incomplete picture of sharpshooting at Vicksburg for multiple reasons.

The sharpshooters of Ulysses S. Grant's and John C. Pemberton's armies were mostly not set-apart soldiers but instead came from the ranks at large, the common "infantry of the line." While Wilkeson and others despised sharpshooters, a significant number of men on both sides took to sharpshooting quite eagerly. Finally, from a military perspective, sharpshooting was not simply random murder but rather an integral part of effective siege craft. Vicksburg's garrison, though outnumbered and with limited ammunition, used sharpshooting as best they could to keep Federal besiegers at bay and delay their approach trenches. Grant's Army of the Tennessee deployed sharpshooters systematically on a large scale. These Union sharpshooters provided covering fire for assaults and fatigue parties, whittled away the defenders' numbers, kept the garrison in a considerable state of unease, and achieved considerable success in suppressing Confederate artillery and musketry throughout the siege.

In many ways, Civil War sharpshooters were analogous to the highly trained and specially armed warriors in modern armies known as snipers. Samuel Pryce used the word "snipers" in his history of the 22nd Iowa, but he completed that work in 1903, sometime after it had entered the American lexicon. During the Civil War, the term was almost unknown in the United States. Civil War armies did include several elite sharpshooter units that prefigured the specialized snipers of today, but few of these took part in the Vicksburg Campaign. Instead, as with many aspects of siege craft at Vicksburg, much of the sharpshooting had to be improvised. Pemberton's garrison included elements from several self-designated sharpshooter battalions, but accounts from the siege suggest that men from these units took part in sharpshooting only as much as other Confederate infantrymen did. Grant's army contained virtually no specially trained or armed sharpshooters. Instead, the task of sharpshooting in both armies fell largely to common soldiers armed with ordinary rifles or muskets.

"Sharpshooter" is a notoriously ambiguous term in Civil War usage. In most cases, it did not refer so much to a particular type of soldier but more often to a particular role any soldier might perform in a battle or siege. Just as a skirmisher referred to any soldier deployed in open order using light infantry or rifle tactics, a sharpshooter could be any soldier detached from the line of battle to target the enemy as effectively as possible. Perhaps not surprisingly, soldiers at Vicksburg often referred to the exchange of small arms fire during the siege as "sharpshooting" and "skirmishing," sometimes using the terms almost interchangeably. Similarly, some accounts describe soldiers doing the firing as "sharpshooters," "skirmishers," and "pickets." Given the pickets' role as the foremost position of their respective armies, sharpshooting during the siege often fell to Union and Confederate soldiers on picket duty.

Sharpshooting at Vicksburg essentially began even before the siege was fully underway, as Pemberton's forces retreated into their defenses and pursuing Federals began to encircle the Confederate Gibraltar. On May 18, Captain James C. Wiggs was guiding a Louisiana regiment along the Graveyard Road when a bullet went zipping over his head. Thinking the shot had come from fellow Confederates, Wiggs stood in his saddle and shouted, "What the Hell are you shooting at?" What followed were shots from what seemed like "a whole Platoon" fired in his direction. "I said Yanks by God and you may bet I galloped down that hill," recounted Wiggs, who had then warned his superiors that Union skirmishers were advancing perilously close.[3]

During Grant's May 19 and May 22 assaults on Vicksburg, Union soldiers, some detailed as sharpshooters and some acting on their own initiative, did their best to provide covering fire for their attacking comrades. Captain James B. Taylor recorded how during the second assault his own 120th Ohio deployed as skirmishes and assisted the 16th Ohio in targeting Rebel gunners. "The enemy did not dare make his appearance on the walls to fire," the Buckeye wrote in his diary, "as our sharpshooters commanded these." In some cases, once the attackers had reached the foot of the enemy earthworks, Rebel defenders had to lean far over or stand atop the parapets, leaving them dangerously exposed. "Then was our sharpshooters' opportunity, and well they made use of it," Samuel C. Jones of the 22nd Iowa recounted. "Many of the Confederates paid with their lives for their foolishness." Whenever possible, the attackers tried to plant their colors atop the enemy works, and in several cases Union sharpshooter fire, either from skirmishers to the rear or from the attackers themselves, helped keep these flags from falling into Rebel hands. Medal of Honor recipient Robert Cox of the 55th Illinois credited sharpshooters for the "hot fire" that kept at bay defenders trying to snag his regiment's flags with bayonets. Samuel Jones's comrade Samuel Pryce told how a dozen of the 22nd Iowa's best shots resolutely defended the colors along the slopes of the Railroad Redoubt: "Here they engaged the confederate sharp-shooters during the entire day, and until after sunset, picking them off like black-birds."[4]

With the failure of both assaults, both sides settled into the business of a siege, the Confederates improving their defenses and the Federals digging the necessary siege works to protect themselves and begin the approaches toward the enemy. Sharpshooters of the two armies fought from behind several kinds of fortification. Yankee and Rebel sources refer numerous times to the use of "rifle pits," a term about as ambiguous as sharpshooter in Civil War usage. At its most basic, a rifle pit could mean any depression in the earth large enough to shelter one or several men, described by one Ohio sergeant as "gopher holes." Sharpshooters on both sides used these especially for picket duty, since they made it possible to take up advance positions in front on their main lines of works. Union sharpshooters also used these cruder fortifications when they wished to venture especially close to Rebel lines. Alternatively, Union soldiers at Vicksburg also referred to more established trenches as rifle pits. One soldier's map depicts long lines that are clearly parallels and half parallels, with the label "Federal Works = Rifle Pits."[5]

In their more elaborate fortifications, Union and Confederate infantry-men at Vicksburg used a number of techniques to create positions from which to fire at the enemy while providing maximum protection for themselves. One of the most common techniques throughout the Civil War was use of a headlog, raised with stakes to sit several inches over the top of a trench or parapet, thus providing a narrow slit through which to fire. To support the headlog, soldiers typically placed perpendicular crossbeams extending behind it, both to elevate the log and to prevent it from rolling down on top of them. At Vicksburg, it was apparently especially common to construct individual firing ports to provide even more protection from enemy fire. Soldiers' accounts and contemporary illustrations depict Union troops using logs and railroad ties with notches cut into one side, laid notched side down atop a parapet, effectively providing a headlog with loopholes. Sergeant William Eddington of the 97th Illinois recorded that while digging breastworks they would fill sandbags with dirt, then top the breastworks with a row of sandbags, each placed about two inches apart. "Now we would lay another tier of bags on top of this one and this would leave a small hole through which we would put our guns," Eddington explained. "We would lay more bags on top of these until we had them away over our heads so that we were entirely hid from the Rebels."[6]

From behind their various forms of cover, Federals and Confederates began the sharpshooters' war in earnest, keeping close watches along the tops of enemy works for a chance at a lethal shot. From their trenches, recorded Wilbur Crummer of the 45th Illinois, "[O]ur sharpshooters were continually on the lookout for the hidden enemy." Marksmen on both sides ensured that neither besieger nor besieged could carelessly expose themselves. "Not a man in the trenches on either side could show his head above the breastworks without being picked off by the sharpshooters," Crummer duly noted. Battery commander Anthony Burton attested to the danger from Confederate fire: "The rebel sharpshooters are equally attentive as our own to any head or body incautiously exposed to their view." Lieutenant Colonel Jefferson Brumback of the 95th Ohio concurred, writing his wife, "Bullets from rebel sharpshooters are continually flying over my head as they aim at every man who shows his." Confederate staff officer William Drennan recounted his own close encounter with one of his Yankee counterparts. Hazarding a look at the enemy with his field glasses, the Mississippian had barely focused his lenses "before a sharpshooter spied me, and *here come the Minnie balls whistling at me.*" A rattled Drennan recorded, "Had I remained there any length of time he would have struck me."[7]

Perhaps no element of the sharpshooters' war at Vicksburg was as intense as the cat-and-mouse encounters between opposing marksmen. Between the lines, Wilbur Crummer recorded, "[M]any a duel was had here between the pickets of the opposing armies." It was in these counter-sniper duels that Union and Confederate sharpshooters tried to eliminate one another in their ongoing fight to dominate the battle lines with musketry. Hunting enemy marksmen involved considerable risk, as one could just as easily become the hunted. Lieutenant Jared Young Sanders recorded the death of a comrade in the 26th Louisiana, "a brave & gallant soldier," in one such encounter. The Louisianan and a Yankee sharpshooter fired simultaneously at one another. What became of the Union marksman is unknown, but Sanders's comrade "fell with his gun empty as soon as he pulled the trigger." Other sharpshooters were lucky enough to walk away from such duels. Jefferson Brumback recorded that on one particular day his regiment's only casualty had been "one of our best shots and best men." The Ohio marksman had been firing behind a tree and had attracted the attention of several Rebel riflemen. "He became careless and exposed himself unnecessarily," Brumback wrote, causing him to take a bullet to the elbow, "a severe but probably not fatal wound." Major George Crosley described a similar incident in which one of the 3rd Iowa's soldiers suffered a wound to the face. "He had just fired through a loop hole in top of rifle pit and Rebel sharp-shooter fired at the spot where the smoke issued," Crosley noted in his diary. "Such incidents are of daily occurrence along our lines."[8]

Soldiers in the Vicksburg trenches often used the time-honored trick of holding up hats as targets to attract shots from opposing marksmen. Some fighting men did this to amuse themselves amid the tedium of the siege. An Ohio veteran recalled how "many of the boys put their hats on ramrods and held them up to have the same perforated by the enemy sharpshooters." According to the 22nd Iowa's Samuel Pryce, "The rival combatants when not trying to kill each other held shooting matches to see who were the best shots." Yanks and Rebs hoisted their hats on sticks, and the "sharps-shooters watched with Argus-eyes" for these chances to test their marksmanship and amuse one another. Holding up hats as targets could also serve a more practical and lethal purpose by drawing the fire of enemy sharpshooters in order to expose them to counter-sniper fire. One Union regiment took the ruse a step further by mounting a hat and coat on a stick; these were soon "riddled with bullets." When the curious Confederates peered over their breastworks to see the result, "a hundred bullets flew at them" in reply.[9]

Historically, one of sharpshooters' prime roles in warfare has been to pick off high-value targets such as enemy officers, thereby disrupting command and control on the battlefield. In turn, officers throughout time have often proved easy marks for enemy marksmen, both by their uniforms and by their active presence leading in combat. At Vicksburg, leaders of the blue and gray quickly realized that they especially had to beware the "body snatchers." It was a Union sharpshooter on June 27 who claimed the life of Brigadier General Martin E. Green, one of two Confederate generals killed during the siege of Vicksburg. Apparently frustrated that his troops had become so cowed by Union fire, Green sought to set the example by grabbing a musket to take a shot at the Yankees. The Confederate brigadier had assured his men that "a bullet has not been molded that will kill me," but before Green could take his shot, a Union ball through the head did just that. Officers in Grant's army also had to learn to avoid making targets of themselves. "Many a second lieutenant has fallen victim to the sharpshooter because of his fresh uniform, while officers of more experience have escaped under slouched hats and old blouses," an Ohio soldier observed. "All are equal here," a Pennsylvania sergeant wrote his wife, "the general keeps as low as the private."[10]

At the beginning of the Vicksburg siege, Grant's army lacked many of the resources befitting a besieging force, such as a sizable engineer corps or a train of siege artillery. However, as with so many other aspects of the siege, the Army of the Tennessee made up for these deficiencies with characteristic self-confidence and adaptability. When it came to the tasks of sapping and sharpshooting, the common Union soldier at Vicksburg took on the work that European armies might assign to specialist troops. The besiegers worked throughout the siege, as one regimental history put it, "with a spade in one hand and a gun in the other." Grant's army achieved a steady volume of fire by systematically deploying entire brigades and regiments as sharpshooters, with each regiment typically rotating its companies through the duty. "This Sharpshooting is not hard work," Wisconsin soldier Edward Potter noted in his diary, "as there is only one Co[mpany] on duty at once and relieved every 2 hours." Regiments evidently had a great degree of latitude in choosing what rotation scheme to use. Colonel William H. Raynor's 56th Ohio, for instance, deployed two companies at a time to the rifle pits, relieving each shift ever six hours.[11]

Union sharpshooter activity settled into a predictable schedule with successive details of blue-coated marksmen keeping the air alive with Minié balls as long as there was enough daylight for shooting. "Enemy's sharpshooters opened a brisk fire about 4 1/2 A.M.," Lieutenant Lewis Guion wrote in the logbook of Company D, 26th Louisiana. The following day, he recorded, "Firing began as usual this morning mostly from the sharpshooters in the valley," this time in his own diary. "A continual fire is kept up by the Sharpshooters along the whole line from morning untill [sic] dark," wrote an Indiana soldier. "[O]ur line is 12 miles long." Loading and firing in the Mississippi sun was hot work, and at least some soldiers managed to take a midday break from sharpshooting. "The principal firing is done in the mornings and evenings," Colonel Raynor observed, "the middle of the day being too hot for such warm work."[12]

As dangerous as sharpshooting was, it became so commonplace throughout the 47-day siege that some combatants began remarking on it as casually as they might mention the weather. Just as with the weather, they might observe whether the firing had been particularly light or heavy on a given day. "The sharp-shooting was slow but constant—unceasing all day," observed William Tunnard, regimental historian of the 3rd Louisiana. "Sharp shooting and cannonading as usual this morning—continued all day," William Clack of the 43rd Tennessee recorded in a short May 24 diary entry. Almost a month later, he could report, "Sharp shooters are pecking away as usual this morning." John Fuller of the 31st Louisiana commented on the level of rifle and artillery fire in nearly every one of his diary entries during the siege, as well as other happenings, although on some days it seemed like the only thing worth writing about. Covering eight straight days—May 23–30—Fuller summed up the proceedings in the same three words: "Nothing but sharpshooting."[13]

"Nothing very important going on today," a Minnesota artillery sergeant recorded in one diary entry, "aside from the usual racket kept up by the sharpshooters." Sharpshooting became such a constant feature of the siege of Vicksburg that the sound of gunshots, along with the louder din of artillery, seemed ubiquitous throughout the daylight hours, an aspect on which numerous combatants commented. "The sharp crack of the rifle . . . is always heard, as the sharpshooter plies his trade," a 15th Illinois soldier wrote home, "and after some loud shout tells that some one had made a good shot." Confederate veteran William Tunnard wrote of how the soldier's day "opened with the usual music of sharpshooting and cannonading," recalling how in one firefight the "rifles of the regiment sang a merry tune." The steady crack of rifles reminded many soldiers from the Old Northwest of the sound of felling timber back home. "The Sharp Shooting this morning resembles in my imagination a party of wood choppers at work," mused an Illinoisan. An Iowa soldier writing his wife reckoned it sounded "just like a chopping frolic where the axes are going continually." An Ohio Buckeye likewise suggested, "The noise is similar to a large force of lumbermen at work in the pine forests, a continual chopping, and every few moments the dull heavy sound of a tree falling."[14]

While Union soldiers on active sharpshooting duty kept this "racket a-going," Wisconsin veteran Hosea Rood explained, troops immediately supporting them in reserve could rest and relax. "My gentle readers cannot see, I presume, how we could sleep when army muskets were being shot off a few feet from our heads at the rate of three or four a minute throughout the day," wrote Rood. "But we did sleep soundly—after getting used to it."[15]

Affording some respite from the tedium of siege work were informal truces Federals and Confederates sometimes arranged with one another. Throughout the Civil War, American soldiers in blue and gray fraternized between lines, taking advantage of the chance to talk, swap newspapers, and trade for coveted items such as coffee and tobacco. At Vicksburg, the contending armies' long-term proximity gave besiegers and besieged ample opportunities to fraternize. Such truces and meetings often took place after nightfall, most of the shooting having ceased and it being safer to expose oneself, though some episodes at Vicksburg apparently did take place during the day. As with similar occurrences throughout the war, witnesses marveled at the sight of deadly enemies meeting amicably during lulls in the fighting. Joseph Bowker of the 42nd Ohio found it "strange that men, who an hour before were doing their utmost to kill each other, should, when darkness sets in, freely converse with each other and sometimes even meet half way and trade tobacco for hard bread." During a formal truce between the lines, Colonel Raynor similarly observed how "both parties came out of their works, shook hands, and met without any evidence of bitter feeling."[16]

A sharpshooter's bullet ended at least one Vicksburg truce on a sour note, albeit not fatally. On May 25, Lieutenant Sanders and his fellow Louisianans took part in a formal truce between the lines, presumably to allow the retrieval of Federal dead and wounded from the assault three days prior. Toward the end of the parley, most of Sanders's men had returned to their defenses while he himself stood atop the parapet. Suddenly, a Union sharpshooter "took a *deliberate fire* at me—the ball passed harmlessly by," wrote Sanders. "It was an infamous act." Given that truce was evidently ending, it is possible the sharpshooter had deliberately fired over Sanders's head as a way of chivvying him back behind the breastworks. Nevertheless, if the units involved were still formally operating under a flag of truce, then the shot was not only unchivalrous but an unlawful act under military law.[17]

Most truces between Yankees and Rebels ended on far better terms. A Confederate veteran from Missouri recorded that the opposing sides conscientiously gave "due notice" when they once more had to open fire, shouting out such warnings as "Lie down, Rebs, we're going to shoot" and "Squat, Yanks, we must commence firing again." As courteously and brotherly as Union and Confederate soldiers treated one another during such interludes, these truces do not seem to have substantially curbed the earnestness of the sharpshooters' war. Instead, truces offered only pauses before Yanks and Rebs returned to the business of picking off one another and avoiding been picked off themselves.[18]

As lethal as sharpshooters could be, their work did not rack up the large body counts that the assaults of May 19 and 22 did. It is hardly surprising that the sharpshooters' war was not bloodier. Certainly not every soldier who took to the trenches was a dead shot with his musket or rifle. Moreover, both besiegers and besieged at Vicksburg fought behind an impressive array of siege works designed to protect them and generally did their best not to make targets of themselves. "[W]e did not expose our selves to the view of the other fellows any more than was absolutely necessary," Hosea Rood noted, "and it was indeed rare that we ever saw a head above the long line of yellow clay on the other side." For every shot that killed or wounded, thousands more missed the mark. "It is wonderful how few shots even of sharpshooters take effect," Jefferson Brumback wrote. The Ohio colonel supposed it took "a man's weight in bullets to kill a man in battles and sieges," an estimation made by numerous Civil War soldiers. From the rifle pits, Minnesota artilleryman Thomas Gordon wryly commented, "[T]housands of bullets are fired at imaginary Johnnies."[19]

"Some of my readers may wonder what we shot at, when nothing was to be seen," the 12th Wisconsin's Hosea Rood wrote decades after the war. "Well, we shot at various things." If no heads presented themselves over the Confederate defenses, Union sharpshooters kept their bullets singing just over the tops of the enemy breastworks. Such shots might catch an unlucky Rebel poking his head above the parapet or might strike the garrison's camps behind the lines. Some Federals fired their weapons at a 45-degree angle toward Vicksburg, supposing that they could drop bullets like miniature artillery salvos into the city itself. Any horse, mule, or other animal so unfortunate as to wander between the lines quickly became a target for both sides. "In fact, we fired at all sorts of marks," Rood summed up, "anything to keep up the leaden hail and the noise of battle."[20] As well protected and hunkered down as Vicksburg's garrison was, Union sharpshooting was hardly going to single-handedly decimate the Rebels' numbers. Nevertheless, Confederate accounts do show sometimes daily losses to Union sniping, often in ones or twos or threes, creating a discouraging drain on the garrison's manpower and demonstrating that sharpshooters continued to make life dangerous for the beleaguered defenders.

Union sharpshooting amounted to more than simply random killing or the sum of Confederate casualties inflicted. Rather, the "leaden hail" that Rood and thousands of fellow U.S. soldiers kept flying over enemy heads was an integral part of subjugating "the rebel Sevastopol." The job of the artillery was to pound Vicksburg's garrison, artillery, and defenses. The goal of soldiers digging the saps and approach trenches was to inch the besieging lines ever closer toward the enemy, increasing the deadliness of Union firepower and the prospects of a future assault. The goal of the Army of the Tennessee's thousands of ad hoc sharpshooters was to keep the Rebels' heads down so that that they could not shoot the gunners and the diggers. As Justin Solonick argues in his landmark study of U.S. siege craft at Vicksburg, "[I]t was not the accuracy of Union small arms fire that suppressed Confederate sharpshooters and artillery but rather the sheer volume of lead that allowed the federal infantrymen to achieve fire superiority." Civil War tacticians may not have spoken of suppressing fire or fire superiority, but this modern terminology describes exactly the purpose and achievement of Union sharpshooters at Vicksburg.[21]

The plainspoken general who had led his Army of the Tennessee to the gates of Vicksburg understood the purpose of the sharpshooters' war. "I have the town closely invested and our Rifle Pitts up so close to the enemy that they cannot show their heads without being shot at short enough range to kill a squirrel," Ulysses Grant wrote his wife Julia. "They dare not show a single gun on the whole line of their works." Moreover, the common soldiers of Grant's army manning the rifle pits knew well and appreciated their role in the siege. The sharpshooters, Joseph Bowker observed, "must do good execution whenever a rebel is bold enough to show his head." William Reid of the 15th Illinois observed, "By day our riflemen keep the rebel works clear of anything that is living." From their loopholes Union troops scanned the tops of Confederate breastworks, Morgan Ebenezer Wescott wrote his parents back in Wisconsin, "and if a Johnny sho[w]s his head he gets a salute." More graphically, Ohio veteran Frank Mason described how sharpshooters stood poised "ready to shatter any head that appeared above the enemy's parapet." Osborn Oldroyd, another Buckeye, included a bit of doggerel in his Vicksburg account that illustrated Union fire superiority with similar colorfulness: "Should a rebel show his pate,/ To withdraw he'll prove too late."[22]

Accounts from the Army of the Tennessee illustrate how well Grant's men understood the importance of protecting their comrades by suppressing Confederate fire. Gun crews were particularly vulnerable to sharpshooters, and Union fire superiority helped ensure that the besieging artillery was free to shell the Vicksburg defenses at will. Lieutenant Colonel Brumback explained to his wife that the sharpshooters "keep down the enemy's riflemen, so that our batteries can play." The day after providing suppressing fire for the May 22 assault, 120th Ohio's James Taylor again deployed his company as skirmishers, this time to protect the Chicago Mercantile Battery while the gunners dug in a new position.[23]

Pemberton's Vicksburg garrison boasted a substantial train of artillery, but the volume of Union sharpshooter fire achieved great success in blunting the Rebels' ability to use those guns. Early in the siege, Carlos Colby of the 97th Illinois noted that picket duty now "consists in acting as sharp shooters to keep the enemy from loading their Artly." Fellow Prairie Stater William Reid wrote his father that "our riflemen" had made it "death for any one to load or sight the cannon." He explained that the Confederate gunners had to settle for loading their heavy artillery under the cover of darkness and only firing off one shot at random during the day. As dangerous as Union riflemen were to Confederate artillery, they had to beware bunching up too much and thus making themselves tempting enough targets for an enemy gun crew to hazard a shot. Reid, an enthusiastic sharpshooter, considered this "a very great compliment for they will never fire a cannon at you unless you are bothering them very much." Among Confederate veterans, William Tunnard deemed Union sharpshooting "particularly accurate and deadly," recounting how on one occasion five crewmen were hit trying to fire a single cannon.[24]

Perhaps the most significant contribution Union sharpshooters' suppressing fire made to the siege operations was protecting their comrades digging the saps and approach trenches. It was the latter's battle waged with pick and shovel that tightened the noose around the "Gibraltar of the West," each day increasing the viability of a successful storming of the Vicksburg defenses. Just as sharpshooting helped shield Union gunners, it also helped protect Union diggers. Theodorus Northrup of the 23rd Wisconsin wrote that if the Rebels "showed themselves to fire on the dig[g]ers the pickets would give them a pressing invitation to retire." Nathan M. Baker, chaplain of the 116th Illinois, likewise recorded how the pickets fired "with great spirit, the object being to keep the enemy down so they could not fire on our working parties." Baker himself ventured into the trenches and observed how sap rollers protected the diggers as they worked their way toward the enemy. The barrier ensured that to get a clear shot into the sap, "a rebel would have to expose his whole body, and that they well know would be certain death to any who should attempt it."[25]

For soldiers on both sides, simple math illustrated Union fire superiority over the Confederate defenders. The Army of the Tennessee's greater numbers ensured that the blue-clad sharpshooters could overwhelm their Confederate counterparts at any given point along the lines. From their rifle pits, William Reid wrote his father, he and his comrades in the 15th Illinois could bring half a dozen rifles to bear against any one Rebel marksman who "dared to fire." Badger Stater Theodorus Northrup observed that as soon as any Confederate poked his head over the works, "more than 20 balls was sent at it." William Tunnard offered one of the largest ratios illustrating Yankee fire superiority. It had been "foolhardy" for any defender to expose himself above the parapet, the Louisiana veteran wrote, "as a hundred rifles immediately directed their missiles upon the man thus showing himself."[26]

Logistics helped shape the course of the sharpshooters' war. Grant's Army of the Tennessee enjoyed a steady stream of supplies via the Mississippi, providing the infantry with enough cartridges to burn to their hearts' content. According to Carlos Colby, men in the rifle pits could fire away "as often as a man wished to shoot," with most men going through "fifty to one hundred rounds a day" before being relieved. "Our men on average shoot away fifty rounds of cartri[d]ge," Colby also wrote, "which is at least ten times as much as the enemy, and the same way with the artillery." Hosea Rood similarly recounted that during the daylight hours "it was not uncommon for a man to use up from fifty to one hundred cartridges." Lucius Barber of the 15th Illinois reported that some managed to fire over 200 rounds in a day. Encouragement to blaze away came from no less than U. S. Grant himself. According to Barber, one day during the siege the commanding general "rode along the line and told the boys that he had plenty of ammunition and not to be afraid to use it."[27]

While Union sharpshooters could fire away with abandon, Confederate officers elected to conserve ammunition and limited how often their men could fire. Lewis Guion noted, "The men lie low all day in the trenches & rarely return the fire, as we have orders to save ammunition, our artillery never opens except in the charges." Ashbel Smith, colonel of the 2nd Texas, reported that his men were anxious "to return shot for shot, and with interest," but he had to obey the "daily . . . orders and admonitions" to save ammunition. By the final week of the siege, Smith's Texans had 54 rounds per man for their Enfields. With little chance of resupply, garrison commanders elected to retain enough powder and ball to meet any future Union attacks. Some Confederates tried to put a brave face on their ability to counter Yankee sharpshooters. "The fire from our trenches upon the enemy was slow and deliberate," reported Captain Amariah C. Roberds, commanding the 23rd Alabama. "We did not waste our powder, but no Abolitionist could show his head without danger from ball or buckshot." Some Union soldiers also concluded that the enemy must be deliberately holding their fire. "The rebels are growing very saving of their ammunition of late," William Reid observed in a June 5 diary entry, "and never fire except when we press them extra hard." Fellow 15th Illinois soldier Carlos Colby likewise reported, "The rebs are very spareing of their ammunition, they do not fire unless it to some purpose consequently we have but few men wounded."[28]

The Confederates' limited ammunition supply factored into Union dominance in the sharpshooters' war, but it was not necessarily the deciding factor. After Vicksburg's surrender, Confederate brigade commander Stephen D. Lee suggested in his official report that it would have been better to allow the garrison to return fire more aggressively. It had indeed been necessary to conserve ammunition, Lee allowed, but in hindsight he was "inclined to think caution in this respect was pushed rather to an extreme, and that a little more firing would have proved beneficial." Operating under the firing limits imposed on them, Confederate sharpshooters had still made themselves dangerous to the besiegers. However, even had the defenders been allowed to use more ammunition, they still would have had to contend with their more numerous Union adversaries and their bountiful ammunition supply. Taking a shot at the enemy still entailed putting oneself in harm's way, and in the defenders' trenches this was often too risky to attempt. Enemy sharpshooters were "extremely vigilant," Brigadier General Francis A. Shoup noted in his record of the siege, "and when one exposes himself in the least a number of guns are discharged simultaneously." Multiple accounts from both sides illustrate how through sheer numbers Federal infantry, backed up by aggressive artillery bombardments, managed to overwhelm and pin down the garrison through volume of fire.[29]

Outnumbered and outgunned, Confederate sharpshooters had still proved formidable enough not only to make the besiegers wary but to earn the Yankees' respect as well. Southern papers proudly boasted of the exploits of a one-eyed marksman in the 30th Alabama named Elliott, who "has already immortalized himself in the Yankee army." Known as the best shot in his state, Elliott reportedly used a Belgian rifle whose shots produced a unique whistling sound, prompting Union soldiers within earshot of his report to shout, "Look out, boys, there is old one-eye!" in warning. "Some of the Alabamians could perforate the bull's eye with great accuracy," Samuel Pryce wrote, "but the Texas 'rangers' were the best marksmen," ostensibly because they were "[t]rained to shoot wild buffalo on the dreamy landscapes of the 'panhandle.'" William Reid similarly attributed Rebel marksmanship to a strong hunting culture. The Illinoisan noted that the enemy sharpshooters "often make good shots, for they carry the same rifles that they have used ever since they first began to hunt squirrels in their native homes." In turn, some Confederates assumed their Yankee counterparts had also brought exceptional weapons to the sharpshooters' war. William Tunnard credited Union sharpshooters with "unerring precision" with "their splendid, long-range guns." In fact, both sides' sharpshooters fought primarily with the same standard-issue rifle and rifle-muskets as each other; what feats they achieved in marksmanship were more attributable to native or recently acquired skill than to specialized weaponry.[30]

One Confederate officer scored a small victory against the besiegers using an ordinary rifle with unconventional ammunition. Union forces had created a unique rolling sap to approach the 3rd Louisiana Redan. They mounted a train car bed onto wheels and stacked it with cotton bales, making it impervious to musketry. Lieutenant W. M. Washburn thought of trying to set the sap on fire by filling the hollow bases of Enfield bullets with cotton saturated with turpentine. Washburn fired three of his improvised incendiary rounds into the "hated object" while his comrades intently watched for the result. After some time with no flames appearing, those men not standing guard returned to camp in disappointment. Then someone cried out that the sap was indeed burning. Smoke was issuing from the cotton bales, which soon burst into flames. Five companies of Louisianans sprang to the breastworks and began "a contestant and rapid fire" that prevented the besiegers from extinguishing the flames. "The achievement was a source of general satisfaction and rejoicing," William Tunnard remembered in the regimental history. "The Yankees could not understand how their movable breastwork was thus given to destruction, under their very eyes."[31]

Lieutenant Washburn's destruction of the rolling sap offered a bright spot for the often-beleaguered garrison. While suppressing Confederate musketry was Union sharpshooters' most significant contribution to siege operations at Vicksburg, their fire also helped erode enemy morale. Pemberton's garrison remained remarkably resilient and hopeful throughout the siege, yet the daily threat of Yankee riflemen made life in the trenches understandably unnerving and wearisome for the defenders. In a May 27 diary entry, Captain Gabriel Killgore of the 17th Louisiana lamented, "This is now the 10th day that we have been cooped up here under an incessant fire of almost all kinds of firearms." Fellow Louisianan Jared Sanders voiced his own frustration at being under siege: "This is quite a school for patience. We are shut in from the world & and are a *constant* target for the hostile soldiery outside." The threat of Union sharpshooters not only made life dangerous for the garrison but added to their discomfort as well. "I pitied our poor soldiers the night of the rain storm," staff officer Henry Ginder wrote his wife, "lying in it all night [and] unable to do anything else next morning for fear of the Yankee sharpshooters, who expend more ammunition in one day than we have on hand."[32]

While Pemberton's men endured being cooped-up targets, many of Grant's soldiers thrilled to take part in the sharpshooters' war. William Reid, the Illinois sharpshooter who took it as a compliment if the enemy returned his fire, recorded how his comrades "enjoyed themselves by shooting at the rebel in and around the forts, some half mile away." Entire units worked shifts on sharpshooter duty, but some soldiers eagerly took part on their own time, as George Ditto of the 5th Iowa noted: "Many of the men consider the sharp shooting fun and many when not otherwise engaged will take their pockets full of ammunition & go to [the] skirmish line." With plentiful ammunition, enthusiastic riflemen could hone their target shooting. "If this siege is to last a month, there will be a whole army of trained sharpshooters," Osborn Oldroyd boasted, "for the practice we are getting is making us skilled marksmen."[33]

Not all soldiers shared in the enthusiasm for sharpshooting. To Edward Potter of the 29th Wisconsin, "[T]his going out once or twice a day to shoot at human beings like ourselves seems strong business to me yet the boys all like better to shoot at a man than to shoot at the loop holes of the Fort." Potter's account not only places him among those Civil War soldiers who felt ambivalently about killing in combat but illustrates that he perceived he was in the minority in that regard. Most of his comrades seemed to enjoy sharpshooting against the enemy. Moreover, Potter indicates that it was possible to engage in sharpshooting by firing at loopholes and other points from which the enemy might fire to keep the defenders' heads down, but most of Potter's comrades evidently preferred shooting to kill than simply providing suppressing fire.[34]

Sharpshooting proved so popular in the Army of the Tennessee that some officers took part along with the enlisted men. Chaplain Nathan M. Baker of the 116th Illinois, one of the Civil War's "fighting chaplains," not only explored the rifle pits and saps but sniped from them as well. On one occasion, Baker laid down behind a stout log to exchange "compliments" with the Rebels. "[F]ive times I fired deliberately, each time at a head which was incautiously exposed," the chaplain recorded in his diary, "and once, I fired at a man's arm which he raised to its full length above the ditch while loading his gun, which he had just fired at me." Baker often fought alongside his friend Captain Thomas White, and the pair experienced several close calls in their skirmishes with Confederate marksmen. In one such instance, White had worked an opening between some sandbags with a pick handle. No sooner had he put his eye to the improvised loophole, a Confederate bullet zipped through, striking White under the right eye. Baker feared his friend's wound would prove mortal, but White survived, only to be killed the following year during the fight for Atlanta.[35]

One of the most active sharpshooting officers in Grant's army was Lieutenant Colonel William E. Strong, a member of General James B. McPherson's staff. Just as Southerner papers extolled the marksmanship of "Old One-Eye," *Harper's Weekly* celebrated the exploits of Lieutenant Colonel Strong, including an artist's rendering of the Badger Stater plying the sharpshooter's trade on its front page. The staff officer, "a fine shot," helped other Seventeenth Corps sharpshooters silence Confederate artillery on their front, prompting a Rebel marksman to crawl out from the works to engage them. Strong turned to the old sharpshooter's trick and placed his hat on the bank in front of him. The Confederate obligingly put a bullet through the inviting target. "The moment was the rebel's last: he had exposed his head in shooting," *Harper's* triumphantly reported. "And the sharp-shooting officer now wears an airy hat."[36]

Perhaps no officer in the Army of the Tennessee fought in the sharpshooter's war at Vicksburg as energetically as Henry C. Foster, second lieutenant in the 23rd Indiana. Foster earned the nickname "Coonskin" for the iconic frontier headgear he eccentrically chose to wear. In the opening weeks of the siege, Foster would venture between the lines with several days' worth of food, fashion a well-protected shooting position, and lie in wait for targets. Such tactics, Solonick suggests, mark Foster as "perhaps the closest thing to a modern sniper lurking in the trenches around Vicksburg." In early June, Coonskin Foster and his comrades began work on "Coonskin's Tower" on the approach to the 3rd Louisiana Redan. The Hoosiers built the tower out of sturdy railroad ties, apparently filling the interior with earth. "Learned in backwoods lore," Foster's colonel wrote of him, "he knew how to construct the genuine pioneer log-cabin." Rising as high as forty feet by some accounts, Coonskin's Tower allowed those who climbed its ladder to look down and fire into Confederate defenses. Standing out against the skyline, Coonskin's Tower was also an obvious target for Rebel marksmen who riddled its timbers with musket balls. To maintain his watch on the enemy, Foster rigged a mirror to the far side of his shooting platform that allowed him to observe the defenders without exposing himself. When a target presented itself, Foster could quickly take aim, fire, and drop back behind cover before anyone could take a shot at him. Union soldiers authored conflicting accounts of the fate of Coonskin's Tower. Some sources claim that Confederate guns smashed it to "smithereens" or enemy musketry made it untenable, while other men insisted Foster and his comrades kept it standing. Federal sharpshooters' ability to keep enemy artillery silent seems to have helped protect the tower from destruction. In fact, photographic evidence proves that Coonskin's Tower survived the siege intact, a unique testament to Yankee ingenuity.[37]

On July 4, 1863, Vicksburg's surrender silenced the rifles and artillery. Union soldiers marched into city they had campaigned so many months to conquer. Confederate prisoners, having subsisted on reduced rations during the siege, fed on Federal provisions. The spirit of brotherhood and comradery between the opposing sides that had kindled episodically during the siege appeared in full force as Yankees and Rebels intermingled. The day after the surrender, Missouri Rebel Theodore Fisher recorded in his diary, "The wharf is filled with Confederate and Federal soldiers conversing as if no hostilities ever existed." Wilbur Crummer's comrades in the 45th Illinois reported that paroled Confederates told how Union sharpshooting had taken a "right smart" toll on them and yet still expressed their desire that "'we'uns' and 'you'uns' could have this war ended and live together in peace." The former besiegers and besieged "felt they were countrymen." Yet the war was not over, and these American soldiers were still officially enemies. Many of Pemberton's garrison would find their way back into Confederate ranks, and the hardy westerners of Grant, Sherman, and McPherson would fight their way farther into the heart of Dixie. Soldiers who had fought one another among Vicksburg's hills and ravines would face off again across battle lines, skirmish lines, and siege lines.[38]

Sharpshooting represented more than simply random killing across opposing trench lines. Rather, the contest between the sharpshooters of Grant's and Pemberton's armies played critical roles in the practice of siege warfare. Confederate marksmen fought to keep the besiegers at bay and, though constrained by limited supplies and orders to husband their ammunition, had nonetheless made themselves a considerable threat to the enemy. That threat contributed to the policy by Grant and his generals to deploy Union infantrymen *en masse* as sharpshooters to diminish the defenders' firepower. Fighting from its rifle pits and breastworks, the Army of the Tennessee achieved considerable success in suppressing Rebel fire, which in turn had helped other siege operations play their own roles in reducing the Confederate Gibraltar. Union sharpshooting further contributed to that goal by wearing down the embattled garrison both in numbers and morale. Union and Confederate soldiers fought as sharpshooters as part of their duty, but many also eagerly took part in a thrilling but dangerous battle of marksmanship and wits. Few of the men in blue and gray scanning enemy lines with fingers on triggers were specially trained or equipped as sharpshooters. Ordinary soldiers with ordinary weapons had fought the sharpshooters' war in summer 1863 and in doing so wrote one of the most dramatic chapters in the siege of Vicksburg.

Notes

1. Samuel D. Pryce, *Vanishing Footprints: The Twenty-Second Iowa Volunteer Infantry in the Civil War*, ed. Jeffry C. Burden (Iowa City, IA: Camp Pope Bookshop, 2008), 134.

2. Frank Wilkeson, *Recollections of a Private Soldier in the Army of the Potomac* (New York: G. P. Putnam's Sons, 1887), 120–21.

3. Quoted in Allan C. Richard Jr. and Mary Margaret Higginbotham Richard, *The Defense of Vicksburg: A Louisiana Chronicle* (College Station: Texas A&M University Press, 2004), 147.

4. James B. Taylor diary, May 22, 1863, 120th Ohio Regimental File, Vicksburg National Military Park (hereafter cited as VNMP); Samuel C. Jones, *Reminiscences of the Twenty-Second Iowa Volunteer Infantry* (Iowa City, IA: S. C. Jones, 1907), 39; quoted in Walter F. Beyer and Oscar F. Keydel, comp., *Deeds of Valor: How America's Heroes Won the Medal of Honor* (Detroit: Perrien-Keydel, 1901), 196; Pryce, *Vanishing Footprints*, 119.

5. Elias Moore diary, May 23, 1863, 114th Ohio Regimental File, VNMP; Cornelius DuBois to V. E. Howell, March 9, 1903, 33rd Illinois Regimental File, VNMP.

6. Frank H. Mason, *The Forty-Second Ohio Infantry: A History of the Organization and Services of that Regiment in the War of the Rebellion* (Cleveland: Cobb, Andrews, 1876), 228.

7. Wilbur F. Crummer, *With Grant at Fort Donelson, Shiloh, and Vicksburg* (Oak Park, IL: E. C. Crummer, 1915), 128, 144; Anthony B. Burton diary, May 24, 1863, 5th Ohio Independent Battery, Diaries and Letters Files, VNMP; Jefferson Brumback to "My dear Kate," May 23, 1863, 95th Ohio Regimental File, VNMP; William A. Drennan diary, June 14, 1863, Diaries and Letters Files, VNMP. Original emphasis.

8. Crummer, *With Grant at Fort Donelson, Shiloh, and Vicksburg*, 115; Jared Young Sanders II, *Diary in Gray: The Civil War Letters and Diary of Jared Young Sanders, II*, ed. Mary Elizabeth Sanders (Baton Rouge: Louisiana Genealogical & Historical Society, 1994), 26; Jefferson Brumback to Kate Brumback, May 23, 1863; G. W. Crosley diary, June 12, 1863, 3rd Iowa Regimental File, VNMP.

9. E. L. Hawk to W. T. Rigby, April 21, 1914, 114th Ohio Regimental File, VNMP; Pryce, *Vanishing Footprints*, 134; Osborn H. Oldroyd, *A Soldier's Story of the Siege of Vicksburg* (Springfield, IL: n.p., 1885), 35.

10. Phillip Thomas Tucker, *Westerners in Gray: The Men and Missions of the Elite Fifth Missouri Regiment* (Jefferson, NC: McFarland, 1995), 242; Carlos W. Colby, "Bullets, Hardtack, and Mud: A Soldier's View of the Vicksburg Campaign," ed. John S. Painter, *Journal of the West* 4, no. 2 (April 1965): 160; Oldroyd, *A Soldier's Story of the Siege of Vicksburg*, 59; William Taylor to Jane Taylor, June 28, 1863, 100th Pennsylvania Regimental File, VNMP.

11. James A. Fowler and Miles M. Miller, *History of the Thirtieth Iowa Infantry Volunteers* (Mediapolis, IA: T. A. Merrill, 1908), 30; Edward N. Potter diary, May 28, 1863, Wisconsin Veterans Museum; William H. Raynor diary, May 25, 1863, 56th Ohio Regimental File, VNMP.

12. Lewis Guion quoted in Richard and Richard, *The Defense of Vicksburg*, 156–57; Augustus G. Sinks diary, May 24, 1863, 46th Indiana Regimental File, VNMP; William H. Raynor diary, June 11, 1863, 56th Ohio Regimental File, VNMP.

13. William H. Tunnard, *A Southern Record: The History of the Third Regiment Louisiana Infantry* (Baton Rouge: n.p., 1866), 264; William R. Clack diary, May 24 and June 21, 1863, Diaries and Letters Files, VNMP; John Fuller diary, 31st Louisiana Regimental File, VNMP.

14. William Reid to "Dear Father," June 8, 1863, 15th Illinois Infantry, Diaries and Letters Files, VNMP; Tunnard, *A Southern Record*, 244, 248; Thomas Gordon diary, June 23, 1863, 1st Minnesota Battery File, VNMP; Orange Parret diary, June 3, 1863, 77th Illinois Regimental File, VNMP; Taylor Peirce to Catharine Peirce, June 13, 1863, in *Dear Catharine, Dear Taylor: The Civil War Letters of a Union Soldier and His Wife*, ed. Richard L. Kiper (Lawrence: University Press of Kansas, 2002), 115–16; Joseph Bowker diary, June 21, 1863, 42nd Ohio Regimental File, VNMP.

15. Hosea W. Rood, *Story of the Service of Company E, and of the Twelfth Wisconsin Regiment, Veteran Volunteer Infantry, in the War of the Rebellion* (Milwaukee: Swain & Tate, 1893), 193.

16. Joseph Bowker diary, June 8, 1863, 42nd Ohio Regimental File, VNMP; William H. Raynor diary, May 25, 1863, 56th Ohio Regimental File, VNMP.

17. Sanders, *Diary in Gray*, 21.

18. Robert S. Bevier, *History of the First and Second Missouri Confederate Brigades, 1861–1865* (St. Louis: Bryan, Brand, 1879), 211.

19. Rood, *Story of the Service*, 192; Jefferson Brumback to Kate Brumback, June 11, 1863; Gordon diary, June 10, 1863.

20. Rood, *Story of the Service*, 192–93.

21. C. J. Durham diary, May 24, 1863, 11th Indiana Regimental File, VNMP; Justin S. Solonick, *Engineering Victory: The Union Siege of Vicksburg* (Carbondale: Southern Illinois University Press, 2015), 135.

22. Grant to Julia Dent Grant, June 15, 1863, in *The Papers of Ulysses S. Grant*, ed. John Y. Simon (Carbondale: Southern Illinois University Press, 1979), 8:377; Joseph Bowker diary, May 24, 1863, 42nd Ohio Regimental File, VNMP; William Reid to "Dear Father," June 24, 1863, Diaries and Letters Files, VNMP; M. Ebenezer Wescott to "Dear Parents," June 20, 1863, in *Civil War Letters, 1861 to 1865: Written by a Boy in Blue to His Mother* (Mora, MN: n.p., 1909), n.p.; Mason, *The Forty-Second Ohio Infantry*, 228; Oldroyd, *A Soldier's Story of the Siege of Vicksburg*, 46.

23. Jefferson Brumback to Kate Brumback, June 11, 1863; James B. Taylor diary, May 23, 1863.

24. Colby, "Bullets, Hardtack, and Mud," 151; William Reid to "Dear Father," June 8, 1863; Ibid., June 11, 1863; Tunnard, *A Southern Record*, 238.

25. Theodorus Northrup to "Ever Dear Mother," June 14, 1863, 23rd Wisconsin Regimental File, VNMP; N. M. Baker diary, June 13, 1863, 116th Illinois Regimental Files, VNMP.

26. William Reid to "Dear Father," June 24, 1863; Theodorus Northrup to "Friend Ira," May 26, 1863; Tunnard, *A Southern Record*, 238.

27. Colby, "Bullets, Hardtack, and Mud," 152, 156; Rood, *Story of the Service*, 196; Lucius W. Barber, *Army Memoirs of Lucius W. Barber, Company "D," 15th Illinois Volunteer Infantry* (Chicago: J. M. W. Jones, 1894), 112.

28. Quoted in Richard and Richard, *The Defense of Vicksburg*, 165; U.S. War Department, *The War of the Rebellion: A Compilation of the Official Records of the Union and Confederate Armies*, 128 vols. (Washington, DC: Government Printing Office, 1880–1901), series 1, vol. 24, pt. 2:391–92. Hereafter cited as *OR*. All references are to series 1 unless otherwise indicated; Ibid., vol. 24, pt. 2:353; William Reid diary, June 5, 1863, 15th Illinois Infantry, Diaries and Letters Files, VNMP; Colby, "Bullets, Hardtack, and Mud," 158.

29. *OR*, vol. 24, pt. 2, 398; Ibid., vol. 24, pt. 2, 408.

30. "The Siege of Vicksburg," *Charleston Mercury*, 8 June 1863; Pryce, *Vanishing Footprints*, 135; William Reid to "Dear Father," June 11, 1863; Tunnard, *A Southern Record*, 236–37.

31. Tunnard, *A Southern Record*, 246–48.

32. Quoted in Richard and Richard, *The Defense of Vicksburg*, 169; Sanders, *Diary in Gray*, 23; Henry Ginder to Mary Ginder, June 12, 1863, in Richard and Richard, *The Defense of Vicksburg*, 195.

33. Reid diary, June 10, 1863; George Ditto Diary, June 6, 1863, Abraham Lincoln Presidential Library; Oldroyd, *A Soldier's Story of the Siege of Vicksburg*, 34.

34. Edward N. Potter diary, June 6, 1863.

35. Baker diary, May 29, 1863; Ibid., June 27, 1863; Solonick, *Engineering Victory*, 138.

36. "The Siege of Vicksburg," *Harper's Weekly*, 27 June 1863.

37. Solonick, *Engineering Victory*, 128–32; Lt. Col. W. P. Davis, quoted in Andrew Hickenlooper, "The Vicksburg Mine," in *Battles and Leaders of the Civil War*, ed. Robert Underwood Johnson and Clarence Clough Buel (New York: Century, 1888), 3:2:543; Oldroyd, *A Soldier's Story of the Siege of Vicksburg*, 47, 49.

38. Theodore D. Fisher diary, July 5, 1863, 1st Missouri Infantry, Diaries and Letters Files, VNMP; Crummer, *With Grant at Fort Donelson, Shiloh, and Vicksburg*, 159–60.

4

NIGHTS AT VICKSBURG

Steven E. Woodworth

The daylight hours were dangerous during the Vicksburg siege. Thousands of troops of both armies, acting as sharpshooters, eagerly scanned enemy positions for possible targets. A man who raised himself above the rim of his trench or rifle pit, or who peered through a gun port in the earthworks, could count on becoming, within seconds, the target of several bullets. "As soon as a man sticks his head above the top of the hill," wrote an Iowa soldier during the siege, "hiss comes a bullet at him."[1]

Artillery was also active by day as targets offered themselves in the opposing positions. Experienced gunners had the range and had their guns well sighted in. Their fire was generally accurate, sometimes amazingly so. Some progress could be made on the Union approach trenches by day, at least until the head-of-sap got too close to the Confederate works, but for the most part, the days of the Vicksburg siege were times of lying low, keeping under cover, or at most peering toward the enemy's position over one's gunsights.

Not so the nights. The nocturnal interludes of the Vicksburg siege were the most fluid and dynamic part of the six-week deadlock around the perimeter of the Confederate stronghold. Whereas the daylight hours were static and predictably deadly, the periods between dusk and dawn placed soldiers in situations ranging from the natural immunity of darkness, to an unnatural immunity due to the foe's indifference, to outright fraternization with the enemy—but always with the possibility that a small but deadly battle might break out on the darkened slopes of no-man's-land.

Night was the time when the most serious and dangerous work was done on the Union approach trenches. The Federals could always make better progress in the dark than they could in the daylight when great caution had to be taken to avoid the least exposure above the trench rim. As the approaches edged closer to the Confederate works, daylight work became prohibitively dangerous, and all further digging had to be done at night.[2] Along with the relative safety came the added benefit that such laborious work was much more comfortable by night than under the heat of the midsummer Mississippi sun. When light was needed for such nocturnal excavations, there was nothing to do but rely on the moon. On May 26 a soldier of the 8th Illinois noted that his regiment dug trenches only during the three hours of good moonlight the preceding night.[3]

Nights on the Vicksburg lines were a strange mix of war and peace. They were quiet only in contrast to the much louder noise of the days. Union artillery, including the gunboats and mortar boats in the river, continued to bombard Vicksburg and its defenses throughout the nights. The fire of the mortars, with their high parabolic trajectories marked by the light of burning fuses on their shells, was especially pleasant to watch for those who were not its targets.[4] The Confederate artillery was also sometimes active at night, though more sparing of its ammunition. Lieutenant William Reid of the 15th Illinois was impressed with the accuracy of Confederate artillery fire directed toward a Union work detail between the lines on the night of June 17–18.[5] And despite the many informal truces around the Confederate perimeter, there was still enough rifle fire that an Iowa soldier noted on June 16 that the sound of cannon and musketry was continuous "both day and night."[6]

Night infantry action was also possible because of Union forays into no-man's-land to advance the siege works. At 7 P.M. on the evening of June 14, the 33rd Wisconsin was ordered into line along its own rifle pits, supplied with a standard combat load of sixty rounds of ammunition per man. Through the evening hours the Union artillery kept up a heavier than usual fire, and the mortar boats in the river were also unusually active. At 10 P.M. the order came for the regiment to advance into no-man's-land in line of battle. The troops moved forward about 200 yards across a crest in their front and were ordered to lie down just in front of it. There they waited through the rest of the night as a covering force protecting Union fatigue parties digging a new line of works just behind them. The Wisconsin men had no opportunity to burn any of their sixty cartridges that night, but the possibility of combat at any moment kept everyone on edge.[7]

Confederates sometimes tried to use the hours of darkness to smuggle needed supplies into Vicksburg. Food was needed but too bulky for smuggling. Percussion caps were another matter. On the night of May 29–30, a picket detail of the 15th Illinois detected movement in a canebrake along one of the roads leading into Vicksburg. They gave a challenge and, when the movement continued, fired a volley. Two Rebels emerged from the cane, surrendering. Sensing that more were present, the Illinoisans plunged into the thicket and pulled out nine others. All but one of the Confederates wore a pack containing 20,000 caps, badly needed by Pemberton's army and which the captured Rebels had been trying to slip past Union lines.[8]

By contrast, many Confederate enlisted men along the Vicksburg line were willing to engage in conversation or even trade with their daytime enemies. The siege was only a few days old in late May when Gould Molineaux of the 8th Illinois commented on the wholesale nocturnal fraternization. Every night, as darkness fell, the shooting stopped, and the men who had just been trying to kill each other began talking. He described the siege as "shooting with vengeance all day and talk it over at night & war through the day & peace at night." This went on, Molineaux noted, "until [the Confederate] officers stopped it."[9]

Sometimes Confederates tried to use the nightly fraternization to advance their own propaganda message. Jacob Ritner of the 25th Iowa wrote his wife on May 30 regarding the previous night's discussions, "One fellow tried to make us a speech." The Confederate orator claimed he and his comrades had nothing against the people of the Northwest and did not want to fight them. The South's quarrel, he claimed, was with the Yankees. "If we would go home they would give us the free navigation of the river." Ritner and his comrades were unimpressed. "I told him we did not ask them to give us the river we were going to take it that we would have the free navigation of the river and not go home either till we got ready," Ritner recounted. He added, "So you see we talk friendly at night and shoot at each other all day."[10]

More often, Confederates expressed discouragement in the nighttime confabs between the lines. On June 16 Iowa soldier Taylor Peirce wrote to his wife, "The reble soldiers are all tired of the war and if it was not for their leaders this war would close in a month for they all acknowledge that they can never whip us and would be glad to lay down their arms."[11]

By mid-June opposing soldiers in some sectors had a regular system of signaling their desire to talk or trade. That same June 16, Wisconsin soldier Samuel Kirkpatrick wrote his family, "When we go out on picket, when we hear one whisel, we answer him, and he preposes to leave his arms and meet half way and have a talk." Kirkpatrick expected his family to be incredulous at such reports, but he assured them it was true. "We will meat and spend a hour or two talking," he explained, adding that knives and canteens were among the popular items of exchange.[12] A brisk trade also went on in coffee and tobacco. A much more valued and unusual item changed hands, apparently as a free gift, when a soldier of the 54th Ohio received a picture of his sweetheart that the Rebels had captured from his tent when they had overrun the 54th's camp at the Battle of Shiloh.[13]

Lieutenant William Reid of Waukegan, Illinois, along with several of his men from Company I, 15th Illinois, "had quite a long talk with the rebels of the 52nd Georgia regiment." The Georgians, they learned, were from the southern part of that state, but they had relations living in Lake County, Illinois, where Waukegan was located. Reid mused in his diary that one of the Rebels with whom he had talked might be his uncle.[14]

By late June, Kirkpatrick noted that men of his regiment conversed with the Rebels all night and even gave them some of their hardtack. The gift or exchange of hardtack, though definitely an aspect of fraternization that worked in favor of the Confederates, was not a unique case at all, but occurred in a number of sectors, driven not by low morale on the Union side but rather by confidence and pity. The Federals had plenty of food, and the Rebels were on short rations.[15]

Despite the occasional insignificant amounts of food Confederates might have gained, these exchanges of goods and information were, in their nature, inherently disadvantageous to the defenders, and the chief opponents of such activity were Confederate officers. Sometimes, however, even Union officers acted on a belief that people who were enemies ought to be enemies round the clock and ordered their men to break off fraternization and resume hostile activity. The soldiers obeyed but contrived to keep faith with their off-duty friends across the way. When officers demanded the troops resume firing, wrote Wisconsin soldier Arthur Robinson, "We hail them with 'Johnny, look out for we are going to shoot,' and they do the same to us."[16]

On one occasion, however, a friendly nighttime conversation across the lines turned sour. The men of the 76th Ohio were in the habit of sitting on top of their breastworks at night to exchange jibes and comments with the Confederates opposite them, who sat atop their own works a few yards away. Each side had a glib-tongued spokesman who did most of its talking. Both sides generally laughed at the witty remarks. One night, however, the Ohio spokesman inadvertently revealed the difference between the limits that applied to good-natured jibes in his own state and the more restrictive limits on such statements in the South. As one of his comrades in the 76th said, "He let his wit run away with his discretion." In later years, even some of his fellow Ohioans thought the remark had been "neither fitting nor nice." The Confederate response was more forceful. "We were lolling on top of the works taking things easy and listening to the conversation," wrote Ohioan Charles Willison, "when this insult was passed over to our friends across the way. Suddenly, over there, there was a flash and before we realized a volley of grape and cannister whistled uncomfortably close overhead." Perhaps the Confederate cannon had been deliberately sighted high. "The danger was past before we could move," Willison added, but he and his comrades lost no time tumbling helter-skelter onto the safe side of their breastworks. "Luckily no one was hit."[17]

Low Confederate morale could lead to an unwillingness to take any active measure to defend against the progress of the Union siege. By June 23, the 29th Wisconsin's pickets were posted little more than fifteen yards from the foremost Confederate outposts. "But a mutual understanding seems to exist that neither party shall fire first," a Wisconsin soldier wrote his family, "and as yet we have not been molested." Even with such an understanding, it was not considered safe to get too close to the enemy. A couple of nights earlier, one of the Wisconsin soldiers had blundered in the darkness right among a number of Rebels. Diving back into the night, he crouched flat to the ground and "crawfished his way" back to Union lines.[18]

On June 26, Iowa soldier Nathan Dye wrote his friends back home describing an even more complete collapse of Confederate morale. Rebel defenders in front of his regiment had for some time had an agreement not to shoot if the Federals would not shoot at them. Thus freed of the need to maintain any cover at all, the Union fatigue parties had dug closer and closer to the Confederate fortifications every night, while Rebels made no effort to stop them. With the rival parties now within easy speaking distance, the graycoats commented from time to time that their blue-clad opponents were wasting their time. "It is of no use to dig," they said. It was "work for nothing" because the Confederates knew "that there is no show for them, but they are bound to hold out till the last." Sometimes the Rebels' resignation reached almost ludicrous degrees. When Iowa fatigue parties found that Confederate pickets were posted where the Iowans wanted to dig, they would call out that fact, and the Rebel pickets would fall back "without grumbling."[19]

The same low Confederate morale reflected in a willingness to enter into fraternization that was, for the most part, favorable to the steady approach of the besieging army, was also displayed in nocturnal desertions. "All through the siege," recalled a Union soldier, "every once in a while we would hear a rebel from between our lines and the rebel lines calling in a suppressed voice, say yank don't shoot I want to come over and surrender and the officer in charge would answer all right come ahead and word would be passed down the line not to shoot."[20] Gould Molineaux noted on May 25 that "two or three" Confederate deserters entered the lines of the 8th Illinois in a single night.[21]

Sometimes fraternization eased the process of crossing the lines. Wisconsin soldier James Newton noted in his diary entry of June 5 that it was becoming common for soldiers of the opposing armies to meet in no-man's-land at night for conversation and coffee, adding, "It very often happens too that the rebels do not go back again, preferring to stop with our men until they can be sent north."[22] Two brothers in Missouri regiments, one Union, the other Confederate, met one night between the lines, and the Confederate brother decided to come over to the Union side and surrender so he could "go home and see the old folks."[23] Confederate soldiers who took the oath of allegiance were free to live out the war north of the Ohio River.

However, as Union lines crept critically close to the Confederate defenses, the tension between war and peace, the camaraderie of men enduring similar hardships, and the duty of soldiers to resist the enemy became more pronounced. A sector of the front that had been characterized by a de facto nightly truce could change to a tense and potentially deadly situation with little warning. Violent nighttime clashes were not rare, especially in the later weeks of the siege. Another Wisconsin soldier wrote, "Not a night passes without a fracas with the enemy."[24]

Sometimes the cause of the nighttime clash was lingering animosity from the events of the preceding day or several preceding days. The 33rd Wisconsin found itself in line opposite the 1st Missouri (Confederate), part of the high-morale Confederate Missouri Brigade. The Missourians became angry at the success the Wisconsin men were having in sharpshooting and, in conversations across no-man's-land, had threatened to give the Federals "h-ll." On the night of June 23, as one wing of the 33rd was pushing its sap closer to the defenses, the Missourians launched "quite a spirited attack" against them. Colonel Jonathan Moore, in command of the 33rd, was at the point attacked and took over direction of the defense. With no visual signals possible in the darkness, Moore, a prewar constable and later sheriff of Platteville, Wisconsin, had to shout loudly over the din of battle to make his commands heard. After he bellowed an order "for the men to retain their fire until the enemy were close enough to burn them with our powder," the Rebels pulled back, and the Wisconsin soldiers concluded that the prospect of a close-range volley had deterred them from further attack.[25]

On the night of June 26–27, the 46th Indiana regiment experienced a tense situation that could easily have resulted in serious bloodshed. At the same time, it was not without its own ludicrous character as well. "We had quite an exciting time last evening," Indiana soldier Aurelius Voorhis wrote in his diary the next day. Shortly after nightfall, the Indiana pickets had moved up very close to the Confederate fortifications. "This did not suit the rebs, so an officer of theirs got up and told our men to fall back to the former line." That was not consistent with the Hoosiers' orders from their own officers, so they "paid no attention to him." The Confederate officer repeated his orders, with the same lack of effect. So the Confederates pulled their own pickets back into their entrenched line, an obvious prelude to opening fire. Then the Rebel officer again ordered "our pickets to fall back or they would help them to do so." At this, the Indiana pickets fell back to the cover of a small hollow a short distance to the rear, and the rest of the regiment turned out and formed battle line along its rifle pits. A silent standoff followed, but after a few minutes the Confederates redeployed their picket line just where it had been before. So the Indiana fatigue party went back out and started digging again, just where it had been before. The Rebels fired two shots over the heads of the working party, harming no one, and the digging went on.[26]

The next night it seemed as if sweet reasonableness—and low Confederate morale—was going to prevail in front of the 46th Indiana. The fatigue party for the night of June 27–28 returned to camp in the morning, reporting that the Rebels had "proposed not to fire on our working parties if we would not fire on them." The besiegers, who had the task of digging right up to the foot of the Confederate works, were naturally quite agreeable to that arrangement. But on the evening of June 28, the Hoosier fatigue party had scarcely started work before word came back to the 46th's camp that the Confederates "had ordered us to stop working or they would fire." Additional companies of Hoosiers moved out through the darkness in line of battle, but the Rebels did not fire, and the work party kept on digging.[27]

Two nights later, the tension ratcheted up again. On this night, Voorhis and his comrade Tom Stuart formed one of a dozen or so pairs of soldiers assigned to serve as outposts protecting the working party. At first the night seemed peaceful enough, and Voorhis was thinking of his friends and family back home and wondering what they were thinking "when all at once the rebels fired on our working party."[28]

Snatching up his rifle, he dived for the ground, but finding the position a little too exposed even when lying prone, he and Stuart crawfished back to a hollow where the other outposts were rallying. To Stuart, that seemed too cowardly, so he crawled back up to their previous position and loosed a shot at the Rebels. "The flash of his gun brought half a dozen balls whizzing around us," Voorhis recounted, and the sergeant of the detail ordered Stuart to get back down in the hollow. The shooting died out on both sides, and the night became as quiet as before. Not knowing what they should do about the flare-up of firing they had just seen and heard, the Hoosier outpost troops reflected that it was almost midnight, when they were scheduled to be relieved by troops of their regiment's Company G and the restless Rebels in the vicinity would be someone else's problem. After relief, Voorhis returned to the camp of the 46th, turned in, and went right to sleep. The night remained quiet, and he did not wake up "until the shooting for the day commenced."[29]

A Wisconsin soldier had a far more disturbing experience during a nocturnal skirmish about that stage of the siege. One night about the end of June, Michael Haffey of Company C, 33rd Wisconsin, opposite those pesky Missourians, was on duty with his company, which was providing flank cover for three other companies digging approaches practically at the foot of the Confederate works. When the Rebels attempted to drive off the diggers, the lieutenant commanding Company C ordered his men into line and said they were going to move to the support of neighboring Company H. Due to his height, Haffey's place in line was on the extreme left of the company, which, since Company C was the 33rd's color company, put him right beside the color-bearer—except that on this night they had left the colors and color-bearer back in camp. So Haffey had nothing but darkness on his left.

The lieutenant ordered the company to form single file, instead of the usual two-file line, and then he ordered "left face," and "double-quick march." Or at least that is what Haffey thought he heard. Trotting into what he remembered as a "very dark" night, he was carrying his rifle in his right hand at "trail arms" when he tripped over something and fell forward against a dirt embankment. He had barely time to ask himself where he was before a gunport opened in the embankment several feet above his head and a cannon roared. "The concussion lifted me off the ground," he recalled. "Before [he] had time to think," which under the circumstances may have been several seconds, a cannon on the opposite line of works thundered a reply. Haffey was later sure the shot had passed directly between his legs before burying itself in the dirt embankment. At any rate, it "nearly covered [him] with dirt."

Haffey needed no more hints to know it was time to move and quickly. He rolled down the slope of the embankment into the fort's shallow ditch. There he found what had tripped him. The Confederates had strung telegraph wire between a number of stakes to trip attackers, and it had worked perfectly on Michael Haffey. His company was nowhere to be seen, so he continued to work his way to the rear, scooting backward on his belly and thankful that the way back to camp was all downhill and fairly steep. He had not gone far before the muzzle flash from another discharge of the cannon he had nearly blundered into caught him in the open and lit him up. A ragged volley of shots from the Confederate parapet told him he had been seen, but he kept scooting, and the darkness swallowed him up again.

Back at the 33rd's camp, he found the colonel but no Company C. Eager to locate his missing company, the colonel had Haffey lead the major out to the place where he had last seen the company. Sure enough, there it was, just where it had been when Haffey had left-faced and trotted off into the inky blackness toward the Confederate works. The major set them to digging, and that night they dug the section of trench they occupied until the end of the siege, only a few yards from the Rebel works.[30]

Sometimes even when the approach trenches had reached to the very foot of the Confederate works, fraternization continued at night. Elisha Stockwell of the 14th Wisconsin noted that even when little more than ten yards separated Union and Confederate works in his sector, the two sides remained on mostly friendly terms at night. "Moonlight nights they used to agree to have a talk," Stockwell wrote, "and both sides would get up on the breastworks and blackguard each other and laugh and sing songs for an hour at a time, then get down and commence shooting again," presumably when daylight came.[31]

At times the proximity of the opposing lines led to accidental encounters that had the potential to be deadly or friendly. A Union captain was making the rounds of his pickets one night when he accidently strayed into Confederate territory and suddenly found himself face to face with a Rebel captain and his picket detail. Quickly recovering from his surprise, the Union captain pointed his cocked revolver at his counterpart's head and threatened to blow the Confederate captain's brains out if the Rebels tried to take him prisoner. The Confederates promised on their honor to let him go free, but the Rebel captain suggested they sit down for a friendly chat first. They did and had a nice conversation. After exchanging copies of the latest newspapers from the rival siege lines, they shook hands, and the Federal captain went back to his side of the lines.[32]

The nights of the Vicksburg siege showed the operation in its most varied, dynamic, and often surprising form. They also displayed the key difference in morale between the two sides. Confederate morale in late May was not as weak as Grant had hoped and was still stout enough to beat off a direct assault, but over the weeks that followed, morale among the Vicksburg garrison succumbed to the regular, mostly nightly approaches of the Army of the Tennessee even more rapidly than did the key city's earthen defenses. As the night encounters in no-man's-land revealed, the low morale of Vicksburg defenders significantly speeded and eased the work of the besiegers in accomplishing their final purpose.

Notes

1. Taylor Peirce, *Dear Catharine, Dear Taylor: The Civil War Letters of a Union Soldier and His Wife* (Lawrence: University Press of Kansas, 2002), 115.

2. George B. Carter to Bill Carter, June 23, 1863, George B. Carter Letters, Wisconsin Historical Society.

3. Gould D. Molineaux diary, May 26, 1863, Augustana College Library, Rock Island, Illinois.

4. Samuel C. Kirkpatrick to family, June 16, 1863, Kirkpatrick Letters, Wisconsin Historical Society; James W. Jessee, *Civil War Diaries of James W. Jessee, 1861–1865, Company K, 8th Regiment of Illinois Volunteer Infantry*, ed. William P. LaBount (Normal, IL: McLean County Genealogical Society, 1997), chap. 3, p. 23.

5. William M. Reid diary, June 18, 1863, Abraham Lincoln Presidential Library.

6. Peirce, *Dear Catharine, Dear Taylor*, 116.

7. Arthur J. Robinson, *Memorandum and Anecdotes of the Civil War, 1862 to 1865* (Harrisburg, PA, 1912; pamphlet in holdings of the Wisconsin Historical Society), 28.

8. William M. Reid diary, May 30, 1863, Abraham Lincoln Presidential Library.

9. Gould D. Molineaux diary, May 25, 1863, Augustana College Library, Rock Island, Illinois.

10. Jacob Ritner and Emeline Ritner, *Love and Valor: Civil War Letters between Captain Jacob and Emeline Ritner*, ed. Charles F. Larimer (Western Springs, IL: Sigourney Press, 2000), 173–75.

11. Peirce, *Dear Catharine, Dear Taylor*, 116.

12. Samuel C. Kirkpatrick to family, June 16, 1863, Kirkpatrick Letters, Wisconsin Historical Society.

13. Robinson, *Memorandum and Anecdotes of the Civil War, 1862 to 1865*, 29; Lucien B. Crooker, Henry S. Nourse, and John G. Brown, *The 55th Illinois, 1861–1865* (Huntington, WV: Blue Acorn Press, 1993), 251.

14. William M. Reid diary, June 16, 1863, Abraham Lincoln Presidential Library.

15. Samuel C. Kirkpatrick to family, June 23, 1863, Kirkpatrick Letters, Wisconsin Historical Society; Peirce, *Dear Catharine, Dear Taylor*, 116; Isaac H. Elliott, *History of the Thirty-third Regiment Illinois Veteran Volunteer Infantry in the Civil War* (Gibson City, IL: Regimental Association of the Thirty-third Illinois, 1902), 45; Crooker et al., *55th Illinois*, 251.

16. Robinson, *Memorandum and Anecdotes*, 29.

17. Charles A. Willison, *Reminiscences of a Boy's Service in the 76th Ohio* (Manasha, WI: G. Banta Publishing Company, 1908), 60.

18. William K. Barney to "all at Home," June 23, 1862, William K. Barney Letters, Wisconsin Historical Society.

19. Nathan G. Dye to "Dear friends," June 26, 1863, Nathan G. Dye Papers, Perkins Library, Duke University.

20. William Wiley, *The Civil War Diary of a Common Soldier*, ed. Terrence J. Winschell (Baton Rouge: Louisiana State University Press, 2001), 53.

21. Gould D. Molineaux diary, May 25, 1863, Augustana College Library, Rock Island, Illinois.

22. James K. Newton, *A Wisconsin Boy in Dixie: The Selected Letters of James K. Newton*, ed. Stephen E. Ambrose (Madison: University of Wisconsin Press, 1961), 76.

23. Charles Dana Miller, *The Struggle for the Life of the Republic: A Civil War Narrative by Brevet Major Charles Dana Miller, 76th Ohio Volunteer Infantry*, ed. Stewart Bennett and Barbara Tillery (Kent, OH: Kent State University Press, 2004), 103.

24. George B. Carter to Bill Carter, June 23, 1863, George B. Carter Letters, Wisconsin Historical Society.

25. Ibid.

26. Aurelius Lyman Voorhis diary, June 27, 1863, Indiana Historical Society.

27. Ibid., June 28, 1863.

28. Ibid., June 30, 1863.

29. Ibid.

30. Michael Haffey, autobiographical notes, Wisconsin Historical Society.

31. Elisha Stockwell, *Private Elisha Stockwell, Jr., Sees the Civil War*, ed. Byron R. Abernethy (Norman: University of Oklahoma Press, 1985), 63.

32. Miller, *Struggle for the Life of the Republic*, 104.

5
―

ANDREW HICKENLOOPER AND
THE VICKSBURG MINES

Justin S. Solonick

M ajor General Ulysses S. Grant's inability to breach the Vicksburg defenses via a frontal assault on May 22 forced the Union commander to find another way to take the Confederate Gibraltar. As a result, on May 25, 1863, Grant handed down Special Orders No. 140, a formal directive that ordered his subordinate commanders to immediately begin digging zigzag approach trenches against Vicksburg. Thus, the picks and shovels that accompanied the Army of the Tennessee quickly replaced the rifle-muskets and bayonets that failed to bring Vicksburg to its knees some three days earlier. As one Union soldier stated, "It now became very evident that the works at Vicksburg could not be carried by storm. . . . There was but one resource left, and that was to dig them out. . . . Henceforth, spades would be trumps."[1]

Despite the fact that Grant waited until May 25 to dispense Special Orders No. 140, the Midwesterners serving in the Army of the Tennessee broke ground the day after the failed assault on May 23. Unfortunately, the Army of the Tennessee contained few professionally trained military engineers. As a result, their ability to successfully detonate two mines underneath the Vicksburg defenses reflected a blend of West Point engineering siege theory combined with Midwestern common soldier improvisation and adaptation.[2]

Throughout the siege, the Union troops dug thirteen major approaches toward the Vicksburg defenders. Although the corps commanders maintained overall responsibility for their respective sectors, the approaches earned the name of the division or brigade commander that managed the actual digging. The army's chief engineer, Captain Frederick E. Prime, oversaw the entire project until illness forced him to hand over his command to Captain Cyrus B. Comstock on June 21. These trenches cut across the no-man's-land between the lines and allowed the attackers to approach the

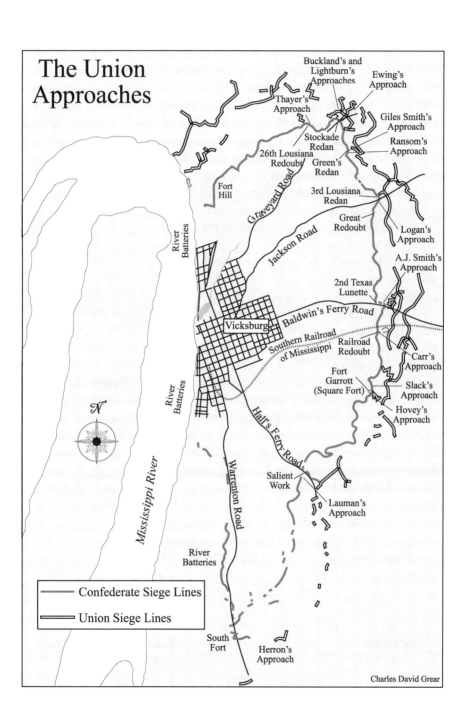

The Union
Approaches

Buckland's and
Lightburn's
Approaches

Ewing's
Approach

Thayer's
Approach

Giles Smith's
Approach

Stockade
Redan

Ransom's
Approach

26th Lousiana
Redoubt

Green's
Redan

3rd Lousiana
Redan

Fort
Hill

Great
Redoubt

Logan's
Approach

Graveyard Road

Jackson Road

A.J. Smith's
Approach

River
Batteries

2nd Texas
Lunette

Vicksburg

Baldwin's Ferry Road

Southern Railroad
of Mississippi

Railroad
Redoubt

Carr's
Approach

Fort
Garrott
(Square Fort)

Slack's
Approach

River
Batteries

Hovey's
Approach

Hall's Ferry Road

Salient
Work

Warrenton Road

Lauman's
Approach

Mississippi River

River
Batteries

——— Confederate Siege Lines

=== Union Siege Lines

South
Fort

Herron's
Approach

Charles David Grear

Confederate earthworks under relative cover. Once the Union troops reached the Rebel defenses, they began to sink mines beneath the enemy works.[3]

The siege tactic of undermining an enemy's fortifications dates back to antiquity. In order to bring down the stout stone walls protecting an ancient city, besieging miners, also known as sappers, dug tunnels directly underneath the enemy works, shoring the subterranean cavity with large wooden timbers in order to prevent cave-ins. Once directly underneath the wall of the beleaguered city, miners built a chamber revetted with wood and filled with combustible materials. Then the sappers would set the chamber alight and scramble to safety. The burning of the shoring timbers would cause the chamber and the stone walls above it to collapse, causing a breach in the city wall that a besieging force of infantry could then exploit.[4]

With the advent of gunpowder, however, this tactic changed. Better and heavier siege artillery, developed during the seventeenth century, forced an evolution in fortification design. The angled-bastion fortress, with its low, thick earthen walls and interlocking fields of fire, became the European standard that influenced fortification design in the New World until the late nineteenth century. Keeping pace with changing defensive measures, offensive siege tactics also evolved. The concept of "bringing down" a stone wall during antiquity gave way to "blowing up" the earthen Vaubanian ramparts of the Enlightenment era, a practice that continued through and beyond the American Civil War.[5]

Albert O. Marshall of the 33rd Illinois, part of Brigadier General Eugene A. Carr's division on the southern part of the Union line, reflected on the mining activities that occurred at Vicksburg some two decades after the summer of 1863. According to Marshall, it became known throughout the Union ranks that "General Grant [had] consented that the soldier who first [completed] the excavations under an important rebel fort may try the experiment of blowing it up." This news supposedly generated a wave of enthusiasm throughout the Army of the Tennessee, and as Marshall described, "[T]he soldiers [became] anxious to win this race first." Whether or not Major General Ulysses S. Grant did in fact initiate such a friendly competition remains uncertain. Nevertheless, the can-do attitude of the Army of the Tennessee, which had carried the blue-clad westerners to the gates of Vicksburg, continued to generate momentum throughout the army as it embarked on mining operations against the Gibraltar of the Confederacy.[6]

Unfortunately for Marshall, Carr's division would not be the first to sink mines underneath the Confederate works. That honor would fall to Major General John A. Logan's division of the Seventeenth Corps, which, until late June, had been digging a zigzag approach trench that hugged the Jackson

Road as it neared Vicksburg. The division's plan, however, did not go unopposed. Prior to the siege, the Confederates under the guidance of their own chief engineer, Major Samuel Lockett, who graduated from West Point in 1859, had constructed one of their most formidable forts in this road's path in order to prevent easy access into the city. To the Confederates, it was dubbed the 3rd Louisiana Redan, after the regiment that manned its defenses. To the Union troops digging toward the obstruction, it was simply Fort Hill. Since Federal solid shot and Parrott shells had failed to obliterate the fort with multiple aliases, it was now time to try another tactic. As Wilber F. Crummer of the 45th Illinois wrote after the war, "Fort Hill is said to be the key to Vicksburg. We have tried to turn this key, and have as often failed—in fact, the lock is not an easy one, but we soon shall try the burglar's plan, and with the aid of powder blow up the lock to 'smithereens.'"[7]

After having traversed some "one thousand five hundred feet" in "less than thirty days," the Federals excavating Logan's Approach finally reached the 3rd Louisiana Redan on June 22. At 9 A.M. the following day, Union troops began to undermine the Rebel works. In brief, this involved tunneling underneath the enemy defenses and there digging a series of galleries and branches that ended in chambers. Once these excavations were completed, sappers packed the chambers with powder, backfilled the branches and galleries with earth, and tamped the opening in order to force the subsequent explosion upward to effect a breach that Union infantry could exploit. As Albert O. Marshall of the 33rd Illinois summarized, "The object was to run the tunnel under the enemy's fort and then when ready, a wagon load of powder could be taken in and the fort blown out of existence. That is the idea. Time will tell how it succeeds."[8]

This herculean feat fell upon the shoulders of Captain Andrew A. Hickenlooper. Hickenlooper, an Ohioan, was not a professional military engineer. During the nineteenth century, the United States Military Academy at West Point (USMA) served as the citadel of America's engineering knowledge. Within the institution's walls, Dennis Hart Mahan, the author of numerous treatises pertaining to military engineering, disseminated knowledge to cadets about the latest European advancements in military engineering theory. Mahan, a graduate of the USMA class of 1824, taught engineering at the academy for some forty-one years until his death in 1871. In fact, almost every graduate of the USMA who fought during the Civil War had taken a class with Mahan at one point in time or another. Meanwhile, West Point welcomed James C. Duane into its teaching ranks in 1859. Duane, a graduate of the USMA class of 1848, compiled a text titled *Manual for Engineer Troops* and taught the practical hands-on aspects of siege tactics. Unfortunately,

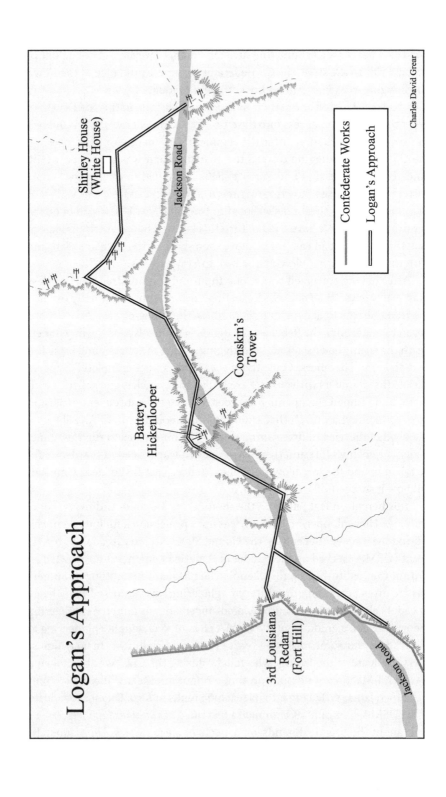

Logan's Approach

Shirley House (White House)

Jackson Road

Coonskin's Tower

Battery Hickenlooper

3rd Louisiana Redan (Fort Hill)

Jackson Road

— Confederate Works

— Logan's Approach

Charles David Grear

Hickenlooper could not claim a lineage to the West Point pedigree. Prior to the war, the Buckeye native performed services as a civil engineer in Cincinnati and lacked knowledge of the nuances of siege tactics. Once the war broke out, Hickenlooper became the captain of the 5th Ohio Independent Battery of Light Artillery. He served in this capacity at the Battle of Shiloh in April 1862, and during the siege of Corinth later that spring. Subsequently, the shortage of engineers began to become more apparent in the Army of the Tennessee, and higher ups transferred Hickenlooper to serve as the chief engineer of James B. McPherson's Seventeenth Corps. Thus, this self-made man in civilian life became a self-taught military engineer while serving the Union.[9]

Despite Marshall's ability to capture the essence of military mining, Captain Andrew Hickenlooper had a large task ahead of him. Military mining during the Civil War lacked precedent. The fact that no American mine had ever successfully been detonated during wartime throughout the country's young history lends further credence to Marshall's innocent comment that the first Union troops able to reach the Confederate works would be bestowed the honor of "the experiment of blowing it up." This lack of precedent, combined with the lack of engineers and sappers during the siege, forced Hickenlooper to improvise. Recalling this grand undertaking after the war, Hickenlooper proudly declared that the mine on Logan's front was "the first one of the war, and one of but two mines of any importance successfully fired during that unpleasantness." The second mine that Hickenlooper referred to, excluding his later detonation at Vicksburg on July 1, would occur at Petersburg on July 30, 1864. Although not a professionally trained military engineer, Hickenlooper, by this point in the siege, had earned Major General James B. McPherson's complete confidence. According to one onlooker, "General McPherson believed in Hickenlooper, and allowed him to construct the work in his own way."[10]

Traditionally, engineers relied on professionally trained sappers to carry out mining operations, but the lack of such specialized troops in Grant's army forced Hickenlooper to improvise. In response to this problem, the Seventeenth Corps engineer sought help from those with prewar civilian mining experience and made "a call for all men having had practical experience in coal mining." Thirty-five men from the "Lead Mine, 45th Illinois Regiment," and "a number of coal miners in the 124th Ill[inois]" answered the call and were subsequently divided into three reliefs, with each detail assigned an eight-hour shift. Once his miners were divided, Hickenlooper placed the details under the immediate command of Lieutenant Thomas Russell of the 7th Missouri and Sergeant William M. Morris of the 32nd Ohio. Brigadier General Mortimer D. Leggett assumed overall command of the effort.[11]

With nightly fraternization occurring between Union and Confederate pickets, friendly scuttlebutt threatened to leak crucial details about the project. While the Rebels atop the 3rd Louisiana Redan could clearly see that Union mining operations were afoot, the precise Federal timetable and the nature of the mine itself remained something of a closely guarded secret. According to William H. Bently of the 77th Illinois, "Guards were placed at the entrance leading to the mine, with instructions to allow no one to pass under the rank of a general excepting the engineers and workmen carrying on the operations." Equipped with "drills, short handled picks, [and] shovels," each individual relief "worked an hour at a time, two picking, two shoveling, and two handing back the grain-sacks filled with earth." By the end of the day on June 23, a gallery some three feet by four feet had been excavated twelve feet under the 3rd Louisiana Redan. Subsequently, on June 24, Hickenlooper's miners drove their gallery "a distance of 40 feet" and "commenced on [a] branch gallery to the left." This "smaller gallery extended in on the same line 15 feet, while from the end of the main gallery two others were run out on either side at angles of 45 degrees for the distance of 15 feet." In short, Union mining operations on Logan's front progressed quickly, smoothly, and under relative secrecy.[12]

One of the reasons for Hickenlooper's rapid progress lay in the characteristics of the loess soil, or thick layer of loamy, silt like clay partially cemented by natural minerals, in which they were digging. Vicksburg's loess soil allowed the Federal miners to excavate galleries and branches that did not require shoring or bracing, a step that professional military engineers considered the most difficult part of military mining. According to West Point engineer James C. Duane, civilian mining and military mining were two completely different tasks. Typically, civil mining was "carried on at greater depths below the surface of the earth, and in solid rock." Meanwhile, military mining "[was] what may be termed superficial, and consequently the miner [worked] through the more recent formations of earth and sands." The instability of looser soil in military mining required artificial support. As a result, military miners normally had to frame and shore up the mine with "wooden linings" as they advanced under the enemy's position. According to Duane, "It is [in] the adjustment and fittings of these linings that the chief art of the military miner [consisted]."[13]

The Army of the Tennessee's astute engineers recognized the serendipitous circumstances that loess soil afforded, characteristics that allowed them to skip an otherwise tedious, dangerous, and complicated engineering step. According to chief engineers Frederick E. Prime and Cyrus B. Comstock, "The compactness of the alluvial soil, [made] lining for mining galleries unnecessary, these galleries were formed with ease." Hickenlooper, at the forefront of Logan's mine, wrote after the war, "The soil of this locality consisted of a peculiarly tenacious clay, easily cut, self supporting, and not in the least affected by exposure to the atmosphere, thus rendering bracing and sheathing unnecessary." In other words, Vicksburg's loess soil favored the neophyte miners who were handicapped when it came to knowledge of the specifics of framing and sheeting mines in order to prevent cave-ins.[14]

Although Hickenlooper's mine progressed smoothly, Confederate countermeasures threatened Union success, and on June 24 the Union miners underneath the Rebel fort could "hear the conversation and pick-strokes of the Confederates engaged in countermining." In effect, the Rebels defending the 3rd Louisiana Redan attempted to intercept the Federals' mine in order to destroy it before it was detonated. Confederate chief engineer Samuel H. Lockett later recalled the Rebels' attempts to thwart Union progress on this front: "The Third Louisiana was located on a very narrow ridge and had no ditch. The counter-mines for it were therefore started from within by first sinking a vertical shaft, with the intention of working out by an inclined gallery under the enemy's sap." The Confederates were coming for the Union tunnelers.[15]

Relaying the disturbing news back to headquarters, Hickenlooper reported to his superiors that his miners "can hear the rebels at work on counter-mining very distinctly. [They] appear to be above and to the left of our gallery." The Federal miners "became frightened at the noise made in the rebel counter-mine and quit work" for fear of being entombed should the Rebels fire their mine. A concerned Union soldier immediately sent for Hickenlooper, who quickly rushed to the mine and "by . . . presence, example and persuasion induced them to renew their labors with increased energy." With the Union troops back in the mine, "it thereupon became a race to see which side would get in the first blow, that is whether we would be blown out or they blown up." The blue-clad miners won.[16]

Hickenlooper completed the construction portion of his mine on June 25. With his gallery by this time far enough under the Rebel Fort Hill (3rd Louisiana Redan) and with concern for the Confederate countermine, the Seventeenth Corps engineer decided to begin packing his mine with powder. "Having reached a distance of 70 feet," Hickenlooper later reminisced, "and fearing that if we penetrated further the explosion might not destroy the easterly [that is, front] face, and being also admonished that the enemy's countermine if fired might destroy our gallery and thus defeat our purpose, I ordered the whole force in[to the mine]." He proceeded to divide the Union soldiers "into three separate detachments" and "began running branch galleries north, south and west." These "were completed for a distance of about fifteen feet, and properly prepared for the reception of the charge." Now all that remained was to pack the mine with powder, detonate the charge, and exploit the breach. Yet the state of the art of military mining at this time dictated that this would be a difficult and unpredictable task.[17]

Military mining during the mid-nineteenth century was a science based on assumption and trial and error. It existed in a theoretical vacuum. The sieges of recent memory, namely those at Vera Cruz during the Mexican American War and Sebastopol during the Crimean War, had been brought to a successful conclusion without the implementation of mining techniques. At Vera Cruz, the U.S. forces under General Winfield Scott had used their artillery to force Mexican capitulation. At Sebastopol, the French storming of Fort Malakoff, one of the key strongpoints in the Russian fortifications, had signaled the end of this Crimean siege. Thus the sieges of the last twenty years had not yielded any empirical mining data.

Mahan recognized that military mining was still in its infancy and credited the problem to believed it was because of the lack of hands-on experimentation. According to the West Point engineering instructor, "But little advance by experiment has been made in the subject of mines, owing to the time, labor and expense, which a prosecution of the subject demands; and the practice has, therefore, undergone but slight changes since the earliest introduction of this means of attack and defence." For this reason, while it was possible to teach West Point cadets the finer points of choking sap fagots for fascines, weaving gabions for revetment, and excavating zigzag approaches and parallels in the academy's Hudson Valley, experimental mining was impractical due to the associated costs and resulting potential damage.[18]

Nevertheless, during the period between the end of the Mexican American War and the outbreak of the Civil War, some hands-on instruction in mining did occur at West Point. This, however, was reserved for the hundred men designated to Company A, Corps of Engineers, the U.S. Army's elite engineering unit. Training was limited and confined within the parameters of a peacetime military exercise. The engineers built small mock forts, sapped them, destroyed the structures with small mines, and then repeated the process. Unfortunately for theoreticians like Mahan, this exercise was carried out in order to perfect the company's skills in practical engineering, not for the sake of collecting scientific data pertaining to mining.[19]

Lack of experimentation in different soil types, in turn, yielded an imperfect pseudoscience. "The physic-mathematical theory of mines is still very imperfect," Mahan wrote. This was due to "the impracticability of ascertaining the exact effects of the explosion of powder in a medium [soil] which is seldom homogeneous." According to Mahan, the gases that a charge expended needed to overcome three obstacles before the desired crater could be created: the weight of the soil to be blown out of the crater, the "tenacity" of the soil type in question, and the atmospheric pressure pressing down on the surface of the crater radius before the charge exploded. Unfortunately for the military engineer, the lack of practical experimentation in different soil types had, up until that time, yielded little observational data. As a result, the equation that engineers used in Mahan's day to determine the weight of charge needed to blow any crater relied upon "approximations" that were "valuable as only guides that the miner [had] to refer to." Thus, with regard to mine detonation, a larger knowledge gap than usual existed between theory and practice. For the most part, successful mining, or lack thereof, rested on the tenacity and ingenuity of the engineer excavating beneath the enemy's defenses.[20]

Nineteenth-century military mining was a science rooted in assumption. In order to calculate the weight of the charge required to produce a finished opening, engineers needed to determine the volume and weight of the soil to be displaced from the crater. Computing this proved more an art than a science. As Mahan stated, "The form of the crater in ordinary soils has not been exactly ascertained. The only use of the exact determination of this form would be to calculate precisely the quantity of earth thrown from the crater, and by that means the proportion of the charge to the effect to be produced."

Weight of the Charge Necessary to Displace One Cubic Yard of Each Soil Type

	lb.	oz.
Light sandy earth	1	13
Hard sand	2	00
Common earth	1	10
Wet sand	2	2
Earth mixed with pebbles	2	8
Clay mixed with loam	2	8
Rock	3	10

Source: D. H. Mahan, *Summary of the Course of Permanent Fortification and the Attack and Defense of Permanent Works, for the Use of the Cadets of the U.S. Military Academy* (Richmond, VA: West and Johnston, 1863), 256.

Consequently, nineteenth-century engineers working in this pseudoscience theorized as to the shape of the hole that a given charge might yield. According to Mahan, some engineers believed that the blast created a "cone, of which the centre of the powder was taken as the vertex." Meanwhile, other professionals concluded that the blast resulted in "a paraboloid, of which the centre of the powder was the focus." Drawing on these two hypotheses, Mahan taught cadets that, in order to determine the volume of a crater and the weight of the soil to be displaced, one needed to assume that the blast consistently resulted in an inverted, right truncated cone.[21]

In order to determine the weight of charge required to displace a specific volume of soil, Mahan assumed an idealized crater in the form of a truncated cone. To provide a simple method of calculating the volume of the crater, Mahan additionally assumed that the radius of the lower circle, *oc* and *od*, was equal to one-half the radius of the upper circle, *Pa* and *Pb* (also called the crater radius). The line *oP*, a perpendicular line from the location of the charge *o* at the center of the base of the crater to the surface, was called the line of least resistance (hereafter referred to as *l*). This was, in theory, the shortest route that the exploded gas would travel on its journey from the center of the base of the crater to the surface. Mahan defined the lines and as the radius of the explosion. When an engineer blew a crater where the line of least resistance equaled the radius of the finished opening (*oP* = *Pa* = *Pb*), the engineer generated what Mahan termed a "common mine."[22]

In Mahan's theoretical model, the common mine provided a simulated standard. It represented an assumed condition designed to offer a basis of comparison against results in the field and provided engineers with a simple method of calculating the volume of soil to be displaced. This, in turn, permitted the engineer to determine the amount of charge needed to produce the desired result. Hence, in order to determine the amount of charge needed to produce a theoretical common mine, Mahan derived the following equation:

$$c = \frac{11}{6} \, q \, l^3$$

In Mahan's equation, the engineer needed to solve for *c*, the necessary charge (in pounds) required to blow the common mine in question. Meanwhile, the letter *l* referred to the line of least resistance (in yards), and the value *q*, in Mahan's words, represented "the [necessary] quantity [of] powder," measured in pounds, needed "to throw out one cubic yard of any species of soil." Unfortunately for Mahan's engineers, contemporaries knew little about the properties of different soils, and empirical data remained limited. Thus, according to Mahan, *q* was "found by experiment." Despite this shortcoming,

Mahan compiled a table of various soil types and the necessary amount of charge (measured in pounds and ounces) "required to throw out a cubic yard of the soil in question."[23]

Already knowing the depth of the charge and therefore the line of least resistance l, the engineer simply needed to plug in the value of q in order to solve for c. This equation, of course, allowed an engineer to determine only the amount of charge necessary to blow a common mine when only the line of least resistance and the soil type were known.

The common mine, however, was not always the result that the engineer was trying to achieve. When an engineer wanted to blow a shallow mine with a wide opening (one in which the crater radius was greater than the line of least resistance), Mahan instructed students to detonate what he termed an "overcharged mine." Conversely, if an engineer wanted to blow a deep mine with a narrow opening (one in which the crater radius was less than the line of least resistance), Mahan taught cadets to explode what he called an "undercharged mine." Despite the negative implications of their names, both overcharged and undercharged mines were simply definitions derived from the results of different explosions that deviated from Mahan's standard, idealized condition, the common mine. In order to provide an engineer with the ability to determine the charge size required to blow an overcharged or undercharged mine, Mahan derived separate equations for each based on the charge required to explode a common mine. These equations, however, are relatively complex, and it is beyond the scope of this study to examine them in detail. Nevertheless, their existence provides further evidence that, in some cases, the concept of either overcharging or undercharging a mine could have created a desirable result.[24]

Vicksburg's defenses sat atop loess soil. Although Mahan's table did not contain this exact soil type, the composition of loess soil closely resembles what Mahan termed "Clay mixed with loam." According to the table, the charge required to blow out one cubic yard of this type of soil is two pounds, eight ounces (that is, two and a half pounds). Yet, with regard to the Vicksburg siege, Mahan's equations and table of soil types remained of limited value. Because Captain Andrew Hickenlooper, an antebellum civil engineer and wartime self-taught military engineer, was the only soldier to detonate successfully a mine under the Vicksburg defenses, it is unclear how much Mahanian mining theory was used against the Confederate Gibraltar. While First Lieutenant Peter C. Hains, the chief engineer on the Thirteenth Corps front, and chief engineers Frederick E. Prime and Cyrus B. Comstock had been exposed to Mahan's tutelage via their West Point educations, Hickenlooper had not. In addition, although Hickenlooper's superior, McPherson, had graduated from West Point as an engineer, he did not partake in the day-to-day minutiae of siege work. Thus, it is unlikely that the Seventeenth Corps chief engineer used Mahan's equations when packing his mine with gunpowder. This western, homespun engineer improvised.[25]

Despite the inherent problems of the pseudoscience of military mining and his lack of official military engineering training, Hickenlooper prepared the mine to receive its charge and sometime before 9 A.M. on June 25 "deposited 1,500 pounds of powder in three different branch mines (500 in each), and 700 pounds in [the] center; 2,200 pounds in all." Subsequently, he arranged fuses so "as to explode them all at the same instant." Following this step, the engineer tamped the mine "with cross-timbers, sand-bags, &c."[26]

On June 24, Hickenlooper informed McPherson that he would be ready to detonate the mine sometime before 3 P.M. the next day. McPherson relayed this news to Grant, who in turn ordered that the mine be fired at that time. Once the mine exploded, Union troops were to attempt to exploit the breach. In order to keep the Rebel forces that were manning the Vicksburg defenses from reinforcing the Confederates defending the 3rd Louisiana Redan, Grant ordered a general bombardment all along the Union line for approximately fifteen minutes immediately after detonation. Union commanders were to place their troops in the rifle pits and trenches along their respective fronts at 2 P.M. and, with the sound of the mine detonation as their signal, were to unleash a hailstorm of iron and lead against the Vicksburg defenses.[27]

On Logan's front, the blue-clad troops began to make their preparations despite the stifling heat of the Mississippi afternoon, which, according to one Union soldier, "was 102 degrees above zero . . . in the shade." McPherson sketched out the general plan for Logan, who was to take advantage of the hoped-for breach in the line. According to McPherson, "If successful in destroying a portion of the enemy's works, it is important for us to take advantage of it." The division commander was therefore to place his "division under arms at 2 P.M." with General Leggett's brigade "in the trenches with fixed bayonets, [and] . . . advanced as near to the mine as they can go with safety." McPherson further ordered that Leggett's men advance under the cover of sharpshooter fire and be supported by a reserve force of three regiments, two from Brigadier General John E. Smith's brigade and another single regiment from Brigadier General Thomas E. G. Ransom's brigade. In addition, Logan was to assemble "a working party, provided with picks and shovels, [to] be in readiness to make a lodgment on the enemy's works should we succeed in getting in." That is, the working party was to create new Union entrenchments at the farthest point the attackers might reach as a result of the mine explosion. All of this, of course, was contingent on Hickenlooper's mine successfully detonating.[28]

With the general assault plan in place, the specifics of the attack congealed on Logan's front. Leggett placed the 45th Illinois in the front behind "ten picked men from the pioneer corps" under Hickenlooper's direct command who were to remove blast debris from the crater and "move forward and take possession of the fort." Meanwhile "in the left-hand sap," Second Lieutenant Henry C. "Coonskin" Foster, a respected marksman in the army who had earlier in the siege erected a log tower that served as a sharpshooting post along the route of Logan's approach, and a detachment of one hundred men from the 23rd Indiana were situated and given "orders to charge with the Forty-fifth Illinois, provided they attempted to cross the enemy's works." Behind the 45th Illinois and the 23rd Indiana, the remainder of Leggett's brigade waited in close supporting distance.[29]

With the Union preparations in place, Grant's scheduled detonation time, 3 P.M., June 25, approached. Tension filled the air. Colonel William E. Strong of the 12th Wisconsin assisted Hickenlooper in lighting the fuse that held the promise of destroying Fort Hill. "We crept forward together on our hands and knees from the terminus of the covered way," Strong later recalled, "and fired the dozen strands of safety fuse; and how coolly yet eagerly Hickenlooper watched the burning grain until it reached an embankment, and how we hurried back to 'Coon Skin Tower,' and held our watches and counted the seconds! All was quiet along the entire line from right to left, save a shot at long intervals from some wary sharpshooter on the other side." Back at the foot of Coonskin's Tower, "where the head of the charging column rested," Hickenlooper and Strong waited with gut-wrenching anticipation. Private Jerome B. Dawn of the 20th Illinois also recollected the eerie silence that filled the air. "I remember seeing birds fly over us and noted the unusual quiet. . . . The heat was intense. . . . We waited, it seemed to me, a long time." Near Dawn's position, Jenkin Lloyd Jones of the 6th Wisconsin Battery reported a similar stillness. "As the hour approached, all hands were anxiously waiting. Each desirous of witnessing the result. It was dull and very oppressive; all nature seemed drooping, and ominous silence prevailed on both sides; not a flutter of air, not a word was spoken, and you could hear naught but your own silent breath."[30]

Close by, Grant, McPherson, and Logan peered out from the protection of Battery Hickenlooper, an advanced breaching battery along the route of Logan's approach, and awaited the grand spectacle. Three o'clock came and went, and nothing happened. It appeared as if Hickenlooper had failed. Time seemed to move slowly, and three o'clock eventually became 3:30. Meanwhile, back at the base of Coonskin's Tower, Strong observed the composure that cloaked what must by that time have been Hickenlooper's considerable anxiety. Hickenlooper "was leaning carelessly against the base of Coon Skin Tower, with his eyes intently fixed upon the hands of his watch," Strong wrote. "His face was white, and there was an anxious expression about his eyes." Despite his inner turmoil, the engineer adopted a cool demeanor throughout the stressful affair. "His reputation with that army was at stake," Strong later remembered, "and I pitied him from the bottom of my heart. What if it should fail? Three seconds more,—tick! tick! tick!"[31]

Just then, at about 3:30 P.M. on June 25, the first successful mine of the Civil War exploded. According to Strong, "The huge fort, guns caissons, and Rebel troops . . . were lifted high into the air; a glimmer, and then a gleam of light—a flash—a trembling of the ground beneath our feet, and great clouds of dense black smoke puffed up from the crater of the mine, like jets from a geyser!" Standing next to Strong, Hickenlooper observed how "the whole Fort and its connecting earth-works appeared to be gradually moving upward, breaking into fragments, and gradually presenting the appearance of an immense fountain of earth, dust and smoke, through which one could occasionally catch a glimpse of dark objects, men, gun-carriages, shelters etc." Artillerist Jenkin Lloyd Jones, still standing with his guns, reported, "All at once a dead heavy roll . . . and you could see nothing but a black cloud of dirt and powder smoke, throwing the earth 30 or 40 feet in the air, and about half of the wall rolled over the ditch as if turned by a ponderous plow." Waiting in the assault column, Corporal Wilber F. Crummer of the 45th Illinois recalled that "the ground was shaken as by an earthquake."[32]

All around the siege lines, soldiers reported the fantastic sight that Hickenlooper's explosion had wrought. On William T. Sherman's front, a soldier of the 55th Illinois later described the scene. At "about half-past three," the soldier stated, "the parapet was seen to heave, and instantly up rose a huge dark column of earth, mingled with timber, tools [and] bodies of men, in the center of which for a second gleamed a lurid flame wreathed in white smoke." To the south of the blast, on Major General A. J. Smith's front, C. W. Gerard of the 83rd Ohio reported after the war that "the tremor of the exploded mine was felt for miles; the solid ramparts surged outward, and a massive dusty cone, mingled with smoke, rose in air, followed by a thunder-clap of the liberated force."[33]

Meanwhile, in Brigadier General Alvin P. Hovey's front, Richard J. Fuller of the 24th Indiana later recalled seeing "a cloud of black smoke go up like the upheaval of a volcano. It carried with it to the height of a mile, hundreds of tons of earth, and debris and a great number of men. This was followed by a mighty shaking of earth, and the 'Queen of Vicksburg' was no more." Just then, within seconds of the explosion, Union guns all along the siege lines opened fire "as if they were all pulled off by one lanyard." According to William S. Morris of the 31st Illinois, the concussion was awesome: "Blood spurted from the nose and ears of the men at the big guns. Some put their hands to their ears; the sound seemed to penetrate the brain." And, with that, the assault force amassed in Logan's Approach in front of the crater pressed forward.[34]

Hickenlooper, along with engineer Captain Stewart R. Tresilian, led the pioneer detachment into the crater and cleared the debris. The men of the 45th Illinois, who followed close behind, entered the defile and initiated "the battle of Fort Hill . . . a hell within a radius of five hundred feet." Inside the crater, however, the men of the 45th encountered a startling surprise. According to a member of Hickenlooper's pioneers, "This explosion was expected to create a very large breach in the works, which would destroy every impregnable defense and enable our troops to charge through the breach, capturing this impregnable position." This, however, did not turn out to be the case. "The explosion had destroyed about one-half of the redan," Hickenlooper later remembered, and "made of it an inverted cone-shaped crater about fifty feet in diameter and about twenty feet deep." Meanwhile, "the inner rim" of the crater "consisted of a parapet made by the descending earth." The Confederates, responding quickly, "brought a battery into position and manned the wings with a force of infantry," a decision that made "it impossible" for the Federals "to raise even a hand above the crest without having it pierced by a dozen bullets." Although there is no definitive proof that Hickenlooper used Mahan's equation, the resulting crater, with a line of least resistance of twenty feet and a radius of twenty-five feet, suggests that the Seventeenth Corps engineer overcharged his mine. This resulted in a shallow crater with a wide opening.[35]

The Confederates, well aware of the mining project that had proceeded over the previous days, had formed another earthen defensive wall that closed off the rearward mouth of the redan. Consequently, rather than creating a hole in the Rebel defenses, the Union mine had simply blown off the forward face of the redan, leaving the Confederate line uninterrupted. The lead miners now faced another, unbroken defensive line manned by Confederates. Hickenlooper, however, was not fazed. Prior to the attack, the engineer had ordered the construction of prefabricated head-logs, beams placed on top of a trench that protected the heads of men. The head-logs were placed in the crater so they could be brought up in case the attack degenerated into a firefight. Seeing this unfortunate turn of events, Hickenlooper sent back for his logs.[36]

The men of Company K, 20th Illinois, made up Hickenlooper's special pioneer detachment. According to one member of the company, Private Jerome B. Dawn, the group "was selected to lead the charge and prepare the way for the assaulting column, but to go unarmed. The duty assigned them was to clear a passage through our side of the crater and put it in a defensable condition." Two days earlier, on June 23, Captain John A. Edmiston of Company E received orders that he was to be reassigned to Company K for "special duty." During the afternoon, Edmiston, as ordered, led his unarmed detachment to its designated place on the right of Leggett's brigade already formed up in Logan's Approach. According to Captain Edmiston, "we were placed in charge of two logs already prepared, and, as I remember, about ten inches in diameter and 18 or 20 feet along with notches on the under side about every two feet. I divided the company in two platoons and placed a log in charge of each, with instructions to charge into the breach immediately after the explosion, first platoon filing to the left and the second to the right, and place the timbers on the top of the crater." Thus, they were to turn the crater into a defensive position, complete with head-logs. In theory, each log would lie on the lip of the crater with its notched side down. The notches would then form loopholes through which Union soldiers could fire their weapons with relative impunity.[37]

With the Union troops in trouble, Hickenlooper ordered that the men of Company K fetch the logs and cap the earthen redoubt that the explosion from the crater had made. According to one K Company member, R. M. Springer, "The perforated logs . . . brought from the rear and elevated to the crest dividing the contending forces, came up some time after the explosion, and not until more than one attempt had been made by the 45th, and then by the 20th [Illinois], to force their way into the interior of the Fort." Edmiston later recalled the arduous task of hauling up the head-logs. "After the explosion as soon as the debris and earth had some what settled," Edmiston remembered, "we passed into the crater, and under great difficulty, as we had to carry these heavy timbers up the side of the crater through crumbling earth and over obstacles. We succeeded in performing the duty assigned. We experienced no loss. . . . Having accomplished the duty assigned us, we returned to the 20th [Illinois] resumed our places in the line, and participated in the subsequent section in the crater with the regiment." After helping direct the placement of the loopholed timbers, Tresilian noticed that some of the Confederates appeared to be preparing to take the Union position by storm. The engineer acted quickly. He dashed to a nearby Federal battery and obtained ten-pound Parrott shells that he rigged with "five-second fuses" and threw over at the enemy. Tresilian hurled his bombs one after the other, a feat that stopped the Confederate advance in its tracks.[38]

Hickenlooper's head-logs, however, met with only limited success. While adequate against small-arms fire, the prefabricated head protection proved worthless against Confederate artillery that, upon striking the logs, would shatter the pieces, sending sharp splinters into the blue-clad troops. The 45th, however, held until 6 P.M., when Leggett decided to withdraw the lead miners and replace them with the 20th Illinois. This process of regimental rotation for duty in what soldiers dubbed the "Slaughter Pen," the "Death Hole," "Fort Hell," or more simply the "Hell Hole," proceeded throughout the night and into the twenty-sixth of June. A bloody stalemate ensued for over twelve hours. Little was gained.[39]

Although robbed of initial success, the Federal troops of Leggett's brigade "were crowded into this frightful pit like sheep in a slaughter pen" and continued to hold the crater. The close proximity of the fighting and the bunching up of Union troops in the confined killing space of the crater led to horrific casualties. When the smoke cleared, 34 Union soldiers lay dead and another 209 were reported wounded.[40]

The exact size of the June 25 crater remains disputed. Those commenting on the precise measurements of the hole wrote their accounts years after the conflict, leaving one to question their accuracy. As previously stated, Hickenlooper, in his personal reminiscences, claimed the crater was "about fifty feet in diameter and about twenty feet deep." The testimony of other soldiers who served during the fight contradicts Hickenlooper. The 20th Illinois's John A. Edmiston wrote to William T. Rigby, Vicksburg's resident park commissioner, on March 8, 1902, "As I remember, the crater was triangular in shape, the base line along the rebel works about 50 feet in length, the sides about 30; depth [of the crater] about 20 feet with sloping sides, very difficult to surmount." A member of Company K, 20th Illinois, more or less corroborated Edmiston's statement with regard to the crater's width, writing on March 18, 1902, "It [the crater] was about 50 feet from rim to rim, sloping like a large bowl from the bottom up, and quite regular in its interior." Similarly, S. C. Beck of the 124th Illinois and Wilber F. Crummer of the 45th Illinois, both of whom participated in the crater fight, wrote after the war that the crater had a diameter of fifty feet. Yet on March 12, 1902, an unidentified member of Company K contradicted Edmiston's estimate of the crater's depth when he wrote to his former captain that "the pit being full of loose dirt and 10 to 15 feet from bottom to top was a hard thing to climb."[41]

Thus, although accounts pertaining to the exact dimensions of the crater differ, all of the dimensions would suggest that, at least according to Mahan's standards, Hickenlooper overcharged his mine. The resulting shallow hole, with gently sloping sides and a wide opening, appeared ideal. Nevertheless, circumstances beyond Hickenlooper's control turned the crater into a death trap. The explosion pulverized the loess soil into a fine sand, making it nearly impossible for the Union assault force to climb out of the depression. At the same time, the Confederate defensive line at the base of the redan provided the Rebels with a fixed defensive position from which they could pour plunging fire down onto the Union troops.

Meanwhile, others described the size of the crater in relative terms and avoided committing to numerical measurements altogether. Immediately after the fight, Grant wrote to Major General E. O. C. Ord that "the cavity made was sufficiently large to shelter two regiments." This, however, appears to be a mistake. William E. Strong, who lit the fuse with Hickenlooper, stated after the war, "The crater of the mine was cone-shaped, and very much exposed. . . . The cavity made by the explosion was not large enough to hold two regiments, and no formation whatever could be preserved." Other soldiers serving in Logan's division corroborated Strong's observation. According to Wilber Crummer of the 45th Illinois, "The Crater was not large enough to hold more than two Companies at a time; between 60 and 80 men." Similarly, a member of the 31st Illinois wrote after the war, "The crater would not admit more than two companies at once."[42]

Why did the Federal attack fail? In his after-action report, Hickenlooper described the event as a "[p]erfect success." This terse statement, however, referred to the detonation of the mine and the fact that the Union assault party had been able to hold part of the crater. When perceived through this narrow lens, Hickenlooper's rosy view becomes justified. He ably carried out an engineering project that lacked precedent, and the assault force, while not able to exploit the breach, was able to consolidate some of its holdings. Hickenlooper, however, remained in the minority in celebrating the event. Most soldiers, both blue and gray, judged it a failure since the assaulting Union troops were unable to break through the Confederate line. As the 20th Ohio's Osborn Hamiline Oldroyd wrote on June 28, "Nothing, however, was gained by blowing up the fort, except planting the stars and stripes thereon."[43]

Those who perceived the event as a failure searched for reasons. Most blamed Hickenlooper and his pioneers. George Ditto, a pioneer in the 5th Iowa, wrote on June 25, "The blowing up of the fort is not as complete as it was expected to be but is I learn satisfactory. The walls of the fort are very thick and the side was not fully blown out as the charge was not far enough under it." On the other side of the siege lines, Confederate engineer Major Samuel H. Lockett claimed that the mine failed because "the charge was too small to do much damage. Nevertheless, it tore off the vortex of the redan, and made what the federals thought was a practicable breach." Back on the Union side, Albert O. Marshall of the 33rd Illinois drew the same conclusion as Lockett. According to Marshall, "The power-charge had not been large enough to have much effect upon the earth fort." That was of secondary importance, Marshall maintained, because "the real purpose of the experiment, which was to ascertain the effect and determine the amount of powder needed for such a purpose in such ground, was accomplished." Thus, in Marshall's estimation, with little precedent to draw on, the information that the trial yielded outweighed the limited nature of its results. Meanwhile, Frank W. Tupper, serving in Seventeenth Corps headquarters, reported a different reason for the June 25 failure, suggesting that the "powder [was not] put in properly and the hole [was not] closed as it should [have] been."[44]

Rather than simply search for what the Union did wrong, it is more profitable to explore what the Confederates did right. Hickenlooper's explosion and the subsequent charge into the crater did not doom the Federal attack. Instead, Lockett's ingenuity and the foresight that spurred his decision to erect his last-ditch breastwork at the rear of the 3rd Louisiana Redan is what determined the Union failure. As Lockett succinctly reported after the event, "An attempt was made to assault the work immediately after the explosion, but our men, having good cover behind the new parapet, repulsed the assailants with considerable slaughter."[45]

Grant, however, would not allow the crater fight to be a total loss, and after the engagement the Seventeenth Corps chief engineer received orders to construct a breaching battery in the middle of the crater. Although Hickenlooper began the project, it soon became clear that any guns placed in this defile would be dominated by Confederate fire. On learning this, Grant had McPherson bisect the crater with a line of field fortifications that allowed the Federals to hold their minuscule gains for the remainder of the siege. Under Hickenlooper's supervision, the Pioneers erected "a defensive line about midway across the crater," with a firing step cut into the side of the trench facing Confederate lines so men could have cover and still be able to fire towards the enemy. Sappers created a reinforced cover where they hoped to start digging another trench toward the Confederate line. According to Hickenlooper, "The completion of our new line and shelter enabled us to withdraw the force from the face of the crater, and yet securely hold all that we had gained."[46]

Despite the fact that Leggett's brigade could not exploit the breach, Grant telegraphed back to Major General Henry W. Halleck the successful details of the ordeal. On June 26 he informed the commanding general in Washington, "Yesterday, a mine was sprung under the enemy's work most commanding the fort, producing a crater. . . . Our men took immediate possession and still hold it. The fight for it has been incessant, and thus far we have not been able to establish batteries in the breach—Expect to succeed."[47]

Some serving in the rank and file, however, questioned the logic of pressing the fight in the crater. Although Wilber Crummer of the 45th Illinois conceded after the war that the Federals had successfully held the crater, he believed the cost of the engagement outweighed its benefits. Reflecting on the event in 1915, Crummer wrote, "It probably was alright to have made the charge into the crater after the explosion and try to make a breech inside the enemy's lines, but it surely was a serious mistake, either of Gen. Grant or Gen. McPherson, to cause that crater to be held for over 48 hours with the loss of brave men every hour." In retrospect, Grant did in fact make the best of the situation. He consolidated his line in the crater, held onto his limited gains, and kept moving forward toward his ultimate goal—Vicksburg's capitulation.[48]

With this fresh defensive position created, Hickenlooper received his new orders on June 27 to commence a second mine beginning on "the right-hand side of the crater." Anticipating such a directive, Hickenlooper actually had already begun a "covered gallery in [the] center of the crater" on the previous day for the purpose of launching "mines or counter-mines, as the case might require." He finished this project just before sunset on June 26 after suffering the loss of seven pioneers engaged in constructing the gallery. With new orders in hand, the energetic Hickenlooper continued to push his new mine forward in an attempt to blow a second mine underneath what remained of the 3rd Louisiana Redan. This new gallery ran "northwest from [the] covered gallery in [the] crater" toward the "left wing of the [Rebel] fort," the remaining "portion of the redan which had not been seriously affected by [the June 25] explosion."[49]

Despite the successful detonation of the mine, the siege began to take its toll on Hickenlooper. Over the course of the siege, the lack of engineers present with the army became an onerous reality that placed a steady, unrelenting strain on Hickenlooper. Sleep deprivation, exposure to the hot and humid Mississippi climate, and "nervous strain" finally broke the engineer's body, and he remained "sick and confined to tent" from June 29 to July 2. In short, Hickenlooper experienced "a total collapse," one that left him "incapable of physical exertion." While he was never able to pinpoint "the specific character of [his] disease," he attributed it to "nervous prostration." Medical personnel and staff officer colleagues doted over the ailing engineer captain as he slipped in and out of a "comatose condition." Unaware of the exact nature of the engineer officer's serious illness, attendants used common treatments. These included packing his head in ice, applying mustard plasters to his stomach, and administering a strict diet of beef, tea, and whiskey.[50]

Nevertheless, Hickenlooper's condition continued to decline, and several days after the collapse, McPherson informed Grant that the young engineer would probably expire. The commanding general of the Army of the Tennessee, concerned for the fate of the talented Seventeenth Corps engineer, decided to pay him a visit. The unassuming Grant quietly entered the tent and sat down beside the ailing Hickenlooper, who, though sick, was "perfectly conscious." Grant gingerly grasped one of the prostrated engineer's hands, felt his forehead, and asked, "Do you know who I am?" Hickenlooper replied, "Certainly I do, you are General Grant." To this, Grant solemnly responded, "I hope you will soon be better." With that brief exchange, Grant exited the engineer's tent and went about his daily business. Although the situation appeared desperate, Hickenlooper would live. Time out of the sun and confinement to quarters saved the young engineer's life, and on July 2 he was able once again to report for duty.[51]

During Hickenlooper's convalescence, the preparations for the second mine went forward, most likely under the direction of Captain Stewart R. Tresilian, Hickenlooper's right-hand man during the June 25 assault into the crater. By June 29 the Federal miners were well underway on their second mine, which aimed to destroy the remnants of the 3rd Louisiana Redan. The Confederates continued to harass the blue-clad westerners, attempting to impede their progress. In order to protect those coming in and out of the mine, Edmund Newsome, along with seventy-four other members of the 81st Illinois, began constructing "a timber shelter" out of "bundles of long cane" designed to shield workers at the base of the fort from enemy hand grenades. The improvised cane roof worked. According to Newsome, "The enemy continued to favor us with their explosive compliments until night, but our cane roof rolled them down . . . and no one was hurt."[52]

Lockett, seeing that the Confederate hand grenades were falling impotently to the wayside, decided to kick the Rebel defensive measures up a notch. In order to deter those working under the remnants of the redan, he obtained an empty barrel, packed it with 125 pounds of powder, "rolled [it] over the parapet and exploded [the device] with a time-fuse of fifteen seconds." The resulting blast achieved its intended effect. According to Lockett, "The effect of the explosion was very severe, and fragments of sap-rollers, gabions and pieces of timber were thrown into the air, and, I think, some of the enemy's sappers must have been burned and smothered." Nevertheless, the resourceful Federals rebounded and finished their second mine under the remaining northwest segment of the redan on July 1.[53]

Participants in the siege did not record the dimensions of the second set of galleries and branches that formed the subterranean honeycomb under the 3rd Louisiana Redan. Nevertheless, on July 1, Union troops finished packing the mine's chambers with approximately eighteen hundred pounds of powder, some four hundred fewer pounds than the previous June 25 mine. On learning that the mine was ready, McPherson contacted Grant for further instructions. Grant, with his penchant for direct orders, responded promptly and succinctly. The Army of the Tennessee commander ordered the Seventeenth Corps commander to "explode the mines as soon as ready. . . . You need not do more than have rifle-pits filled with sharpshooters. Take all advantage you can, after the explosion, of the breach made, either to advance guns or your sharpshooters." The debacle the first explosion had wrought influenced Grant's orders on July 1. A quiet, practical man of intelligence, Grant would not make the same mistake twice.[54]

Union commanders settled on 3 P.M. as the detonation time, and McPherson handed down Grant's instructions to Logan. Around 11 A.M. on July 1, McPherson instructed Logan, "The mine in your front will be exploded as soon as the proper disposition of troops can be made. It is not intended to make any assault, but simply to have the rifle-pits lined with sharpshooters, and the command under arms, ready to take advantage of any chance in our favor or repel any sortie of the enemy." As ordered, Logan detonated the second mine on his front. This time, events went according to plan. Unlike during the June 25 explosion, the delay between setting match to powder trail to the explosion in the underground chamber did not include the tense extra half hour of waiting.[55]

The explosion obliterated the remainder of the 3rd Louisiana Redan at 3 P.M. as scheduled. "Oh my, what a sight it was," wrote S. C. Beck of the 124th Illinois. "Timbers, dirt, men all in the air at once." Farther to the south in the rifle pits that protected Carr's Approach, Albert O. Marshall of the 33rd Illinois described the memorable event in greater detail. "The entire hill seemed to rise in the air," wrote Marshall. "The more compact pieces of earth and all solid bodies in the fort, such as magazine, timbers and artillery, and even men, were shot up into the air like rockets. The ground beneath our feet trembled as though a fierce earthquake was passing beneath us. As the force of the explosion ended, the loose earth and broken fragments of the destroyed fort fell back, into the opening made, a shapeless mass."[56]

Among those on the Rebel side thrown into the air was a young African American slave named Abe who had been working on a Confederate countermine designed to disrupt Logan's second mining attempt. Of the Rebels working in the countermine, Abe became the only one who "survived his transit." An instant camp celebrity, Abe became the subject of many soldiers' accounts of the siege. According to Seth J. Wells of the 17th Illinois, the blast "threw out several people, one Negro was thrown a hundred and fifty feet, [landing] on his head and shoulders, scarcely hurting himself. He attempted to run back, but a half dozen [leveled] muskets brought him back." According to another version that R. L. Howard of the 124th Illinois penned after the war, Abe, on landing unharmed, "said he went up two miles, saw the stars, met his master—who was one of the white men killed—coming down, etc., the part of which—seeing stars—was doubtless true. He was the hero of the hour, and seemed to enjoy it vastly." News of the remarkable event eventually ascended the ranks, and Logan, on hearing of the miraculous incident, "had his [Abe's] wounds dressed and well cared for."[57]

Reports of the exact dimensions of the resulting July 1 crater vary. According to chief engineer Cyrus B. Comstock, who did not provide the depth of the hole, the blast generated a crater some "30 feet in diameter." Meanwhile, Confederate engineer Samuel H. Lockett in his report stated, "The charge must have been enormous, as the crater made was at least 20 feet deep, 30 feet across in one direction and 50 in another. The earth upheaved was thrown many yards around, but little of it falling back into the crater. . . . The original faces of the redan were almost completely destroyed." At the same time, Jenkin Lloyd Jones of the 6th Wisconsin Battery, part of the Seventeenth Corps, simply recorded in his diary on July 1 that "a large volume was thrown inside making a much wider gap than before." Unfortunately, the conflicting information in Comstock's and Lockett's reports makes it difficult to determine the type of Mahanian mine detonated on July 1. Regardless, the blast proved devastating, and as McPherson would later report to Grant, the detonation "took the rebels by Surprise."[58]

In addition to the damage done to the remainder of the redan, the explosion also cut a large swath out of the retrenchment berm that Lockett had erected across the "gorge of the work"—that is, the extra section of breastwork across the rear of the redan that had stymied the June 25 assault. Fearing a replay of the unsuccessful June 25 attack, the Federals refused to mount another charge. Rather, they raked the new opening with murderous artillery fire.[59]

Lockett, expecting a Union charge into the breach, immediately sprang into action and set to work repairing the damages the mine had wrought to his last-ditch defense line, which now sported a large, gaping hole some twenty feet wide. The Confederate engineer ordered his shell-shocked gray-and-butternut-clad subordinates to obtain shovels and heave dirt into the breach. Union fire, however, proved too hot and negated this effort. Undaunted, Lockett called for sandbags, hoping that these, once filled, would plug the hole. This too failed. Union artillery and rifle fire tore holes in the bags and scattered their contents. With casualties mounting, Lockett improvised an ingenious solution. He scraped together an unspecified quantity of "tent flies and wagon covers," rolled them up with dirt inside, and pushed them into the hole. This solved the problem and sheltered the Confederates from Federal fire. According to the Confederate engineer, "At last we had something between us and the deadly hail of shot and shell and minie-balls."[60]

If Lockett had only known that the Union did not intend to make an attack, he could have waited until nightfall in order to repair his earthworks under the cover of darkness, but he did not. As a result, when the smoke cleared, some one hundred Confederate casualties littered the field. Reflecting on the incident sometime after the war, Lockett wrote that the July 1 explosion "was really the last stirring incident of the siege." From this point forward, until the Rebel garrison surrendered on July 4, the only sounds of war would come from the random report of a sniper's rifle, the belch of cannon and the subsequent thud as its ordnance lost velocity against the Vicksburg defenses, and the steady sound of pickaxes and shovels as approaches along the line continued to press forward toward the Gibraltar of the Confederacy.[61]

Nineteenth-century military mining was a pseudoscience rooted in assumption. While engineering theorists understood the basic principles of their art, the high cost associated with experimental mining led to a lack of empirical data. As a result, Mahan, beginning with the root assumption that all mines yielded a right truncated cone, derived equations that would allow engineers in the field to generate predictable results. Mahan's basis for comparison was the common mine, a crater where the line of least resistance was equal to the crater radius. Everything in Mahan's theoretical realm, from overcharging to undercharging mines, stemmed from this constant standard. Although modern engineers and scientists might scoff at Mahan's pseudoscience, his theories were cutting-edge during the antebellum period.

During the Vicksburg siege, Andrew Hickenlooper, a prewar civil engineer and self-taught military engineer, was the only one to successfully detonate a mine under the Confederate works. Sources do not indicate whether or not Hickenlooper applied Mahanian maxims to either his first mine, which he detonated on June 25, or his second mine, which was detonated by proxy on July 1. While Hickenlooper understood the basic principles of mining, he probably did not use Mahan's equations or exact methodology. Hickenlooper, a homespun frontier engineer and inherent problem-solver who lacked a formal military education, improvised. In addition, the nature of the local loess soil allowed Hickenlooper to skip the most difficult step in military mining—framing and shoring the shaft and subsequent galleries and chambers.

According to Mahanian definitions, Hickenlooper overcharged the June 25 mine. This, however, despite the negative connotation of its name, was not bad. The blast generated a shallow hole with a wide opening that appeared ideal. The crater's theoretical parameters, however, were deceptive. Behind the blast radius at the base of the redan, Confederate chief engineer Major Samuel H. Lockett had created a fixed defensive position that thwarted the Federal advance. In addition, the explosion pulverized the loess soil, turning the crater's walls into a fine sand that made it difficult for the attackers to climb out of the hole. Thus, although Hickenlooper successfully detonated his first mine, the subsequent attack failed.

Following the failed assault on June 25, the Federals under Hickenlooper's command prepared a second mine, which was detonated on July 1. Conflicting accounts make it difficult to determine what type of Mahanian mine Hickenlooper created with his second blast. Although this explosion destroyed what remained of the 3rd Louisiana Redan, Grant feared a replay of the failed charge into the crater, and a subsequent attack never occurred. Hickenlooper's efforts, however, were not in vain. The detonation of this second mine confirmed Grant's belief that his neophyte western sappers could successfully undermine the Confederate defenses and influenced the general's plan for the rest of the siege. With the various Union approaches now, in some places, only yards from the Confederate defenses, Grant decided to bring the siege to a successful conclusion. As a result, on July 1, the general decided to launch a full-scale frontal assault against the Rebel entrenchments on July 6. Soldiers and engineers, whose approaches sported galleries by July 6, would pack the dugouts with powder. Then, upon Grant's order, soldiers would blow these mines, artillerymen would fire their final rounds, and soldiers, assembled all along the trenches beneath the Confederate parapets, would attack. With the killing ground of no-man's-land that had derailed the May 22 attack literally behind them, the Army of the Tennessee could take Vicksburg.[62]

The attack, however, never came. With a Confederate relief force nowhere in sight, Vicksburg's commanding general, John C. Pemberton realized that he could not fend off an assault of this magnitude. As a result, on July 3, Pemberton dispatched Major General John Bowen and Lieutenant Colonel Louis M. Montgomery with a letter to Grant feeling out peace terms. Grant, however, wanted to talk to Pemberton in person. Pemberton, in response, rode out and met Grant. But, a misunderstanding had occurred. Grant believed that Pemberton had initiated the surrender conversation. Meanwhile, Pemberton's subordinates had led him to understand that Grant had been the one to propose the meeting. As a result, when Grant presented Pemberton with his usual terms of unconditional surrender, Pemberton refused to comply. Fortunately, the two generals agreed to let their subordinates talk in private, and the armies reached a more amicable settlement. Grant's formal written surrender proposal reached Pemberton, now back within the walls of Vicksburg, at 10 P.M. that evening. Pemberton, realizing that he had no other option, agreed to Grant's terms and his army formally surrendered on July 4.[63]

Notes

Portions of this chapter have been reproduced from Justin Solonick, *Engineering Victory: The Union Siege of Vicksburg* (Carbondale: Southern Illinois University Press, 2015).

1. Justin Solonick, *Engineering Victory: The Union Siege of Vicksburg* (Carbondale: Southern Illinois University Press, 2015), 39, 43; U.S. War Department, *The War of the Rebellion: A Compilation of the Official Records of the Union and Confederate Armies*, 128 vols. (Washington, DC: Government Publishing Office, 1880–1901), series 1, vol. 24, pt. 3, 341–42, 348. Hereafter cited as *OR*. All references are to series 1 unless otherwise indicated. William H. Bently, *History of the 77th Illinois Volunteer Infantry. Sept. 2, 1862–July 10, 1865* (Peoria, IL: Edward Hine, 1883), 162–63.

2. Solonick, *Engineering Victory*, 3–5, 43–45, 225–29.

3. Solonick, *Engineering Victory*, 81–82, 225–29; *OR*, vol. 24, pt. 2, 171–75; Edwin C. Bearss, *Unvexed to the Sea*, vol. 3 of *The Campaign for Vicksburg* (Dayton: Morningside House, 1996), 885–957; Adam Badeau, *Military History of Ulysses S. Grant, from April, 1861 to April, 1865*, vol. 1. (New York: D. Appleton, 1881), 338–39.

4. Kenneth Wiggins, *Siege Mines and Underground Warfare* (Buckinghamshire, UK: Shire Publications), 5–26.

5. Ibid., 30–47; David Chandler, *Art of War in the Age of Marlborough* (Kent, UK: Spellmount Limited, 1990), 234–71; Robert A. Doughty and Ira Gruber et al., *Warfare in the Western World: Military Operations from 1600 to 1700*, vol. 1 (Lexington, MA: Heath, 1996), 36–39.

6. Albert O. Marshall, *Army Life: From a Soldier's Journal*, 2nd ed. (Joliet, IL: printed for the author, 184), 258.

7. Wilber F. Crummer, *Grant at Fort Donelson, Shiloh and Vicksburg and an Appreciation of General U. S. Grant* (Oak Park, IL: E. C. Crummer and Co., 1915), 136.

8. Andrew Hickenlooper, "Our Volunteer Engineers," in *Military Order of the Loyal Legion of the United States*, vol. 3 (Wilmington, NC: Broadfoot, 1991), 311; *OR*, vol. 24, pt. 2, 202. According to the *Official Records*, Hickenlooper reached the Third Louisiana Redan on June 22, but harassment from Confederate grenades forced him to begin mining operations on June 23. Andrew Hickenlooper, "Vicksburg Mine," in *Battles and Leaders of the Civil War* (New York: Thomas Yoseloff, 1956), 541. After the war, Hickenlooper stated that mining operations commenced on the night of June 22. D. H. Mahan, *Summary of the Course of Permanent Fortification and the*

Attack and Defense of Permanent Works, for the Use of the Cadets of the U.S. Military Academy (Richmond, VA: West and Johnston, 1863), 251; J. C. Duane, *Manual for Engineer Troops* (New York: D. Van Nostrand, 1862), 208; Mahan, *Summary*, 251; A. Marshall, *Army Life*, 256.

9. Solonick, *Engineering Victory*, 13–22, 46–49; Andrew Hickenlooper, "Personal Reminiscences," vol. 1, Hickenlooper Collection, MSS fH628, box 1, folder 3, 5–38, Cincinnati Museum Center, Cincinnati, Ohio.

10. A. Marshall, *Army Life*, 258; Hickenlooper, "Our Volunteer Engineers," 311; William E. Strong, "The Campaign against Vicksburg," in *Military Order of the Loyal Legion of the United States*, 11:338.

11. Andrew Hickenlooper, "Personal Reminiscences," 145–46; Crummer, *Grant at Fort Donelson*, 136; A. Newland, "Surrender of Vicksburg. Marching into the City on the Glorious Fourth, 1863," *National Tribune*, August 27, 1903; *OR*, vol. 24, pt. 2, 202. Hickenlooper's report in the *OR* states that thirty-five miners volunteered. After the war, Hickenlooper wrote in his "Personal Reminiscences" that forty men stepped forward. Hickenlooper, "Vicksburg Mine," 541; Thomas M. Stevenson, *History of the 78th Regiment O.V.V.I. from Its Muster to Its Muster Out Comprising Its Organization, Marches and Skirmishes* (Zanesville, OH: Hugh Dunne, 1865), 252.

12. Bently, *History of the 77th Illinois*, 173; Hickenlooper, "Vicksburg Mine," 541. Here, Hickenlooper stated that the gallery was four feet wide and five feet high; *OR*, vol. 24, pt. 2, 202; Hickenlooper, "Personal Reminiscences," 146. Hickenlooper later claimed in his "Personal Reminiscences" that this gallery was 3½ feet wide by 4½ feet high.

13. Duane, *Manual*, 207.

14. *OR*, vol. 24, pt. 2, 177; Hickenlooper, "Personal Reminiscences," 146.

15. Hickenlooper, "Personal Reminiscences," 146; S. H. Lockett, "Defense of Vicksburg," In *Battles and Leaders of the Civil War* (New York: Thomas Yoseloff, 1956), 3:491.

16. *OR*, vol. 24, pt. 2, 202; Hickenlooper, "Personal Reminiscences," 146.

17. Hickenlooper, "Personal Reminiscences," 146.

18. Mahan, *Summary*, 252.

19. Walter G. Bartholomew file, Corps of Engineers, USMA Library, Special Collections, United States Military Academy, West Point, New York.

20. Mahan, *Summary*, 254.

21. Ibid., 251.

22. Ibid.

23. Ibid., 256.

24. Ibid., 251, 254–58.

25. Ibid., 256.

26. *OR*, vol. 24, pt. 2, 202; Andrew Hickenlooper to "My Dear Sister," June 26, 1863, Hickenlooper Collection, MSS fH628, box 11, folder 12, Cincinnati Museum Center, Cincinnati, Ohio.

27. Steven E. Woodworth, *Nothing but Victory: The Army of the Tennessee, 1861–1865* (New York: Knopf, 2005), 358; *OR*, vol. 24, pt. 3, 438–41.

28. Alonzo Brown, *History of the Fourth Regiment of Minnesota Infantry Volunteers during the Great Rebellion 1861–1865* (St. Paul, MN: Pioneer Press Company, 1892), 227; *OR*, vol. 24, pt. 3, 440.

29. Hickenlooper, "Vicksburg Mine," 542; *OR*, vol. 24, pt. 2, 294; Hickenlooper, "Personal Reminiscences," 147; Solonick, *Engineering Victory*, 128–133.

30. Strong, "Campaign against Vicksburg," 339; Hickenlooper, "Personal Reminiscences," 148; Jerome B. Dawn to unknown recipient, March 13, 1902, Twentieth Illinois Infantry File, Vicksburg National Military Park (hereafter cited as VNMP); Jones, *Artilleryman's Diary*, 73.

31. Hickenlooper, "Personal Reminiscences," 147–48; Hickenlooper, "Vicksburg Mine," 542; Strong, "Campaign against Vicksburg," 341; Solonick, *Engineering Victory*, 150.

32. Strong, "Campaign against Vicksburg," 341; Hickenlooper, "Personal Reminiscences," 140; Jenkin Lloyd Jones, *An Artilleryman's Diary* (Madison: Wisconsin Historical Commission, 1914), 73; Crummer, *Grant at Fort Donelson*, 137.

33. A Committee of the Regiment, *Story of the Fifty-Fifth Regiment Illinois Volunteer Infantry in the Civil War 1861–1865* (n.p., 1887), 252; Clinton W. Gerard, *A Diary: The Eighty-Third Ohio Vol. Inf. in the War, 1862–1865* (Cincinnati: n.p., 1890), 51.

34. Richard J. Fuller, *A History of the Trials and Hardships of the Twenty-Fourth Indiana Volunteer Infantry* (Indianapolis: Indianapolis Printing Co., 1913), 74; Jones, *Artilleryman's Diary*, 73; W. S. Morris, L. D. Hartwell Jr., and J. B. Kuykendall, *History 31st Regiment: Illinois Volunteer Organized by John A. Logan* (Carbondale: Southern Illinois University Press, 1998), 73.

35. Morris, Hartwell, and Kuykendall, *History 31st Regiment*, 74; James F. Coyle to Captain John A. Edmiston, April 11, 1902, Twentieth Illinois Infantry File, VNMP; Hickenlooper, "Personal Reminiscences," 148.

36. Woodworth, *Nothing but Victory*, 442.

37. Jerome B. Dawn to unknown recipient, March 13, 1902; unknown soldier to "Comrade Edmiston," March 1, 1902, Twentieth Illinois Infantry File, VNMP; John A. Edmiston to Wm. T. Rigby, March 8, 1902, Twentieth Illinois Infantry File, VNMP.

38. R. M. Springer to Captain J. A. Edmiston, March 18, 1902, Twentieth Illinois Infantry File, VNMP; John A. Edmiston to Wm. T. Rigby, March 8, 1902, Twentieth Illinois Infantry File, VNMP; *OR*, vol. 24, pt. 2, 208.

39. Woodworth, *Nothing but Victory*, 444; Richard L. Howard, *History of the 124th Regiment Illinois Infantry, Volunteers, Otherwise Known as the Hundred and Two Dozen, from August, 1862 to August, 1865* (Springfield, IL: H. W. Rokker, 1880), 116; Strong, "Campaign against Vicksburg," 342; Crummer, *Grant at Fort Donelson*, 139; R. M. Springer to Captain J. A. Edmiston, March 18, 1902; Woodworth, *Nothing but Victory*, 445; Green B. Raum, "With the Western Army: Tightening the Coils," *National Tribune*, January 16, 1902.

40. Strong, "Campaign against Vicksburg," 342; Woodworth, *Nothing but Victory*, 445.

41. Hickenlooper, "Personal Reminiscences," 148; John A. Edmiston to Wm. T. Rigby, March 8, 1902, Twentieth Illinois Infantry File, VNMP; R. M. Springer to Captain J. A. Edmiston, March 18, 1902, Twentieth Illinois File, VNMP; S. C. Beck, *A True Sketch of his Army Life*, 124th Infantry, Manuscript File, Old Court House Museum, Vicksburg, MS, 14; Wilber F. Crummer to Captain W. T. Rigby, October 21, 1902, Forty-Fifth Illinois File, VNMP; Unknown recipient to J. A. Edmiston, March 12, 1902, Twentieth Illinois Infantry File, VNMP.

42. *OR*, vol. 24, pt. 3, 441; Strong, "Campaign against Vicksburg," 341; Wilber F. Crummer to Captain W. T. Rigby, October 21, 1902, Forty-Fifth Illinois Infantry File, VNMP; Crummer, *Grant at Fort Donelson*, 137; Morris, Hartwell, and Kuykendall, *History 31st Regiment*, 73–74.

43. *OR*, vol. 24, pt. 2, 202; Oldroyd, *Soldier's Story*, 68.

44. George Ditto diary, June 25, 1863, SC 2192, Abraham Lincoln Presidential Library, Springfield, Illinois; Lockett, "Defense of Vicksburg," 491; A. Marshall, *Army Life*, 258; F. W. Tupper to "Dear Parents," June 30, 1863, SC 1567, F. W. Tupper Letters, Abraham Lincoln Presidential Library, Springfield, Illinois.

45. *OR*, vol. 24, pt. 2, 333.

46. Woodworth, *Nothing but Victory*, 445; *OR*, vol. 24, pt. 2, 202; Hickenlooper, "Personal Reminiscences," 149–50.

47. John Y. Simon, ed., *The Papers of Ulysses S. Grant* (Carbondale: Southern Illinois University Press), 8:431–32.

48. Crummer, *Grant at Fort Donelson*, 142.

49. *OR*, vol. 24, pt. 3, 444; ibid., pt. 2, 202–3; Hickenlooper, "Vicksburg Mine," 542; Hickenlooper, "Personal Reminiscences," 150.

50. Hickenlooper, "Personal Reminiscences," 150–51; *OR*, vol. 24, pt. 2, 203.

51. Hickenlooper, "Personal Reminiscences," 150–51; *OR*, vol. 24, pt. 2, 203.

52. *OR*, vol. 24, pt. 2, 334; Edmund Newsome, *Experience in the War of the Great Rebellion by a Soldier of the Eighty First Regiment Illinois Volunteer Infantry August 1862-August 1865*, 2nd ed. (Carbondale, IL: n.p., 1880), 21–22.

53. *OR*, vol. 24, pt. 2, 334–35.

54. Ibid., 178; *OR*, vol. 24, pt. 3, 456.

55. *OR*, vol. 24, pt. 2, 178; *OR*, vol. 24, pt. 3, 456–57.

56. Ibid., pt. 2, 178; S. C. Beck, *A True Sketch of his Army Life*, 124th Infantry, Manuscript File, Old Court House Museum, Vicksburg, MS, 15; A. Marshall, *Army Life*, 259.

57. Howard, *History of the 124th*, 118; Seth J. Wells, *The Siege of Vicksburg from the Diary of Seth J. Wells* (Detroit: Wm. H. Rowe, 1915), 85; Stevenson, *History of the 78th Regiment*, 252; S. C. Beck, *A True Sketch of His Army Life*, 124th Infantry, Manuscript File, Old Court House Museum, Vicksburg, MS, 16; A. Newland, "Surrender of Vicksburg. Marching into the City on the Glorious Fourth, 1863," *National Tribune*, August 27, 1903; Joseph Stockton, *War Diary of Brevet Brigadier General Joseph Stockton* (Chicago: John T. Stockton, 1910), 18.

58. *OR*, vol. 24, pt. 2, 178, 334; Jones, *Artilleryman's Diary*, 75; Simon, *Papers of Ulysses S. Grant*, 449.

59. *OR*, vol. 24, pt. 2, 334; Lockett, "Defense of Vicksburg," 491–92.

60. *OR*, vol. 24, pt. 2, 334; Lockett, "Defense of Vicksburg," 491–92.

61. Lockett, "Defense of Vicksburg," 491–92.

62. Solonick, *Engineering Victory*, 202–5; Lockett, "Defense of Vicksburg;" *OR*, vol. 24, pt. 2, 174–75, 177, 186; pt. 3, 458–59; Bearss, *Unvexed to the Sea*, 891, 898–901, 904; A. Marshall, *Army Life*, 259; Captain Frank Swigart, "Vicksburg Campaign," *National Tribune*, August 9, 1888; Charles A. Hobbs, "Vanquishing Vicksburg: The Campaign Which Ended in the Surrender of America's Gibraltar," *National Tribune*, April 14, 1892; Strong, "Campaign against Vicksburg," 343.

63. Solonick, *Engineering Victory*, 206–9; Warren E. Grabau, *Ninety-Eight Days: A Geographer's View of the Vicksburg Campaign* (Knoxville: University of Tennessee Press, 2000), 495–99; J. H. Craven, "Fighting Them Over: What Our Veterans Have to Say about Their Old Campaigns; Vicksburg; The Offer to Surrender," *National Tribune*, October 30, 1884; T. B. Marshall, *History of the Eighty-Third Ohio Volunteer Infantry: The Greyhound Regiment* (Cincinnati: Eighty-Third Ohio Volunteer Infantry Association, 1912), 93; Ulysses S. Grant, *Personal Memoirs of Ulysses S. Grant*, (New York: Charles L. Webster, 1885), 1:543–63; *OR*, vol. 24, pt. 3, 446; Chaplain N. M. Barker, July 3, 1863, 116th Illinois File, VNMP; Howard, *History of the 124th*, 120; Michael B. Ballard, *Grant at Vicksburg: The General and the Siege* (Carbondale: Southern Illinois University Press, 2013), 149.

Ulysses Simpson Grant, commander of the Union Army of the Tennessee during the Vicksburg Campaign, in discussion with John Clifford Pemberton, commander of the Confederate Army of Mississippi that defended Vicksburg, Mississippi. Library of Congress.

Union lieutenant colonel John A. Rawlins served as Ulysses S. Grant's assistant adjutant general and chief of staff during the siege. Library of Congress.

Union lieutenant colonel James Harrison Wilson served on the staff of
Ulysses S. Grant and was a biographer of John A. Rawlins. Library of Congress.

Monument dedicated to the 57th Ohio Infantry at Vicksburg
Military Park. Personal Collection of Jonathan Steplyk.

Monument dedicated to the 72nd Ohio Infantry at Vicksburg Military Park. Personal Collection of Jonathan Steplyk.

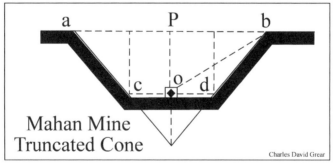

Mahan's perception of the idealized crater in the form of a right truncated cone. From D. H. Mahan, *Summary of the Course of Permanent Fortification and the Attack and Defense of Permanent Works, for the Use of the Cadets of the U.S. Military Academy* (Richmond, VA: West and Johnston, 1863), 251.

Confederate general Joseph E. Johnston realized defending Jackson was a futile gesture and escaped during the night of July 17. Personal collection of Richard Holloway.

Union major general William T. Sherman eagerly anticipated the opportunity to trap Johnston at Jackson. Library of Congress.

Union major general Francis P. Blair's timely arrival into Jackson emboldened the Federals to assault the trenches on July 12. Personal collection of Richard Holloway.

Drawing of a scene Joseph B. Polley described: a Texan "feeling for a furlough." *Confederate Veteran* 5 (1897): 104.

6

A COMMUNITY BESIEGED: CIVILIANS
OF THE VICKSBURG CAMPAIGN

John J. Gaines

As the Union and Confederate forces drew closer to the town of Vicksburg, the residents of the community grew increasingly concerned about the brewing storm. They had no doubt read about civilians witnessing other battles through the continuing newspaper exchanges of the struggling Confederacy. In those accounts, an occasional civilian found themselves in the midst of the battlefield as the gangling lines meandered around the field and nearer to the civilians huddled in basements or root cellars, subjecting the occupants to a terrifying ordeal usually lasting several hours. For the most part though, such engagements only placed the local residents in danger for a few hours, or at most a couple of days in the event of an extended battle. A relatively short engagement was not to be for the people of Vicksburg, however. Civilians at Vicksburg endured months of intermittent danger that resulted in the crescendo of a forty-seven-day siege with intermittent shells falling and exploding throughout the community.

The people of Vicksburg were realists, though, an aspect of their collective personality that enabled the clear majority of them to survive the siege that threatened their town. Though they were divided on secession prior to the war, once Mississippi left the Union, the members of the community accepted their lot and attempted to make their way through the war years as best as they could. That same notion of pragmatism aided the community as they confronted General Ulysses S. Grant's besieging force from May through July of 1863. Rather than relying completely on the Confederate defenders under the command of General John Pemberton to provide for their safety, many of the resourceful residents of Vicksburg endeavored to secure themselves in a multitude of hand-dug caves.

The early attacks on the town of Vicksburg in the summer of 1862 caused panic in the residents unaccustomed to witnessing an artillery exchange.

The Union gunboats shelled the town to secure the Mississippi River in the early hours of the morning on June 26, 1862. Though they were awakened by exploding artillery projectiles falling on the Confederate positions, the residents were not taken completely by surprise. They largely understood that the war would pay them a direct visit given their proximity to the Mississippi River and the importance of the waterway to both the new Confederate nation and the United States. During the initial shelling, most of Vicksburg's civilians fled the town and remained a safe distance from the falling ordnance. When the gunboats departed a few days later, most of the community returned only to endure the periodic shelling to dislodge the Confederate forces over the next month. Fortunately for the community, late July 1862 brought a dramatic drop in the level of the river and forced Admiral David D. Farragut to leave the area and give the town a much-needed reprieve.[1]

The blooming flowers of the next spring brought the rising levels of the Mississippi, as well as news of the returning Union forces as Grant openly moved overland toward the city and Farragut returned with his gunboats. As Grant neared the city, and the Confederates took positions in their emerging fortifications, many of the civilians realized they were trapped in the crossfire of the two opposing forces. As Confederate forces poured into the city, the pending fight sparked some civilians into attempting to relocate to safer confines. Some attempted to leave the town by road, but they discovered Grant's forces stationed along the surrounding roads and elected to retreat to Vicksburg. As both forces settled into their positions, artillery streamed overhead from both directions as Union artillery fired thousands of rounds into the city, targeting Pemberton's defensive forces.[2]

Outside the newly besieged community, the rest of the country eagerly watched for news of the happenings within Vicksburg. Unfortunately, very little information emerged from the surrounded community itself. As a result, newspaper editors sought out reports from unchecked local populations, and at times, embellished and likely even wholly created stories for their readers on the events. Editors on both sides of the conflict spread news that supported their stance on the war, often foregoing documenting the real situation in Vicksburg. In a newspaper exchange from the *Chattanooga Rebel*, the editor of the *Alexandria Gazette* noted that the Union forces surrounding Vicksburg were extremely apprehensive due to "the fact that certain death awaits them; their officers acknowledged certain defeat or annihilation." In an attempt to offer a quick disclaimer, at the end of the piece, the editor of the *Rebel* stated: "[T]his is contradicted in other quarters."[3] While this was likely a fictional report, it is revealing that the Southern editor focused on one of the few advantages of the Confederate garrison occupying the town of Vicksburg. In that scenario, the Union forces faced the prospect of streaming into a city of well-fortified Confederates. Although Union forces heavily outnumbered Pemberton's garrison, the possibility of fighting street by street, house by house, was likely very worrisome to many Federal soldiers.

Northern editors likewise played up the advantages that the Union troops held, though at times falsifying the story a bit. The *Daily Freeman* featured one of these falsified, but revealing, reports. The editor claimed that General Grant had twice offered the women and children of the besieged city the chance to evacuate and was met with their refusal. The editor followed up in asserting that after the Union forces heavily shelled the city again, the women and children asked Grant for another chance to flee the city. The general allegedly refused and remarked: "He only wished there were fifty thousand more of them and they would soon surrender."[4] Though the account of Grant offering to allow the women and children to evacuate did not seem to have actually occurred, much like the editor of the *Chattanooga Rebel*, the *Daily Freeman* sought to bolster the morale of their own readers by focusing on the advantages of their respective affiliates. In this case, one of the major challenges facing the besieged Confederates and civilians occupying the city of Vicksburg was the lack of incoming supplies and the stark possibility of starvation facing the impromptu community.

While the Union artillerists targeted the Confederate military units within the town, they also found an advantage in firing into the civilian-occupied areas of the town. By panicking the masses, they would at least give Pemberton an additional concern over the usual issues of safeguarding his soldiers. But that led to the view in the larger Confederate nation that the invading Yankees were merciless butchers that targeted civilians and military forces alike. The local press released reports that were repeated in the newspaper exchanges that depicted the Union cannon purposely firing on the civilian population that had remained in town. A writer in the Richmond *Daily Dispatch* proclaimed to his readers, "[M]en, women, and children, both black and white, went screaming through the streets, seeking a place of safety—some dressed and others almost nude. Mothers were running, with little babes in their arms crying 'where will I go,' and some would crouch under the first hill while the shell was bursting above them."[5] The initial shelling of the Vicksburg fortifications along with the ordnance that fell into the civilian community seemed to catch the population by complete surprise. With no place to find substantial shelter, the populace panicked upon realizing that they were not safe in their town. The war had arrived on their doorsteps, and like many people throughout the warring country, they had prepared over the course of several months with the expectation that the town would directly experience some combat but were startled into reality as forces arrived and shots began to be exchanged.[6]

Understanding that the siege of Vicksburg centered on the ability of the besieged population to sustain themselves over the duration of the event, Federal forces endeavored to eliminate any supplies that might allow the Confederate soldiers and civilians to withstand the affair. The *Daily Freeman* documented the strategy by relating portions of a letter from a Union soldier dated June 1, 1863. The Federal trooper stated: "It was made our powerful but imperative duty to destroy everything, corn, cotton, meats . . ." and any other goods that might aid the surrounded community. He went on to claim: "This is bringing the war home to their people and making them realize their own crime in bringing its calamities upon the country."[7] Although such measures fall within the concept of hard war, some other editors, especially those from the South, focused on those accounts guaranteed to incite animosity among their Southern readers. The editor of the *Abington Virginian* claimed that on the lead up to the siege, Federal soldiers were "tearing jewelry from citizens, gutting residences," and other crimes while moving toward Vicksburg.[8] As with many newspaper accounts during the war, this was very likely a mix of reality and elaboration with the obvious goal of prodding the readership to anger.

The frequency and destruction of the explosions shocked the local population and livestock. The *Daily Dispatch* reported that "even the stock, and almost everything in the city was in panic-stricken and fled. Horses, mules, cows, dogs & c., could be seen speeding though the town, out of reach of the missiles."[9] In response to the Union gunboats, Confederate batteries fired back. During the artillery duels over the next few weeks, there was some damage to local homes because of the inaccuracy of period artillery. Though the shelling flew wildly into town, the Union artillerists were able to keep much of their fire confined to the Confederate emplacements. During the early bombardment, only one white civilian resident of Vicksburg, Mrs. Patience Gamble, was killed by exploding artillery.[10]

As soon as Confederate forces flooded in and overwhelmed the town, logistical issues became apparent. On May 17, the Confederate army moved into the town, bringing all of the supplies they could possibly handle with them. They brought livestock, rice, vegetables, and even sugar from the surrounding countryside in order to stock supplies for the impending siege. In addition to the imported foodstuffs, members of the impromptu garrison both purchased and covertly appropriated food from the civilian community. The short-lived market did not last very long as both civilians and Confederate soldiers realized that food would be in short supply if the siege endured for longer than a couple weeks. Quickly, the demand for goods overwhelmed the reserves of the town and pushed prices upward. Butter reached "$1.50 a pound and flour was virtually unavailable."[11] The garrison planned to remain in town under Pemberton's command in the hopes of denying the river to Grant and David D. Porter's combined forces. Unfortunately, the Confederate troops that marched into Vicksburg maintained only about six weeks' worth of rations in reserves, not including the estimated goods that would be required to provide for the civilian population. Once the siege started, those rations and the cashiered foodstuffs of the civilian population quickly dwindled.[12]

In the first couple of weeks of the siege, it quickly became obvious that food would immediately become a central issue for the besieged, civilian and military alike. About ten days into the siege, Confederate quartermasters cut food rations for their men. A few days later, on June 4, Confederate officers ordered all rations and civilian food supplies to be confiscated and doled out to all inhabitants of the besieged city in an effort to stretch the supplies for as long as possible.[13]

Already accustomed to occasional shortages and open to possible innovation, the besieged populace sought out any source of nutrition. One of the first alternative rations was sourced from a cache of black-eyed peas. Prior to the siege, several livestock owners in the city had accumulated a sizable store of the peas to use as animal feed. In an effort to introduce some variety, millers ground the black-eyed peas into meal. Attempting to stay ahead of the food shortages, bakers substituted the black-eyed pea meal for flour and distributed the loaves to the masses. Following several days of subsisting largely on the bread made from the unique meal, many of the soldiers and civilians that had consumed the bread became ill. The gastric irritation soon overruled the blandness of ordinary boiled black-eyed peas, so cooks quickly resumed distributing a steady stream of boiled black-eyed peas instead.[14]

Just as the lack of food weighed on the civilians of Vicksburg, Confederate soldiers likewise endured the privations. Requests for additional foodstuffs came from every station of the besieged forces. General Pemberton sent a very concerned message to General Joseph E. Johnston proclaiming, "I am waiting most anxiously to know your intentions; have heard nothing of you or from you since 25th of May. I shall endeavor to hold out as long as we have anything to eat."[15] The soldiers in the trenches expressed similar laments concerning the lack of food. Though Pemberton was quite a bit more diplomatic in his request, an anonymous letter from one of the men was far more demanding. As noted in the letter, the men were on less than subsistence rations. "We are, and have been, kept close in the trenches day and night, not allowed to forage any at all, and, even if permitted, there is nothing to be had among the citizens." The writer went on to threaten, "This army is now ripe for mutiny, unless it can be fed."[16] While Pemberton's forces did not appear to come close to a mutiny, their desperation for supplies echoed that of the civilian population.

As the hungry residents exhausted regular sources of meat as the humid days of the siege crawled by, mules became a menu item. Although it was an adjustment, some of the residents eagerly consumed the new fare with it reportedly selling for as much as a dollar a pound. When the supply of mule dwindled for some and was economically out of reach for others, a few adventurous residents of the impromptu community turned to rat. One diarist reported, "rats are hanging dressed in the market for sale with mule meat,—there is nothing else."[17] Though the alternative nutritional sources might at first seem fairly revolting, to those in desperate situations with few resources available, the early skepticism over such fare would quickly dissipate. Sheer need of sustenance drove the residents to uncover new sources of caloric intake lest they starve to death during the ever-lengthening siege.

Try as they might, those alternative sources were not enough to provide for the daily needs of the hungry population. As the days went on and supplies dwindled, both soldiers and civilians began to show symptoms of malnutrition and in some cases of scurvy. During the ensuing weeks, "fewer and fewer horses, mules, and dogs were seen wandering about Vicksburg. Shoe leather became the last resort of sustenance for many adults."[18] By the end of the siege, a great many of the residents were on the verge of starvation, and the incoming Union forces were shocked at the appearance of the newly freed occupants following Pemberton's surrender.[19]

In addition to the threats faced by the residents in terms of scant food supplies, they also regularly endured the risk of incoming artillery shells. Much like the other civilians that found themselves near the battles scattered through the Confederacy and United States, the people of Vicksburg manifested a variety of reactions to the close proximity of the combatants. Some residents predictably attempted to find safety for themselves and their families as well as their slaves. Without the benefit of many basements or natural shelters, the people of the community had only a few choices. The option of leaving the town had been negated by the encircling Union troops. The only other alternatives were to remain in their homes and hope that an errant artillery shell did not explode near the residence during the engagement or to establish some sort of shelter of their own. Most occupants of the town chose to do the latter and dug elaborate caves within the hills of the town.[20]

A few stubborn residents chose to remain in their homes. One of the more well-known residents that opted for this route was Emma Balfour and her household. Though she recognized the danger of the situation, for the most part she refused to leave her home for the duration of the siege except for occasionally venturing into the shelter of the caves. In her diary, Balfour captured the situation that many residents faced after finding they were unable to evacuate. "What is to become of all the living things in this place when the boats begin shelling—God only knows. Shut up as in a trap, no ingress or egress—and thousands of women and children who have fled here for safety."[21]

Remembering the lessons of the earlier bombardments of the initial assaults of the summer before, many residents took to underground shelters or the tiny caves that had been dug in preparation for those short-lived assaults. On May 20, 1863, Union gunboats brought several mortars in range to begin shelling the Confederate works. As they began firing, the citizenry fled into the scattered caves of the city, with several people killed on their way to shelter. During the attack, Balfour wrote: "As all this rushed over me and the sense of suffocation from being underground the certainty that there was no escape that we were hemmed in, caged, for one moment my heart seemed to stand still then in my faith and courage rose to meet the emergency, and I have felt prepared ever since and cheerful."[22]

Balfour's home was next door to the home occupied by General Pemberton for his headquarters. After her first sojourn into the caves, Balfour usually refused to leave her home during future shelling.[23] It is possible, however, that Balfour took some security in the choice of Pemberton's headquarters. Pemberton's officers would have likely selected a location that was relatively safer than the rows of homes facing the river, as well as unseen directly by Federal gunners. Balfour conceivably found solace in such a realization and believed that she had the same chance of being hit with an artillery shell by remaining in her home during shelling as she did in most places in the locale.

Like most of the people of Vicksburg, Balfour grew accustomed to the shelling as the days crept past. Amazingly, unlike the other residents of the town, Balfour did not flee to the caves during shelling and seemed to accept whatever her fate might be. She later confided in her diary that if a shell passed high overhead, she would simply "stand still." Others might fly by and explode before the witness was aware of it. Balfour appeared to suggest that nothing could be done to avoid the shrapnel anyway, so the residents should go about their business if they were not inside the caves during artillery fire.[24]

In some ways, however, she also gave the impression that she might have been willing to die and become a cause célèbre for the hopeful nation of the Confederacy. She evinced the determined resolve of many of the residents. In her diary she later noted: "The general impression is that they fire at the city ... thinking that they will wear out the women and children and sick and General Pemberton will be forced to surrender the place on that account, but they little know the spirit of Vicksburg's women and children if they expect this. Rather than let them know they are causing us any suffering we would be content to suffer martyrdom."[25] She was ready to die for the cause, as noted by her words as well as her refusal to leave her home during the worst of the shelling, and in this she differed from many of the other residents of the community. The willingness of most of the other citizens to live in the caves for the duration of the siege suggests that they were not as devoted to the cause as Balfour and remained more realistic about their situations.

Though she refused to go into the caves to seek shelter with the exception of a couple of times, Balfour willingly moved around her home during shelling in hopes of finding a modicum of shelter. Fortunately for historians, Balfour's refusal to descend into the caves allowed her to observe the shelling on a regular basis. On May 31, she wrote that the shelling continued throughout the night and did not allow the occupants of the house to get any rest. As the shells exploded, the fragments rained down, further adding to the concern of the residents. Balfour commented with some regularity that she expected to be hit by one of the exploding shells and killed during the siege, a thought many other members of the community likely had. At midnight, Balfour and the rest of the occupants retreated to the downstairs dining room for a modicum of security. As that did not seem sound when the artillery began firing from the southeast as well, the group moved to the parlor in the interior of the dwelling in the hopes of avoiding a direct blast. At that, the group remained fretful that a shell might fall through the roof.[26]

Despite her near complete refusal to seek shelter in the caves, most of the civilians of the community embraced a greater degree of self-preservation and regularly fled to the earthen shelters. The immediate risk of being injured or killed by the shelling wisely overruled any sense of inflated pride of such enlightened residents. Some of the stronger residents that were used to manual labor even sparked a temporary real estate trade in excavating the cave lodgings along with some citizens acting as agents in buying and selling the caves for others.[27]

The civilians of the community feared the smaller artillery shells that regularly flew overhead, but they were petrified of the enormous 220-pound mortar shells fired from the Union gunboats. The Parrott shells likewise terrified the populace due to the unique sound that they made while flying through the Mississippi skies. Resident Mary Loughborough noted in her diary that while she was in her well-apportioned cave, a battery of Parrotts opened up from the Union lines. She immediately called the servants into the cave and saw a shell impact the ground nearby and fail to explode. Another shell amazingly flew directly into the cave, landing among the occupants. Like the previous round, this one too failed to explode, only lying on the floor with wafts of smoke dissipating from the fuse. As the shell sat in the room, Loughborough handed one of the other occupants a blanket as a meager means of protection from the impending blast. They remained frozen for a few seconds

> with our eyes fixed in terror on the missile of death, when George, the servant boy, rushed forward, seized the shell, and threw it into the street, running swiftly in the opposite direction.
>
> Fortunately, the fuse had become nearly extinguished, and the shell nearly harmless—remaining near the mouth of the cave, as a trophy of the fearlessness of the servant and our remarkable escape. Very thankful was I for our preservation, which was the theme of conversation for a day among our cave neighbors. The incident of the blanket was also related; and all laughed heartily at my wise supposition that the blanket could be any protection from the heavy fragments of shells.[28]

Though this remained a very close call, Loughborough, like most of the other residents of the community, made quite an effort to remain as safe as possible during an incredibly dangerous period for the riverfront town. It is also impressive that the residents of the area retained a sense of humor to deal with their predicament. Another citizen used humor to make light of the nutritional privations shared by the community. They wrote up a fake hotel menu from the supposed Hotel De Vicksburg that noted dishes such as "Mule Head Stuffed A La Mode" or "mule rump stuffed with rice," served along with liquors: "Mississippi water, vintage of 1498," or "spring water, Vicksburg brand."[29]

In a strategic move, those constructing the caves did so with the openings facing away from the river so that shrapnel would not fly into the dwelling after an explosion. The hope was that since the shells flew in a direct line from the river, having the openings facing away would prevent the shells from flying right inside. Some residents even constructed an earthen berm in front of their caves so that the blast from an errant shell that landed at the opening would be deflected, blocking any fragments from the explosion from entering the cave and harming the occupants. Though it was not a foolproof system, it did keep the civilians safe from the Union siege.[30]

During the early weeks of the siege, most of the caves remained simple affairs with a basic dugout that allowed their owners to take temporary refuge from the incoming artillery. Later, civilians increasingly began to bring the comforts of home into the new underground bunkers through gradual expansions of the underground dwellings. Linda Lord described her family's bunker: "The cave ran about twenty feet underground, and communicated at right angles with a wing which opened on the front of the hill, giving us free circulation of air." In addition to the efforts to allow for airflow, Loughborough's family attempted to gain some relief from the tight quarters of the cave by setting up a small dining area just outside the entrance that they might enjoy when shells were not falling. Near the dining area, the family also had an open-air kitchen and fireplace complete with cooking implements. [31] They used the outdoor kitchen to prevent heat from building up in the enclosed caves. However, the cooking done in these areas was carried out in a sporadic fashion, delayed by the random incoming shells from the Union gunboats.

Inside the cave, the family had dug various closets for supplies along with some "niches for candles, books, and flowers. . . . Our cave was strongly boarded at the entrances, and we had procured some mattresses which made comfortable beds. For a time we slept in the tent, and only used the cave for shelter."[32] Like the Lords, many Vicksburg residents expanded their cave systems and attempted to bring the comforts of home into their underground shelters. With an exception of the very few reckless folks, residents endured long periods of shelling within their bunkers and emerged briefly just outside the entrance during the lulls in the artillery shot. They expected a lengthy siege.

To the grudging relief of many of the residents of the town, Pemberton surrendered his forces to Grant on July 4, 1863. Following the surrender, many of the Union forces took pity on the Confederate troops and civilians, offering them personal rations. The *Camden Confederate*, a South Carolina newspaper, objectively pointed out the humanity of the often-despised General Grant in revealing that following the surrender, the general "sent boat loads of supplies and furnished the garrison" and civilian inhabitants of the city.[33]

Upon hearing that a cease-fire had been ordered by the commanding generals, Mary Loughborough took her first stroll outside the cave in relative safety. Many of the cave dwellers had only ventured outside their caves for very brief periods during the shelling and had always remained vigilant to the possibility of incoming artillery fire. Staying in their shelters for as long as possible, the residents simply could not make careful observations of their surroundings. Finally able to leave the cave safely, Mary recorded her careful observations in her diary:

> I put on my bonnet and sullied forth beyond the terrace, for the first time since I entered. On the hill above us, the earth was literally

covered with fragments of shell—Parrott, shrapnel, canister; besides lead in all shapes and forms, and a long kind of solid shot, shaped like a small Parrott shell. Minie balls lay in every direction, flattened, dented, and bent from the contact with trees and pieces of wood in their flight. The grass seemed deadened—the ground ploughed into furrows in many places; while scattered over all, like giants' pepper, in numberless quantity, were shrapnel balls. I could now see how very near to the rifle pits my cave lay: only a small ravine between the two hills separated us.[34]

When Pemberton finally ordered his men to stack their arms in surrender to the Union forces entering the town of Vicksburg, his men also distributed the remaining Confederate stocks of supplies to the citizens. During the siege, the rations had been restricted drastically to make them last for an unknown period, so a moderate stockpile remained in hopes of carrying the besieged through a continuing occupation.[35]

In addition to releasing rations to both the Confederate garrison and townspeople of Vicksburg, Federal troops also stepped in to aid the community in recovering from the siege. In a letter to his brother dated July 16, 1863, William Christie of the 1st Minnesota Light Artillery Battery remarked that the Federals used gangs of African Americans to clean the streets and haul away refuse while Union soldiers filled ditches and closed some caves in part as a means of stemming outbreaks of disease in the waterfront community. While working throughout the city, Christie's group stumbled upon a store of provisions hidden under the home of a civilian in town. He angrily exclaimed in his letter that "he was drawing rations from our commissar" and had hidden "fifteen barrels of flour, several of sugar and a great quantity of melossas [sic], he was takin in custody and the goods seized."[36] While Christie was understandably angry at this citizen, the gentleman's motives for hoarding the foodstuffs is open to speculation. Prior to Pemberton's surrender, the timespan for the conclusion of the siege was unknown. Following the siege, drawing rations from the Federal stores, however, provided a formerly besieged resident, suffering at the hands of Federal forces, an opportunity to take something back from those very same Yankees.

Ultimately, the civilians of Vicksburg represented a microcosm of the Confederate public at large. Just as Emma Balfour remained recalcitrant and refused to seek safety during the artillery barrages, so too did many other Confederate citizens in their devotion to the fledgling nation. Balfour set herself up as a martyr for the cause of the Confederacy. Much of the rest of the community, however, remained quite a bit more pragmatic in their efforts to face the war. At the outset, much of the community of Vicksburg opposed or had a more lukewarm view of secession. Once the state left the Union, though, the community lent its support to the infant nation. Likewise, during the siege, a good number of the residents of the town made a halfhearted attempt to leave the site of the impending confrontation. Unfortunately for them, they were too late in their efforts and found themselves trapped in a besieged community and doomed to suffer for the duration of the engagement, much like the civilians of the Confederacy as a whole. The civilians of the community found themselves in a terrible situation (in part due to their own actions) and were resourceful in constructing an elaborate hamlet of caves to serve as bunkers during the near continual artillery duels. Their efforts were rewarded, and less than a couple dozen residents of the town were killed during the shelling over the course of the siege. Like the rest of the former Confederates, they continued to hold a grudge against the North as well as against some of the former Confederate officers.

Though quite a bit of discussion often centers on the perceived bitterness of the residents of Vicksburg following the surrender, at least some of that discussion is myth. An oft-repeated line is that the residents of Vicksburg refused to celebrate the Fourth of July for nearly one hundred years following the surrender out of a sense of absolute bitterness. However, that does not at all seem to be the case. As early as 1877, there are accounts of celebrations of the holiday among the local people of the community.[37] Although some residents likely did not take part in the celebrations of the holiday, enough celebrations did occur that they were reported in the local newspapers. Likewise, the influx of occupation forces during the next two years of the war as well as the occupation during Reconstruction introduced a plethora of single young men to the area, some of whom even found love and eventual marriage partners with the local ladies of the community. Though some animosity very likely lingered within the residents of Vicksburg, a great many let go of old feelings and moved on.

Notes

1. David D. Porter, *The Naval History of the Civil War* (New York: Sherman Publishing Company, 1886; reprint, Mineola, NY: Dover Publications, 1998), 323–25; page citations are to the reprint edition.

2. Andrew F. Smith, *Starving the South: How the North Won the Civil War* (New York: St. Martin's Press, 2011), 101.

3. *Alexandria Gazette* (Washington, DC), June 9, 1863.

4. *Montpelier (VT) Daily Freeman*, June 15, 1863.

5. *Richmond (VA) Daily Dispatch*, July 14, 1862.

6. *Richmond Daily Dispatch*, July 14, 1862.

7. *Montpelier Daily Freeman*, June 15, 1863.

8. *Abington Virginian,* May 29, 1863.

9. *Richmond Daily Dispatch,* July 14, 1862.

10. A. A. Hoehling, *Vicksburg: 47 Days of Siege* (Upper Saddle River, NJ: Prentice Hall, 1969; reprint, Mechanicsburg, PA: Stackpole Books, 1996), 15; page citations are to the reprint edition.

11. Smith, *Starving the South,* 100.

12. Ibid.

13. Ibid., 102.

14. Ibid.

15. U.S. War Department, *The War of the Rebellion: A Compilation of the Official Records of the Union and Confederate Armies,* 128 vols. (Washington, DC: Government Printing Office, 1881–1901), series 1, vol. 24, pt. 3, 982–83.

16. Ibid.

17. Smith, *Starving the South,* 105.

18. Hoehling, *Vicksburg,* 200–201.

19. Ibid.

20. Mary Ann Loughborough, *My Cave Life in Vicksburg* (New York: D. Appleton and Company, 1864), 72.

21. Hoehling, *Vicksburg: 47 Days of Siege,* 21.

22. Timothy B. Smith, *Mississippi in the Civil War: The Home Front* (Jackson, MI: University of Mississippi Press, 2010), 117.

23. Michael B. Ballard, *Pemberton: The General Who Lost Vicksburg* (Jackson: University of Mississippi Press, 1991), 173.

24. Armstead L. Robinson, *Bitter Fruits of Bondage: The Demise of Slavery and the Collapse of the Confederacy, 1861–1865* (Charlottesville: University of Virginia Press, 2005), 216.

25. Andrea Warren, *Under Siege! Three Children at the Civil War Battle for Vicksburg* (New York: Melanie Kroupa Books, 2009), 89.

26. Hoehling, *Vicksburg,* 74.

27. Loughborough, *My Cave Life in Vicksburg,* 72.

28. Ibid., 74–75.

29. *Chicago Tribune,* July 25, 1863.

30. Winston Groom, *Vicksburg, 1863* (New York: Alfred A. Knopf, 2009), 364.

31. Hoehling, *Vicksburg,* 106.

32. Ibid.

33. *Camden (SC) Confederate,* July 10, 1863.

34. Loughborough, *My Cave Life in Vicksburg,* 173–138.

35. Ulysses S. Grant, *Personal Memoires of Ulysses S. Grant,* (New York: Charles L. Webster and Company, 1885; reprint, Old Saybrook, CT: Konecky and Konecky, 1999), 330; page citations are to the reprint edition.

36. William G. Christie to Alexander S. Christie, July 17, 1863, Minnesota Historical Society, St. Paul.

37. *Vicksburg Daily Commercial,* July 3, 1877.

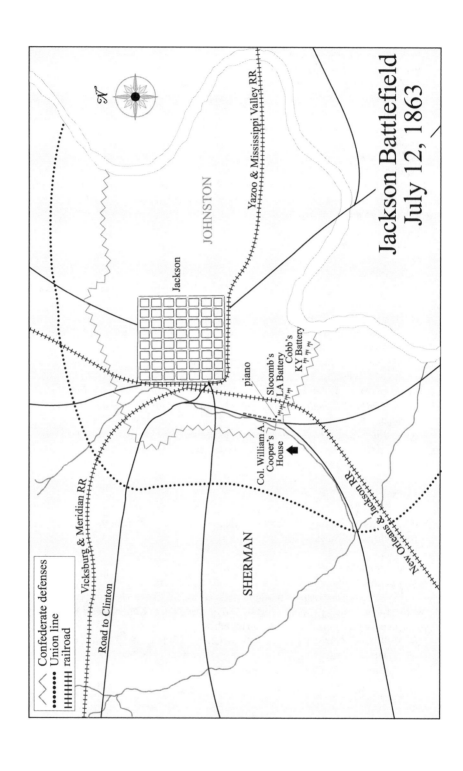

Jackson Battlefield
July 12, 1863

Confederate defenses
Union line
railroad

Road to Clinton

Vicksburg & Meridian RR

SHERMAN

New Orleans & Jackson RR

Col. William A.
Cooper's House

piano

Slocomb's
LA Battery

Cobb's
KY Battery

Jackson

JOHNSTON

Yazoo & Mississippi Valley RR

7

MOURNFUL MELODIES: LOUISIANANS PLAYED
THE SWAN SONG OF THE ARMY OF RELIEF

Richard H. Holloway

The area surrounding Pollard, Alabama, located east of Mobile, was full of criminal mischief in the early months of 1863. It was the epicenter of "great numbers of outlaws of the worst character [who] roved in bands, committing robberies, murder, and all manner of crimes." Deserters and stragglers from the armies both North and South filled the ranks of marauders flocking to this sparsely populated and isolated locale. Fortunately for the neighboring populace, including a large number of refugees removed from Pensacola, Florida, several Confederate units were stationed nearby to protect them if required.[1]

The command consisted mainly of Alabama and Florida units and, the lone group not from that part of the country, the 19th Louisiana Infantry. Describing Pollard, Private George Asbury Bruton of the 19th Louisiana wrote to his sister, "This is the poorest country I ever saw in my life or ever expect to see. Tell Ma I am sorry that I can't say any thing in favor of her old native state but we are camped in the out-edge close to no where. I never saw a goffer [gopher] before I come to this country & I imagin that is all this country is fit for is to rais goffers [gophers]." Despite Bruton's low opinion of his surroundings, these forces served another vital purpose in their assignment to keep an eye on the Yankees at Pensacola; thus the assembled Confederates units were officially deemed an "army of observation."[2]

The Louisianans were added to this garrison in part to recoup their strength after appalling losses nearly a year before at the Battle of Shiloh, Tennessee, where they earned the sobriquet, "Bloody 19th." In addition to their daily drudge of drill and outpost duties, the troops set about raising a vegetable garden and fishing in the Escambia River to supplement their normal ration issue. The garden served to alleviate their physical maladies. Their agricultural efforts soon received praise from the Mobile newspaper, which lauded their work and suggested it "should be appreciated and imitated."[3]

Music was incorporated into the 19th Louisiana with both practical and spiritual results. The 19th's commander, Colonel Wesley Parker Winans was a "lover of music" but primarily formed a regimental band for roll call, dress parade, and drilling. Douglas John Cater, a transfer from the 3rd Texas Cavalry to the 19th, was tabbed as drum major. Four others with rhythmic talents served under him. Benefits for the drummers were relief from musket and guard duty, offset by the need to rise earlier than everyone else for reveille.[4]

While the drumming served to keep the soldiers in step and sound notifications for other duties and events, Cater's boredom led to his successful implementation of a string band, further raising the spirits of the soldiers. The regiment took up money, sending it to Mobile to purchase musical instruments. "We secured," Cater later recalled, "a good violin [for Cater's brother, Rufus], a guitar [for John W. Bonham who also sang lead for the melodious quartet], a base violin [for Lieutenant Frank Smith] and a piccolo [for himself]." Not long afterward, Cater and his new orchestra were serenading young ladies throughout the countryside.[5]

Preparation for resumption of duty at the front lines soon marred the serenity of the concerts. Since only a scarce number of men returned to the regiment after recuperation from their wounds at Shiloh, Winans decided to send one of his officers to bolster their ranks. There was little likelihood able-bodied men from the local community would join a Louisiana unit instead of one of their own state's commands also residing in the vicinity. Captain Hyder Ali Kennedy was selected to head back to Louisiana for the first two months in 1863 in order to sign up men for the 19th's replenishment. He succeeded in enrolling several new recruits before returning.[6]

Orders came to pack up and get ready to move, circuitously, by train starting April 8 and ending May 31 at Jackson, Mississippi. Cater speculated their old army commander, Braxton Bragg either saw the newspaper article about their garden "or remembered where we were sent, and decided he had better use for us and that Pensacola was not liable to be attacked, at least in the near future." Bruton's reasoning for willingly abandoning the Pollard area was more practical as he likened the Alabama female's appearance to the numerous gophers he spotted earlier, "They dont look like the La [girls] do." Apparently, twenty of the unit's soldiers had no qualms about the beauty of the local females and concocted a scheme to marry them. Of the subterfuge played upon the girls, Private Rufus Festus Eddins lamented, "They do not know but what those men they are marrying have wives at home."[7]

During the same time, the 5th Company of Washington (Louisiana) Artillery was passing through Mobile from their leisurely post at Wartrace, Tennessee. Like the 19th Louisiana, the artillerist's detachment from their native Louisiana hindered refilling their ranks. Fortunately, new recruits from New Orleans were in Mobile, and they converged on the battery. Mobile became a safe haven for residents of the Crescent City fleeing their homes prior to its capture by Union forces, thus providing a quick bolstering of forty men to their muster rolls. This welcome influx of eager citizens was supplied courtesy of none other than Union Major General Nathaniel Prentiss Banks who ordered the deportation of all registered enemies of the United States from Federally-occupied New Orleans to any Confederate-held territory by May 15. The battery's members sought to take "full advantage of all the comforts & pleasures" but their commander, Captain Cuthbert Harrison Slocomb, soon collected them back aboard the train to unite with their old brigade, including the 19th Louisiana.[8]

The last time the 19th Louisiana and the Washington Artillery served side by side was at Shiloh, Tennessee, more than a year ago. Both units were part of a makeshift brigade with the Crescent (24th Louisiana) Infantry during the battle's second day. The two units, along with the Crescents, bonded from the fighting they endured. Asking for assistance when it appeared their battery of the Washington Artillery was to be overrun, both infantry groups moved to their defense, and desperate hand-to-hand fighting ensued. Despite the Washington Artillery's best attempts, Union soldiers captured three of their cannons. In his official report on the cause of the losses, the battery's then-commander, Washington Irving Hodgson exclaimed, "[M]y men were broken down, my horses nearly all slain, ammunition out, and sponges all broken and gone."[9]

The two battle-hardened Louisiana units were reunited when the battery arrived in Jackson three days after the foot soldiers. The Washington Artillery opted for a dramatic grand entrance when the train steamed into the city. They organized a parade in the grove of Mrs. Susan S. Oakley, "who will be remembered by the 5th Co. for her kindness & attention to us," noted an unidentified artilleryman. It was likely no coincidence since she operated a "young ladies institute." The battery was also celebrating a banner day in which they received four new twelve-pounder Napoleon cannon along with two James rifles to replace their old ordnance. The fanfare for the members of the 19th Louisiana was much less elaborate. After reuniting with other members of their old brigade, Eddins glumly noted, "We have got back to Mis[sissippi] where we have to drink bad water."[10]

The brigade the 19th and Washington Artillery joined consisted of the 32nd Alabama Infantry, 13th and 20th Louisiana Consolidated Infantry, 14th Louisiana Sharpshooter Battalion, and 16th and 25th Louisiana Consolidated Infantry, all under the command of Brigadier General Daniel Weisiger Adams. The soldiers learned they were ordered there by General Joseph Eggleston Johnston, who was assembling an army for the relief of the Vicksburg garrison. Johnston arrived in Jackson a couple of weeks before the Louisianans and immediately began to formulate a plan to free up the encircled forces inside of beleaguered Vicksburg. In his diary, one soldier inside the city mentioned that "General Johns[t]on is Said to be within 30 miles of here," so hope still existed for the Southern men in the trenches of Vicksburg after Union General Ulysses Simpson Grant invested the city with his massive Federal army.[11]

Johnston continued to receive reinforcements from the far reaches of the Confederacy. Most groups arrived by train, but some used other modes of transportation. Brigadier General William H. "Red" Jackson's three thousand–man cavalry division rode atop their mounts from Spring Hill, Tennessee, four hundred miles away. Others wearily marched on foot to Mississippi's capital. British observer Lieutenant Colonel Arthur Fremantle accompanied some of these troops and noted, "[the] straggling of the Georgians was on the grandest scale conceivable." The Englishman managed to garner a meeting with Johnston, who, he related, was "rather below middle height, spare, soldierlike, and well set up."[12]

Confederate Secretary of War James Alexander Seddon dispatched Johnston to Mississippi on May 9 with orders to take "chief command of the forces, giving to those in the field, as far as practicable, the encouragement and benefit of your personal direction." The general accepted this directive and replied, "I shall go immediately, although unfit for field service." Unfortunately, Johnston arrived too late as the enemy were already positioned between him and Lieutenant General John Clifford Pemberton's forces just east of Vicksburg. Some of Pemberton's soldiers left the confines of the city, attempting to join Johnston, but they were soundly defeated at the Battle of Champion Hill and retreated into their earthen breastworks. Thwarted at rescuing Pemberton, Johnston resolved to assemble a large enough force to attack the Federal rearguard and trap them between the two Southern forces. To accomplish this objective, Johnston waited as long as possible, allowing reinforcements to arrive at his selected staging area in Jackson.[13]

What greeted the Louisiana units in Jackson was a deplorable sight. In an attempt to destroy facilities housing Confederate war materials in mid-May, the Union invaders under Major General William Tecumseh Sherman started fires to burn every building capable of producing war material in the city. Both public and private residences went up in flames despite one of the "most drenching rain storms" the night prior to the city's brief occupation by Federal units. About Jackson, Sherman later announced, "The city . . . is a mass of charred ruins." The residents later dubbed their city "Chimneyville" because the remaining chimneys were the only thing left of many of the burned buildings. Eddins observed upon his entrance to the city, "The Yanks nearly ruined Jackson . . . they burned up $15,000,000 worth of property."[14]

Shortly after pitching their tents in a valley about two hundred yards from the Mississippi capitol building, Cater recalled the 19th Louisiana was ordered to go on provost duty three miles from town. Eddins complained he was "standing guard ev[e]ry other day." A Kentucky native in Major General John Cabell Breckinridge's division with the Louisiana brigade was elated to find their camping spot not far from a small lake and the Pearl River. Although the city "presented quite a desolate appearance" to him, a "great deal of it having lately burned down," the soldier noticed the kindness of the citizens who remained in the city. To combat the perpetually hot weather, many of the Kentucky soldiers engaged in a novel way to expand their rations. He noted, "The boys caught a great many fish out of the lake and river." Two men would go into the shallow part of the lake and "hold a blanket spread out." As other men would splash about on one side, the fish would jump out of the water and right onto the blanket, "thus being caught by the hundreds."[15]

Aside from guard duty, members of the Washington Artillery spent an inordinate amount of time ensuring the unit was as well equipped as possible. Captain Slocomb managed to secure new issues of clothing, refurbished wagons, "camp equipage, artificers tools, etc." From inspection reports, the company replenished its needs and was better equipped than it had been in over a year's time. No doubt the new cannon were the pride of the artillerists and their drill maneuvers practiced to near perfection.

Rumors about Vicksburg began trickling in. As the middle of June approached, Eddins wrote, "[T]here is talk ev[e]ry day of Johonsons [Johnston's] mooving on the Yanks. [T]hey have Vicksburg in a clost [closed] place. [T]hey are within rifel shot of our works and as well fortied [fortified] as we are in some places. The Pontoon Bridges from here this morning. I expect there will be a forward move shortly. I expect our Regt will be left here to guard Jackson." Despite the rest and refitting, Eddins was experiencing the doldrums when he explained, "I don't feel like writing humor this morning." Soon, others in the 19th Louisiana would have a cure for his sagging spirits.[16]

Because of his appreciation of music, Winans ordered the 19th Louisiana's string band instruments safely stored among the baggage of the regiment on their winding travels from Pollard to Jackson. Cater and the other members of the musical group excitedly hauled them out and put them to use. One night, the group somehow secured the use of an ambulance to transport them, along with Adjutant A. Ben Broughton, Captain Jack Hodges, and Sergeant Thomas J. Prude, a few miles outside of town with the purpose of serenading some young ladies. It was a beautiful moonlit night; the men brought out their pieces and took note of their surroundings, bedecked with a plethora of decorative flowers and shrubs. "[T]he folding doors were thrown open by an affable old gentleman, who welcomed us and invited us" inside, so impressed was he with the band's selection of tunes. In the dining room, the bandsmen were delighted to discover a "sumptuous repast" awaiting them. Cater later remembered his brother Rufus saying the dessert cake "was too pretty to cut." Wines, salads, and much more awaited the talented musicians, all surrounding a notable vase inscribed, "Vicksburg, Vicksburg, Vicksburg." Discreetly tucked inside the flower arrangements encircling the vase were dainty notes thanking the soldiers "for the serenade and conveying happy wishes."[17]

Camped nearby, the Washington Artillery was no less inventive with ways to benefit from their surroundings. The battery planned a "Grand Fete . . . in appreciation of the many kindnesses & favors of the ladies of Jackson." They were "determined to have their fun while they can." The artillerymen gathered delicacies and laid them out on Mrs. Oakley's lawn. They set up covered areas for dancing as well. An unidentified battery member recalled, "Our pieces or guns having been thoroughly cleaned & burnished up & also decorated with miniature flags, wreaths, ribbons & flowers are posted at one side of the lawn in the shape of a Crescent." The men even built a bandstand for the musicians to ply the young ladies with their melodic tunes. Not many units could host such a lavish event with an equally sumptuous meal like the members of the Washington Artillery of New Orleans.[18]

While the men under his command were involved in frivolous activities to pass the time, Johnston finally began to realize he was not getting any more additions to his small army, nicknamed the "Army of Relief." He even debated with Confederate President Jefferson Davis concerning the actual number of men he had on hand. The general speculated he had in the neighborhood of 23,000 soldiers fit for duty while the president countered with an amount totaling 34,000 troops. Other governmental officials in Richmond chimed in and confirmed the president's mathematics, but Johnston insisted those numbers were blown out of proportion. Finally, Johnston was told by Confederate Secretary of War Seddon in no uncertain terms, "You must rely upon what you have and the irregular forces in Mississippi." Aware of Johnston's probable approach, Grant instructed his command to build another set of entrenchments outside the one they built facing Vicksburg, this one protecting the Federals from a possible offensive emanating from Jackson. Sherman observed, "We must work smart as Joe Johnston is collecting the shattered forces," while also noting the desperation they were encountering from Pemberton's garrison.[19]

During most of late June, soldiers in Jackson could hear "heavy cannonading" originating from the direction of Vicksburg. However, some men were temporarily distracted from the constant booming upon the late arrival of their army wages. Payments were issued June 30, not leaving much time to spend their funds nor arrange for the money to be sent home with a trustworthy comrade, because on the first day of July, Johnston finally budged from the safe confines of Jackson and headed toward Vicksburg with his army. Cater noted he and his comrades marched all day and reached the outskirts of Clinton more than a dozen miles away. A Kentuckian remembered it was, "The hotest march we have ever made. Many soldiers tumbled down the road from sun-stroke." Some men in Breckinridge's division, including Louisiana soldiers, were a part of the members of the Pioneer Corps prior to their departure. This special group was tasked with finding the nearest sources of potable water. The precious liquid proved elusive and, combined with the rising temperatures, caused the soldiers to tire easily.[20]

To combat the extreme heat, the officers elected to take up the next day's march before daylight. Units like the Louisiana brigade had an artillery battery attached to their force. In a proper line of march, this kicked up an inordinate amount of dust, causing the infantrymen in line behind these units to suffer from sight and breathing deficiencies, not to mention the ignominy of stepping in the waste left in the wake of the horses pulling the artillery pieces. An Alabamian remarked, "Orders issued to allow no music from bands, beating of drums nor any noise above ordinary tone of conversation," a hardship for the musically inclined Louisiana troops. Some men were "falling dead from sunstroke" in spite of their commander's best efforts. Eddins confirmed, "A grate many fell, some stretch on the side of the road." Late in the afternoon, Johnston's exhausted soldiers halted, turned to the side, and stretched out to sleep alongside the road they had just trodden upon.[21]

The Army of Relief, including the 19th Louisiana and Washington Artillery, stayed in a holding pattern for most of July 3 and 4. An exasperated member of the Washington Artillery jotted down how they were "occupied in marching around the country, with seemingly no object in view but to keep moving." One disgruntled Alabama soldier complained, "Our idea of generalship was that if our expedition was intended for a relief of Vicksburg, it should be a bold and quick movement. It was irritating to be dallying along at the rate we were going, but we had implicit confidence in General Johnston and hoped all would turn out well." In a letter to his wife on the 4th of July, well-traveled South Carolina Brigadier General Nathan G. "Shanks" Evans wrote, "Vicksburg holds out nobly. We are now only four miles from them and all of us anxious for the order to advance. The Genl. [Johnston] however is very cautious and is studying the position of the enemy."[22]

After negotiations on July 3, Grant prepared to accept the surrender of Vicksburg's garrison, thus ending the long siege. When Sherman heard the news of the city's impending capitulation, he enthusiastically exclaimed, "Glory Hallelujah! The best Fourth of July since 1776." Soon thereafter Grant instructed Sherman: "I want Johnston broken up as effectually as possible, and the [rail]roads destroyed." Sherman responded, "[T]elegraph me the moment you have Vicksburg in possession, and I will secure all the crossings of [Big] Black River, and move on Jackson or Canton, as you may advise." As an Illinois foot soldier put it on July 5, "We were called out and started on the march toward [Big] Black River at an early hour. We were marched at a very rapid pace as Gen Sherman was trying to steal a march on Gen Johnston before he learned of the fall of Vicksburg."[23]

On the afternoon of July 5, Johnston's command assembled and headed toward Vicksburg. The army advanced about six miles toward Vicksburg along a nearby railroad. One Louisiana soldier commented, "The weather is very dry and the roads a foot deep in dust." An enlisted man serving in the Breckinridge's division proclaimed it "the hardest marching ever" and noted when his unit halted for the evening, they "bivouacked in line of battle on the battle field of 'Champion's Hill.'" The men expected to soon encounter Union resistance the following day and were readying the pontoon boats for quick deployment across the Big Black River. Eddins was fortunate enough to be one of the soldiers to receive mail from home while on the march: "The pleasure it afforded me to read a letter from home, one stating to that peace and plenty rained in my native Isle."[24]

The next day was ominous for the Confederates as word began to spread throughout Johnston's forces of Vicksburg's fall. Cater would recall the impact the loss of the city and its garrison had on him. "Gloom is on every countenance, with Pemberton's army prisoners in the hands of Gen. Grant and the war prolonged." Johnston almost instantaneously "moved his camp on Big Black [River], in the direction of Jackson." At one o'clock in the morning of July 6, one of the soldiers recalled being "aroused from our slumbers and officially informed that Vicksburg had surrendered." Johnston's army reversed their course toward Vicksburg and headed back to Jackson. About

a mile down the path, many of the units had to soon "give the road" to passing wagons and artillery units and allow them to take up position at the
head of the column. Although batteries like the Washington Artillery were
mostly mounted, dust still managed to permeate their lungs and clothes. "No
water—dust, dust, dust," recalled a Louisiana private of the exposure. "My
God it is awful." Occasionally, the Yankees would catch up with a bunch of
Confederates on this retreat. One weary Ohioan managed to help "charge a
line of 'Jonnies' located in a corn-field." He claimed, "We run them out lively"
just before he "gave out."[25]

Continuous forced marching caused elements of Johnston's men to arrive
back in Jackson toward the late evening amid a "heavy rain & storm." Eddins
wrote, "We got back the night of the sixth. [T]he last day we marched nearly
all day and a good portion of the night." During the trip, the Washington
Artillery stopped forward progress on a regular basis to deploy into battery
to confront any perceived rearguard attacks only to limber their cannons
right back up and continue on once the threat dissipated. In a letter home, a
South Carolina infantryman on loan to Johnston reported, "I am back safe
in this City [Jackson] having made one of the hardest marches yesterday in
the annals of war." Eddins wrote, "[W]e arrived in Jackson [and then] we were
ordered to the ditches." British observer Fremantle had earlier described the
breastworks, stating they were "a mild trench . . . dignified by the name of
the fortifications of Jackson."[26]

The units settled into the trenches, and cannons were unlimbered at their
respective gun emplacements in an arc configuration with both flanks resting
on the Pearl River per Johnston's orders. The Louisiana brigade manned the
extreme right side of the Confederate line's left flank, straddling the New
Orleans Railroad. In line from the left were the 16th and 25th Consolidated
Louisiana; 32nd Alabama; 5th Company, Washington Artillery; 19th Louisiana; and 13th and 20th Consolidated Louisiana. The 14th Louisiana Sharpshooter Battalion was stationed nearby with its dependable sharpshooters.
Incredulously, the members of the Washington Artillery "grumbled exceed-
ingly" about their placement in these works. The gunners even complained
as they constructed the gun emplacements initially. They decried the use of
a barricade for protection as they were used to fighting out in the open. They
"asked to be allowed to fight without protection, as they had done on so many
fields before. But nothing availed." As First Lieutenant J. Adolphe Chalaron
explained, most "had never handled anything heavier than a pen," and this
experience became "their first initiation handling picks and shovels."[27]

Slocomb's gunners were not the only ones in the area unfamiliar with
digging implements. As soon as Breckinridge's division established its line,

a party of them scoured the city in search of "negroes to work on the forti-fications." One group managed to corral quite a crowd, "among them a few dandy barbers, who did not fancy wielding the pick and shoving the spade much." One of the Kentucky natives remembered, "We layed around & took it easy while the negroes used the picks, spades & axes." The Army of Relief's commander personally inspected the earthworks and found them "miserably located and not half completed." Johnston ordered four thousand bales of cotton to help augment his defenses. Of Johnston's directions, a Georgian surmised, "I think he is going to make a stand here. He is going to fight the Yanks as old Jackson did the English at New Orleans, behind the cotton bags." Slocomb "erected a strong traverse of cotton bales" around the battery and proclaimed, "Thus we formed quite a comfortable redoubt for ourselves." This area of fortifications was referred to as Fort Breckinridge in honor of their division commander. Second Sergeant James Elijah Carraway of the 19th Louisiana wrote, "[A]ll of the timber and underbrush had been cut down for one quarter of a mile in front of our works."[28]

As the Confederates were preparing their defense of Jackson, Sherman's army trudged along the same route used by Johnston during his withdrawal. The retreating forces nearly drained the entire water supply, and what re-mained was unhealthy. "[T]he Rebels had sought to render the waterholes unfit for use by having tar, turpentine, ashes, and other offensive matter thrown into them. Livestock were brought into creeks and then shot, leaving the rotting carcasses to prevent Union troops from quenching their parched throats." A Texas chaplain tasked with tainting the drinking supply recalled, "[We] threw a dead horse into the balance [of the remaining water] to keep the yankees, who are in pursuit, from getting of it."[29]

"A very fine but abandoned brick residence stood out in front of our works," recalled Carraway. One of Slocomb's gun crew confirmed his state-ment by remarking, "[It was indeed a] splendid mansion . . . which had been deserted by the family, leaving most of the household effects behind." On the 10th, Cater volunteered to join a party of five from Adams's brigade and sharpshoot in front of their position. "I volunteered to go and a musket and cartridges were furnished me," Cater later wrote. He continued, "There were five of us in the squad. We took position in a clump of trees not far from Col. [William A.] Cooper's residence." Exploring the Cooper home and its grounds, Cater speculated, "There was a large cistern under a dwelling in the yard. The water was cool and it seemed the Federals knew that the cistern of good water was there and they wanted it." Of the Yankees, he noted, "Their guns were better than ours and they were doing good execution while our guns could not reach them, only raise the dust twenty or thirty feet in front of them." Not long after the Southerners settled in, one of them was hit by an enemy bullet. Two men were required to drag him to safety, leaving Cater and another man to scramble behind a tree until they could retreat under the cover of darkness. Cater resolved to not volunteer for sharpshooting again "if I could not get a longer ranging gun."[30]

This detachment was firing into the distant ranks of Union Major General Edward O. C. Ord's Thirteenth Corps that managed to pull duty in front of Adams's brigade. Their attention toward the Cooper house caused Johnston to direct it to be burned immediately. A small group comprised of Louisianans was tasked with the job. Cater grabbed a "little piece of broken mirror and about a yard of Brussells carpet for use in camp." Carraway pocketed a piece of one of the "large and costly mirrors" so he could "afterwards behold his own half-starved features and ragged clothes," and he also cut himself a blanket-sized section of the carpet. All the men appropriated a suitable volume from the splendid library. The squad came across a magnificent piano and debated what to do with such a grand item. A "swarthy Creole" from the Washington Artillery "proposed that it be turned over to his battery as most of them were musicians, all of them French." It was agreed upon, and the men picked up the heavy piano and carried it back to their breastworks in the dead of night. The large musical instrument was safely placed among the large cotton bales. After they were gone, the remaining men, much to their chagrin, began to "apply the torch" to the magnificent home.[31]

Bolstered by the reinforcements from the timely arrival of Major General Francis P. Blair Jr.'s division of the Fifteenth Corps, Ord's men made a heavy reconnaissance toward the cistern at the Cooper residence the next day but were met with the deadly fire of one of Slocomb's rifled cannons. This gun was sent out five hundred yards in advance of Fort Breckinridge to hamper the Federal advance. Fortunately, the officer of this weapon had David "Hawkeye" Smith sighting the piece for him; thus the second round "struck one of their [Union's] guns on the muzzle, ruining it entirely." This miraculous shot was from approximately seventeen hundred yards away. After being bloodied heavily, the Northern troops retired to a safe distance. With the onset of evening, the Union troops were treated to a concert of melodies played by the Southerners on the piano and accompanied by hundreds of Louisiana soldiers singing such patriotic songs as "Dixie." Not to be outdone, their Northern counterparts "fired back the national airs."[32]

An hour before noon on July 12, elements of the Thirteenth Corps began to attack the well-defended Confederates, despite orders not to bring on a general engagement by their superiors. Adams anticipated a movement on his section of the works and cautiously transferred his headquarters to the rear of the embrasure. As the Southerners saw the advance develop, Lawrence Pugh of Slocomb's unit made his way to the piano and began playing it enthusiastically. Fellow cannoneer Andy Swain soon pushed him aside, grabbed an ammunition box, flipped it over, and took a turn at the ivory keys. Other men packed around the piano and sang along with the songs. An enthusiastic artilleryman under Adams jumped up on the parapet "like some grand orchestral leader" as the music played. The selection of songs was numerous and included the classic songs, "Auld Lang Syne, Lorena, Dixie, The Mocking Bird and the 'jolly' You Shan't Have Any of My Peanuts."[33]

The force moving on Fort Breckinridge consisted of two divisions from Ord's Thirteenth Corps. He instructed them to "make a reconnaissance, and, if it is necessary to form a line and attack to drive the force in front, do so, so as to keep your connection with the main corps." The Federals dispatched the 5th Ohio Independent Battery to shell the Confederates in the vicinity of Slocomb's battery and Winans's infantry. The Washington Artillery coolly responded to the attack but with only two of their cannon, thus not revealing their remaining arsenal. One of the Yankee brigade commanders hesitated upon receiving the Louisianans' return fire. Ordered to continue forward, Union Colonel Isaac Pugh complied and moved to a cornfield in front of the fort. The other division halted forward progress and dug in while Pugh's men advanced amid a hail of cannon and small arms fire from Slocomb's and Winans's men. Felled trees blocked their progress as a Kentucky artillery unit and the 32nd Alabama managed to get an angle on them to multiply the murderous firing.[34]

As Pugh's men trudged forward, some of the 19th Louisiana "had told the battery 'boys' to send for me," described Cater, "and that I would give them some good music on that piano." Cater responded to Slocomb's call, along with his brother Rufus. As the Southerners enjoyed Cater's playing while the shells and bullets whizzed by, Slocomb caught sound of a Federal movement and "saw them coming at a charge." The Cater brothers quickly scurried back to their post. Winans's regiment held their fire until Slocomb's cannon belched forth a volley in unison. Adams, excited at the prospective slaughter of Pugh's forces, grabbed a musket from one of the men, jumped on the parapet, and fired off a couple of rounds in the direction of the mass of Unionists. Cater reported the deadly rounds took a toll of 260 men dead in their front, 150 prisoners, and 160 wounded. One of the Washington Artillery recounted years later, "'Tis over; with a rush the piano is sought again. Not twenty minutes has sped since its last notes have died away." When Pugh's regiments streamed to the rear, Winans's soldiers emerged from behind the breastworks to collect their spoils of war.[35]

Carraway came upon a wounded Yankee officer who begged the sergeant for a doctor. The Southerner acquiesced. Winans's regimental surgeon, Chauncey F. Philson, "was a wiry, active fellow and nothing gave him more pleasure to visit a field hospital after a battle and aid in the hewing of flesh and sawing of bone." After Carraway called him to attend to the wounded Federal, Philson actually showed compassion instead of "his usual bitter hatred" toward the enemy. Another injured Union soldier brought out a roll book belonging to Carraway's company, captured a year prior at action near Corinth, Mississippi, from one of the sergeant's comrades killed in action. The captive man explained his company would call out the names in the 19th's company roll book and then answer to them to amuse themselves. As evening approached, two Kentucky regiments moved behind Slocomb to cover them in case of another attack.[36]

The only major assault of the siege of Jackson occurred on July 12, and by the 17th Johnston's forces abandoned the city. One of Breckinridge's Kentuckians recalled, "About midnight . . . we folded our tents like the Arabs and quietly stole away." The Confederates burned the bridge they retreated across and moved to Morton, a short distance away. Looting and destruction by the Federal soldiers entering Jackson was rampant until Blair's division arrived to restore order.

Into the next century, Carraway would sit at a local store and relate the story of the piano in the trenches to anyone who would listen. Used as a horse trough by the Yankees after they retook the city, the piano found its way to New Orleans after the war where it remains on display today at the Confederate Memorial Hall Museum. It is a fitting honor for the musical instrument that unintentionally played the swan song of Johnston's Army of Relief.[37]

Notes

1. Rodney B. Huffman, *Steadfast to the Last: The Life and Military Service of William Richardson Hamner Co. A, 19th Louisiana Volunteer Infantry (Pelican Regiment)* (Athens, AL: Rodney B. Huffman, 1999), 45. I thank Todd Wilber for providing me with great sources for this essay, along with Trayce Snow for offering me advice on the content.

2. Ibid.; George Asbury Bruton to sister, September 14, 1862, Richard H. Holloway private collection, Alexandria, LA (hereafter cited as Holloway collection); Arthur W. Bergeron Jr., *Confederate Mobile* (Baton Rouge: Louisiana State University Press, 1991), 56; Rufus Festus Eddins, "Four Years in the Confederate Infantry: The Civil War Letters of Private R. F. Eddins, 19th Louisiana Volunteers," *Texas Gulf Coast Historical and Biographical Record* 7 (November 1971): 24.

3. George Asbury Bruton to brother and sister, November 10, 1862, Holloway collection; William D. Cater, *As It Was: The Story Douglas John Cater's Life* (San Antonio, TX: W. D. Cater, 1981), 152, 157.

4. Cater, *As It Was*, 154–55.

5. Ibid.

6. Andrew B. Booth, *Records of Louisiana Confederate Soldiers and Louisiana Confederate Commands* (Spartanburg, SC: Reprint Company, 1984), 2:536.

7. Cater, *As It Was*, 157–58; Bruton to sister, September 14, 1862, Holloway collection; Eddins, "Four Years in the Confederate Infantry," 29.

8. Nathaniel Cheairs Hughes Jr., *The Pride of the Confederate Artillery: The Washington Artillery in the Army of Tennessee* (Baton Rouge: Louisiana State University Press, 1997), 98, 104; *New Orleans Daily True Delta*, May 1, 1863.

9. Hughes, *Pride of the Confederate Artillery*, 35–42; Huffman, *Steadfast to the Last*, 32–33.

10. Hughes, *The Pride of the Confederate Artillery*, 104; Eddins, "Four Years in the Confederate Infantry," 32–33.

11. Huffman, *Steadfast to the Last*, 49; Arthur W. Bergeron Jr., *Guide to Louisiana Confederate Military Units, 1861–1865* (Baton Rouge: Louisiana State University Press, 1989), 25, 106, 114, 121, 167; Edwin C. Bearss and Warren Grabau, *The Battle of Jackson, May 14, 1863* (Baltimore: Gateway Press, 1981), 9; Gabriel M. Killgore, "Vicksburg Diary: The Journal of Gabriel M. Killgore," *Civil War History* 10 (March 1964): 48; Powell A. Casey, *An Outline of the Civil War Campaigns and Engagements of the Washington Artillery of New Orleans* (Baton Rouge: Louisiana State University Press, 1986), 63.

12. Jim Woodrick, *The Civil War Siege of Jackson Mississippi* (Charleston, SC: History Press, 2016), 30–31.

13. Gilbert Govan and James Livingwood, *A Different Valor: Joseph E. Johnston* (New York: William S. Konecky, 1994), 197, 201–8.

14. H. Grady Howell Jr., *Chimneyville: "Likenesses" of Early Days in Jackson, Mississippi* (Madison, MS: H. Grady Howell Jr., 2007), v, 38, 42; Eddins, "Four Years in the Confederate Infantry," 33.

15. Cater, *As It Was*, 162; Eddins, "Four Years in the Confederate Infantry," 33; John S. Jackman, *Diary of a Confederate Soldier: John S. Jackman of the Orphan Brigade*, ed. William C. Davis (Columbia: University of South Carolina Press 1990), 77.

16. Hughes, *Pride of the Confederate Artillery*, 105; Eddins, "Four Years in the Confederate Infantry," 33–34.

17. Cater, *As It Was*, 163–64.

18. Hughes, *The Pride of the Confederate Artillery*, 105–6.

19. Woodrick, *Civil War Siege of Jackson*, 9; Govan and Livingwood, *Different Valor*, 208.

20. Jackman, *Diary of a Confederate Soldier*, 78; Huffman, *Steadfast to the Last*, 56; Cater, *As It Was*, 164; Booth, *Records of Louisiana Confederate Soldiers*, 2:344.

21. Jackman, *Diary of a Confederate Soldier*, 78; J. P. Cannon, *Bloody Banners and Barefoot Boys: A History of the 27th Regiment Alabama Infantry CSA; The Civil War Memoirs and Diary Entries of J. P. Cannon, M.D.*, ed. Noel Crowson and John V. Brogden (Shippensburg, PA: White Mane Publishers, 1997), 37; William C. Davis, *The*

Orphan Brigade: The Kentucky Confederates Who Couldn't Go Home (Baton Rouge: Louisiana State University Press, 1983), 174; Eddins, "Four Years in the Confederate Infantry," 34.

22. Stuart Salling, *Louisianians in the Western Confederacy: The Adams-Gibson Brigade in the Civil War* (Jefferson, NC: McFarland, 2010), 109; Cannon, *Bloody Banners*, 37; Jason H. Silverman, Samuel N. Thomas Jr., and Beverly D. Evans IV, *Shanks: The Life and Wars of General Nathan G. Evans, CSA* (Cambridge, MA: Da Capo Press, 2002), 151.

23. Terrence J. Winschel, *Triumph and Defeat: The Vicksburg Campaign* (El Dorado Hills, CA: Savas Beatie, 2006), 2:129; William Wiley, *The Civil War Diary of a Common Soldier: William Wiley and the 77th Illinois Infantry*, ed. Terrence J. Winschel (Baton Rouge: Louisiana State University Press, 2001), 62.

24. Robert Patrick, *Reluctant Rebel: The Secret Diary of Robert Patrick, 1861–1865*, ed. F. Jay Taylor (Baton Rouge: Louisiana State University Press, 1959), 119; Jackman, *Diary of a Confederate Soldier*, 78; Eddins, "Four Years in the Confederate Infantry," 34.

25. Cater, *As It Was*, 165; Wesley Thurman Leeper, *Rebels Valiant: Second Arkansas Mounted Rifles (Dismounted)* (Little Rock, AR: Pioneer Press, 1964), 176; Cannon, *Bloody Banners*, 37; Patrick, *Reluctant Rebel*, 120; Jerry Frey, *Grandpa's Gone: The Adventures of Daniel Buchwalter in the Western Army, 1862–1865* (Shippensburg, PA: White Mane Publishing, 1998), 77.

26. Salling, *Louisianians in the Western Confederacy*, 110; Eddins, "Four Years in the Confederate Infantry," 34; David Jackson Logan, *"A Rising Star of Promise": The Civil War Odyssey of David Jackson Logan, 17th South Carolina Volunteers, 1861–1864*, ed. Samuel M. Thomas Jr. and Jason H. Silverman (Campbell, CA: Savas Publishing Company, 1998), 104; H. Grady Howell, *Going to Meet the Yankees: A History of the "Bloody Sixth" Mississippi Infantry, C.S.A.* (Jackson, MS: H. Grady Howell Jr., 1981), 193; H. Grady Howell, *To Live and Die in Dixie: A History of the Third Mississippi Infantry, C.S.A.* (Jackson, MS: H. Grady Howell Jr., 1991), 217.

27. Salling, *Louisianians in the Western Confederacy*, 110–11; Hughes, *Pride of the Confederate Artillery*, 111.

28. Jackman, *Diary of a Confederate Soldier*, 79; Davis, *Orphan Brigade*, 175; Hughes, *Pride of the Confederate Artillery*, 111; Woodrick, *Civil War Siege of Jackson*, 41, 69; James Elijah Carraway, *Reminiscences of the Civil War, 1861–1865: Especially of Company B, Nineteenth Louisiana Regiment*, 1899, Holloway collection.

29. Edwin C. Bearss, *The Siege of Jackson: July 10–17, 1863* (Baltimore: Gateway Press, 1981), 67–68; Woodrick, *Civil War Siege of Jackson*, 50.

30. Carraway, *Reminiscences of the Civil War*, Holloway collection; Cater, *As It Was*, 166–67.

31. William C. Davis, *Breckinridge: Statesman, Soldier, Symbol*, 367; *The Confederate Veteran Magazine*, 43 vols. (reprint, Wilmington, NC: Broadfoot Publishing, 1977), 16:347–48; Cater, *As It Was*, 167; Carraway, *Reminiscences of the Civil War*, Holloway collection; Hughes, *Pride of the Confederate Artillery*, 112–13.

32. Hughes, *Pride of the Confederate Artillery*, 111–12; Woodrick, *Civil War Siege of Jackson*, 57–9; Leeper, *Rebels Valiant*, 177; *Cambridge (WI) News*, July 9, 1909.

33. Hughes, *Pride of the Confederate Artillery*, 113.

34. Woodrick, *Civil War Siege of Jackson*, 67–69.

35. Cater, *As It Was*, 167–69; William Miller Owen, *In Camp and Battle with the Washington Artillery of New Orleans* (reprint, Baton Rouge: Louisiana State University Press, 1999), 418–19.

36. Carraway, *Reminiscences of the Civil War*, Holloway collection; Jackman, *Diary of a Confederate Soldier*, 89.

37. Carraway, *Reminiscences of the Civil War*, Holloway collection; Gervis D. Grainger, *Four Years with the Boys in Gray* (reprint, Dayton, OH: Nabu Press, 1972), 17; Evelyn Hall Lowrance, "History of Petty, Texas, Lamar County" (Paris, TX: n.p., 2011; personal library of Evelyn Hall Lowrance).

8
___

"WEST OF THE MISSISSIPPI TO US IS NEARLY A SEALED BOOK": TRANS-MISSISSIPPIANS AND THE FALL OF VICKSBURG

Charles D. Grear

Young men are initially drawn to war expecting exciting moments, and the American Civil War was no exception. With the first announcements to join the ranks, young men rushed to enlist, and in many cases for those that called the Trans-Mississippi home, to fight far from their homes. As the Civil War stretched into a second year and then a third, Confederate soldiers from west of the Mississippi River lost the zeal for war and began to change their priorities. Soldiers from Texas, Louisiana, and Arkansas began seriously contemplating whether they wanted to continue the struggle. Early in the war, soldiers expected the conflict to be brief, so when Trans-Mississippians received orders transferring them east of the Mississippi River there was little opposition. However, as the war progressed, many western soldiers wanted to return to the Trans-Mississippi, especially when there was a perceived threat to their homes, wives, and children.[1] Trans-Mississippians, though highly motivated to fight for the Confederacy, succumbed to the same despair that many Southern soldiers experienced when the war reached the doorstep of their homes. Vicksburg, Mississippi, represented a bastion that limited the Union army's ability to threaten their homes in the west. The surrender of the "City on the Hill" was a critical moment in their military experience that profoundly influenced their view of the war and forced them to reprioritize their motivation to fight. The fall of Vicksburg and subsequent Union control of the Mississippi River amplified the despair Trans-Mississippians faced, including difficulties sending and receiving letters from home detailing the privations of their wives, children, and family members; isolation from their families when the Union army split the Confederacy; and, most important, the imminent threat to their home west of the Mississippi River.

Though Trans-Mississippians succumbed to the same influences as other Confederate soldiers, they experienced them differently because the distances they served from home were much greater than soldiers from other states. Confederate soldiers from the Trans-Mississippi fought in every theater and in almost every battle of the war, which others cannot claim. These Trans-Mississippians endured the same hardships as other Southern soldiers and agreed to fight far from home for many reasons. Since their states were the most recently settled in the South, they still had extended family members living east of the Mississippi River they wanted to protect. Additionally, by keeping the Union army occupied in the East, they would prevent their enemies from reaching their homes in the West since early in the war their states were not as immediately threatened as those east of the river. When their newly adopted states faced a serious threat to their security in May 1863, Trans-Mississippians began to reprioritize their motivation to fight for the Confederate cause. No longer was it to protect their extended families east of the Mississippi River but to defend their homes and immediate family, because the North finally threatened them. The danger the Union army posed to Trans-Mississippians during the latter half of the war had a devastating impact on their morale.

John Baynes, a scholar of morale and motivation, argues that a soldier's spirit "is concerned with the way in which people react to the conditions of their existence." Maintaining morale is extremely important in warfare, even more important than tactics, because commanders have difficulty getting soldiers to fight well if their hearts are not in the conflict.[2] When the Civil War began, morale was not a concern for the commanders, because the men's heads were full of romantic ideas of battlefield glory. The romance of warfare quickly dissipated once men experienced combat. A "Letter from the 2d Texas [Infantry] Regiment" appearing in the *Houston Tri-Weekly Telegraph* on July 16, 1862, demonstrated that the novelty of war had worn off. In the letter, an unnamed soldier wrote that the "romance of soldiering has pretty nearly worn off, and it has become reduced to facts and figures."[3]

Trans-Mississippians in the Confederate army endured in the perils of combat and witnessed the horrors of war. When the men "saw the elephant," they realized the romantic descriptions of war were false. Few soldiers record these feelings, especially in letters back home, because they did not want their loved ones to worry about their safety or consider them cowards or dishonorable. The carnage of warfare and its impact on the minds and bodies of the young men involved led them to see their motivations to fight from a new perspective. William Kuykendall of the 1st Texas Mounted Rifles recorded his feelings of combat in his diary: "I had now seen 'grim-visaged war' with its masque off. How dreadful in its horried features, a regular charnel house of death. . . . The very atmosphere protested as the foul stench from decaying men and beasts filled the nostrils. Friends whom I had left but two short months before in health and strength in full enjoyment of 'vigerous' manhood had immolated themselves on the altar of their country."[4] Scenes of death and destruction, though rarely acknowledged, had a dramatic impact on the morale of soldiers in the Civil War.

Though the soldiers' enthusiasm diminished, the men continued to fight, but not for the same reasons many of them had enlisted. As the Civil War became protracted, some of the initial motivations of the soldiers disappeared. Their motivations changed, especially those of the men who enlisted to fight east of the Mississippi River. Men with few or no ties in the Cis-Mississippi were the first to reprioritize their motivation. As Trans-Mississippians lost the illusions that had initially motivated them to fight, they had to resort to their basic instincts—the desire to defend their wives, children, and their adopted state—before the Union army could harm the people and land they loved. When morale plummeted, those instincts influenced Trans-Mississippians to recross the Mississippi through any means available, whether it be transfer or desertion.[5]

Trans-Mississippians felt a sense of urgency to return to their home states when they heard news of major Confederate defeats and occupations in the Trans-Mississippi and Western Theaters. One of the earliest was the Battle of Pea Ridge, followed shortly by the Union capture of New Orleans. Fought on March 7 and 8, 1862, the Confederate defeat at Pea Ridge allowed the Union army to secure Missouri and half of Arkansas. This victory isolated both Kansans and Missourians from the Confederacy and threatened Rebel positions within Arkansas and Indian Territory. Soon thereafter, the bloodless capture of New Orleans by the Union navy posed another huge threat. New Orleans was the largest city in the Confederacy; more important, it controlled the mouth of the Mississippi. In the hands of its army and navy, the Union now controlled a significant section of the river, placing an obstacle between the states of Texas, Louisiana, and Arkansas and the men from those states fighting east of the river. Essentially the Union gains threatened to cut off the Trans-Mississippi from the rest of the Confederacy. Samuel A. Goodman of the 13th Texas Infantry expressed his dismay at the loss of the Crescent City to the North: "I believe in less than 30 days the enemy will set foot on Texas coast, N. O.'s [New Orleans] has fallen, Ft. Jackson also and Texas will be visited next."[6] Even at this point, the only significant occupation in the region was northern Arkansas and southern Louisiana, which did not alleviate the concerns the men had for home.

"Oh!" exclaimed Henry Orr of the 12th Texas Cavalry after the battles. "Shall the foul foot of the invader even trace the soil of Texas and bring distress upon its people like they have here! God forbid that they may. I wish I were on its soil today to give my life if necessary for its defense."[7] A dismayed William Thomas Darr of the 10th Texas Infantry commented, "There is still less prospects for us gaining our independence then ever since New Orleans is abandoned and given up with out the firing of a gun."[8] Within a month of the defeat at Pea Ridge, James K. Street of the 9th Texas Infantry wrote about a potential wave of desertion in his regiment. "There is still strong talk of disbanding," Street wrote. "I shouldn't be surprised if we do and if we do I shall make right for Texas."[9]

Pea Ridge and New Orleans affected the morale of Trans-Mississippians, but that influence was not nearly as powerful as the effect of later defeats. On October 5, 1862, the Union navy established a blockade off Galveston that worried all Texans, civilian and soldier. Four days later, U.S. Marines captured the town, and then occupied it for nearly four months. It was the first time Union soldiers had set foot on Texas soil and directly threatened the interior of the state. Soldiers from Texas always expressed their concerns about a Union invasion of their state, as Elijah P. Petty of the 17th Texas Infantry wrote, "My feelings, inclinations and all my yearnings are to be in Texas if she is invaded. My all is there—All that is near and dear to me is there and I want to be there to protect it."[10] Even men east of the Mississippi kept their attention on Texas. John Wesley Rabb of Terry's Texas Rangers wrote of the regiment's concern for the safety of Texas when it received news of the Union blockade of Texas ports. "We here it reported in the regiment that Colonel Wharton is going to do his best to get this Regiment sent back to Texas because the Yanks have come there. The boys want to go back very much."[11] The troops of Terry's Texas Rangers expressed their relief when they heard the Yankees were driven out of the city on New Year's Day, 1863. "We have just herd of the recapture of Galveston by Gen. McGrooder [Magruder]. It does us good to think there is nary a Yankey foot on Texas soil."[12] Another member of the Rangers, Captain Gustave Cook, wrote to his wife, "That was a great little fight you had in Galveston and reflects great credit on all engaged. If you all have any very serious invasion I will try and get back to help you, all I can."[13]

Arkansas's most influential loss was the Union victory at Arkansas Post. Using combined naval and ground assaults, the Union army captured Fort Hindman on January 11, 1863. Though the Confederate defeat did not bring Ulysses S. Grant closer to capturing Vicksburg, it did give his army more than 5,000 Confederate prisoners, 17 cannons, and thousands of small arms.

More importantly, the Union gained the mouth of the Arkansas River, essentially opening an avenue to the state capital of Arkansas. Samuel W. Bishop of the 18th Texas Cavalry recalled, "Strong men were weeping like whipped children. Others were enraged and were cursing."[14] Morale dropped across Arkansas since supply and communication lines were reduced. The price for food rose, civilians suffered, and guerilla warfare broke out in the countryside. The Confederates rebounded from this defeat to strengthen their defenses along the Arkansas River with forts and gunboats, denying the Union army the chance to take Little Rock.[15]

Pea Ridge, New Orleans, Galveston, and Arkansas Post had a deep impact on the morale of all Trans-Mississippians serving outside that region, but not as deep as the July 4, 1863, fall of Vicksburg. Vicksburg was important to both Union and Confederacy. Abraham Lincoln stated the importance of the city and its significance for the Trans-Mississippi: "Let us get Vicksburg and all that country is ours. The war can never be brought to a close until that key is in our pocket."[16] The Mississippi River was key to controlling the West. Inspired by General Winfield Scott's Anaconda Plan, the Union army recognized the river was a major component to its strategy for winning the war. Like the large snake, the Union army and navy would work in concert to squeeze the life out of the Confederacy by establishing a blockade on the southern coast and splitting the nation in half by controlling the river. Vicksburg represented the last major Confederate stronghold on Old Man River. Without Vicksburg, the Union navy could never control the Mississippi.[17]

The Mississippi River, though strategically important to both sides, was especially vital to Trans-Mississippians. Even a year before the Gibraltar of the West fell to the Union army and navy, Trans-Mississippians expressed their concerns over its security. William H. Barcroft of the 3rd Texas Cavalry wrote during the siege of Corinth, Mississippi, "If they whip us here and get possession of these Roads here they will have opportunities in a short time and that will cut us off from home entirely for when they get that place they will have the Miss River almost entirely from head to foot."[18] While fighting to defend his old hometown in Arkansas, Drury Connally of Alf Johnson's Spy Company wrote, "No doubt there is much depending upon the next two fights depending at Richmond and Vicksburg."[19] Other Texans felt the same. Hearing the news of a possible transfer from Louisiana to Vicksburg, Elijah P. Petty of the 17th Texas Infantry wrote, "If at Vicksburg we can stab the enemy to the heart or some other vital point, the hand that is laid upon Texas will paralize so that where ever the most service can be done is the place for me."[20] James Black of the 1st Texas Heavy Artillery Regiment viewed the battle for Vicksburg as the turning point of the war, as he wrote to his wife: "If we can repulse the enemy at Vicksburg I don't think the war will last much longer, but if it should fall into their hands, I fear it will be a long time before peace is made."[21]

To those from the West, the Mississippi River was an important psychological barrier. As long as the Confederacy controlled the river, it was a bulwark between the Trans-Mississippi and the bulk of the Union army. A Texan wrote, "Our lines once broken, whether on the Mississippi or the Arkansas, or the Red River, would have thrown open the approach to the invasion of Texas, by an ever alert and powerful foe."[22] The editor from the *Little Rock (Arkansas) Patriot* colorfully wrote about the importance of the Mississippi town. "Any head with a thimble full of brains ought to know, that should that city be captured . . . the state of Arkansas falls an easy prey necessarily to the combined and various columns of the enemy—The fate of Arkansas rest intimately upon that of Vicksburg."[23] Some men from the 7th Texas Infantry campaigning in Tennessee wanted to rush to Vicksburg's rescue after the Union besieged the city. Cyrus W. Love and several men from Limestone County, Texas, did not "seem to be pleased with the idea of being kept at this place[.] they think they ought to be allowed to go west of the Mississippi."[24] Fellow Texan Erasmus E. Marr from the 10th Texas Infantry prophetically wrote during the same time, "west of the mississippi to us is nearly a sealed book."[25]

Mail was essential to the morale of Trans-Mississippians fighting far from home, but it proved to be a double-edged sword. They wanted to hear about the lives of their families back home and constantly asked their loved ones to write. "Write to me often as you can," Alexis T. Rainey urged from Virginia. "You have no idea how much pleasure it gives me to read a letter from my sweet little wife."[26] Another Texan, T. A. Williams of the 3rd Texas Cavalry, complained to his wife, "When you receive this letter, write to me. I have wrote 4 letters and I have no answer yet. Write soon."[27] The commissary clerk for Mouton's Louisiana division, Felix Pierre Poché, recorded in his diary, "Thoughts of my dear wife and child whose fate is now in the hands of our enemies are always painful, and I will fear continue so until I can have encouraging news from them, and know that they are safely . . . gone through the crisis."[28]

If the Mississippi River fell under the control of the Union navy, almost all Confederate traffic from either side of the river would be cut off. Trans-Mississippians serving in the East would be effectively isolated from their homes and immediate families. The most noticeable effect of the control of the river involved the communications between the Trans-Mississippi Department and the rest of the Confederacy. Before the Union navy had complete authority over the Mississippi, it controlled some of the tributary rivers. Though not severing all communication between the two halves of the South, the Confederate defeat at Vicksburg did affect the amount of mail leaving and entering the region. Concerned Frederick W. Bush of the 1st Arkansas Infantry optimistically wrote from Vicksburg, "I think us Ark boys would fight mighty hard, to keep them from cutting off Communications between us and Arks. . . . I think the Feds are playing out pretty fast, if we can hold Vicksburg all is saved."[29] Captain Khleber Miller Van Zandt of the 7th Texas Infantry "had much rather they were below than above [Port Hudson]. . . . I don't like having our communication with Red River cut off."[30] A few days later he complained to his wife about the lack of correspondence: "I am consequently getting anxious to hear from you again. The fault must be in the mail as no one has had a letter from home since then. I am afraid that our letters will be very slow in passing to & fro as long as the Gunboats are in the river between here and Vicksburgh."[31] Finally, one month later, Van Zandt gave up and accepted the inevitable: "I presume our mail will be very irregular so long as the 'Feds' are between us."[32] Even those from Louisiana, who were closer to home, experienced the impending isolation. A soldier from the 3rd Louisiana Infantry, James Pierson, commented to his wife, "It is said that the Yankees have us flanked if they gain the Yazoo River above here, for then they will march to Jackson, some 25 miles, and then on to the river below Vicksburg, cutting of the communications on all sides."[33]

If partial Union control of the Mississippi hindered communication for the soldiers and families, complete dominance, established by the fall of Vicksburg, cut it off entirely. Jeremiah Caddell of the 4th Texas Infantry commented, "Viseburg [Vicksburg] had fell in to the hands of the Yankie's and there is a bad chance for letters to pass but I hope there will be someway to pass them threw."[34] Caddell was correct, and it had a significant impact on the morale of the Texans and other Westerners. "Our communication with Texas," Maurice Kavanaugh Simmons wrote, "is entirely cutoff & it's a great drawback to my happiness." A few days later Simmons continued, "I really feel lost since the mail with Texas has stopped."[35] John Gardner McNemar, of Waul's Texas Legion, elaborated on the effects of the loss of the Mississippi River a month after the fall of Vicksburg: "Our communication is almost entirely cut off from home. . . . Since the fall of Vixburg everything has bin very gloomy in this part of the army."[36]

Concerned about Arkansas, Alex E. Spence of the 1st Arkansas Infantry wrote home from his regiment's camp near Chattanooga, Tennessee: "I am afraid our chance for hearing from home will be much worse now since the Yankees have got possession of the River. I shall write some of you by every one I see going across & want you all to do the same." He wrote home every chance he got and sent his letters with a soldier or trusted civilian travelling to Arkansas. Despite his pleas for news from home that October, he still had not heard from his loved ones. "I have written you all every chance lately but have recd no letters from home in a *long long* time."[37] Even Rueben Pierson, brother to the aforementioned Louisianan James Pierson, who just returned to Virginia after the Battle of Gettysburg, noted he had difficulty communicating with family back in the Pelican State. "I shall be cut off from all my correspondents if the mail is stopped from crossing the Mississippi. . . . I have not sent you the paper in a long time as mail communication was too uncertain." His greatest concern was for his brothers and sums up the concern throughout the South. "I have not heard a word from Henry or Dave [brothers] since the fall of Vicksburg."[38] Isolated from his home region, Rueben had no idea about the fates of his brothers that fought at Vicksburg. Fortunately for him and his family, the Union army paroled both brothers, and they survived the war.[39]

The lack of communication with their homes demoralized Trans-Mississippians. Van Zandt, the German Texan, knew that the fall of Vicksburg would dishearten men, both in the army and on the home front: "I suppose the fall of Vicksburg and the consequent possession of the whole of the Miss. River by the Feds made you all feel pretty blue, did it not? . . . It is indeed a dark hour to us."[40] Less than five months later, he wrote to his wife from Chattanooga, "I shall take steps to get away from here as soon as practicable. . . . I would not have any hesitancy about resigning, and would adopt it as the least objectionable course to pursue."[41] Benjamin F. Burke of Terry's Texas Rangers elaborated less than a month after the Confederate defeat: "Vicksburg . . . has cut our further communication off from Texas east of the Miss. river. There has never anything happened during the war that I regreted as bad as the fall, of Vicksburg."[42]

Vicksburg had a huge impact on the morale of Trans-Mississippians in every theater of the war. Desertion increased throughout the Confederate army after the simultaneous defeats at Vicksburg and Gettysburg, but to the men from west of the river, Vicksburg had a greater effect because with the loss of the Mississippi River the enemy now blocked their way home.[43] Similarly, Theophilus V. Ware of the 27th Texas Cavalry also recognized the importance of the event and expressed the feelings of thousands of Trans-Mississippians when he wrote, "This little Confederacy is gone up the spout."[44] Once the river fell into the control of the Federals, the men began to fear a Northern invasion into their state. That fear directly affected these soldiers because they felt that the Trans-Mississippi was secure as long as the Mississippi

River was an obstacle to the Union. Dr. John Claver Brightman of the 18th Texas Cavalry worried about a possible Union invasion of Texas. In a letter to his mother and friends still in his hometown, he advised them how best to protect themselves from roving Yankees. "If the Yanks should come to Texas," Brightman wrote, "drive all the negroes before you and burn everything as you go, to destroy their subsistence on the country. Gather yourselves together and form bands and companies so as not to let them scatter out in small robbing parties like they have done in this country."[45]

The day after the fall of Vicksburg, Christian Wilhelm Hander, a captured German soldier from Waul's Texas Legion, recorded in his diary, "What will happen to us, everybody is asking and in unison we say, 'To Texas we want to go.'"[46] Feelings of uncertainty and desires to desert their units and head back to the Lone Star State spread across Texas units, and dozens of men in the 9th Texas Cavalry returned to their homes. James C. Bates wrote from Vernon, Mississippi, on September 3, 1863, "About 30 men have deserted the Brigade within the last two weeks—ten of them from my old co. . . . The men of this Brig are very much dissatisfied & want to get west of the Miss. I look for more desertions as soon as we move from here. They are not tired of the war but *of this state*." Some of the men simply returned to their homes, but many joined other Trans-Mississippi units. Bates explained this to his mother: "You will probably hear before this reaches you of the desertions in this Regt. . . . Saying they will enter the service on that side of the river does paliate their offense, but it is on the other hand, an aggravation of it." Though he did not react in the same manner as his men, Bates had the same feelings of dismay about the loss of Vicksburg, which he summarized when he wrote, "My military aspirations have been long since satisfied & since Texas is threatened I would sooner than not return home." Bates and the men of the 9th Cavalry who remained behind believed that the government would transfer the unit to the Trans-Mississippi once enough men deserted its ranks. They did not get their wish.[47]

Texans in other units east of the Mississippi River expressed their concerns about a vulnerable Texas. Maurice Kavanaugh Simmons of the 2nd Texas Infantry, which surrendered at Vicksburg, resigned his commission to fight under General John Bankhead Magruder in Texas. Simmons wrote, "I joined the service in 1861; was a member of the 2nd Regiment of Texas Infantry; and expected to continue in service 'till the war should end, but three years absence from home has produced many changes. The Wolf [Union army] is at my door & I have but *one Leg* with which to repel him."[48] The Union threat appeared imminent, and Simmons had to protect his home state. Others in the 2nd Texas Infantry decided to leave Vicksburg immediately after it fell because they did not want to wait for the Confederate army to arrange a prisoner exchange. Men such as J. Henry Cravey just wanted to return to Texas. He wrote, "Myself brother Bill and Silvester Head we puld [pulled] out to ourselves. We got to the river all right," built a raft, and "Findla [Finally] we got over the river all right we felt like birds let out of a cage. We was on our way home."[49]

Trans-Mississippians in the units fighting east of the Mississippi had a strong desire to protect their old hometowns, but the idea that their western states were vulnerable influenced the men to change their priorities—from defending the unprotected homes of their early life to protecting the homes of their present and future. In a letter to his sweetheart, Andrew J. Fogle of the 9th Texas Infantry wrote, "They have got now the most of our importante plases now and if they ceap on like they have bin for the last twelve monthes our little Confedrecy will go up."[50] By October 1863, Fogle also wrote about desertion in his regiment for the first time during the war: "Their has bin severl that has Deserted from our Regiment That is one thing that I nevr expect to do: there is severl more talks of Deserting we had one to leave our compney at that was Sipe bush."[51] By November of that year, desertion had become a major problem in the regiment. Even the men sent back to Texas to gather deserters used the opportunity to leave the Cis-Mississippi. Jesse P. Bates noted to his wife, "I am in hopes that James Hooten will act more honorable than many that has gone to Texas and has not returned."[52] Additionally, the 3rd Texas Cavalry experienced increased desertion in the fall of 1863. James Black of the 1st Texas Heavy Artillery stated it best: "The men are still deserting from here occasionally. . . . There is a great deal of dissatisfaction among the troops here. Many of them are whipped since the fall of Vicksburg."[53]

Men serving in Terry's Texas Rangers were no strangers to the demoralizing effects of isolation from Texas. George Washington Littlefield expressed his desires to return to Texas in a letter to his wife at the end of July: "Oh how mutch I wish I was only off for Texas. My heart would be filled with overflowing joy. . . . Just to think that I was off for my home in Texas."[54] Lucky Rangers like Issac Dunbar Affleck were able to serve in the Trans-Mississippi after the fall of Vicksburg. In May 1863, Affleck received a discharge because of a wound he received near Sparta, Tennessee. He spent six months at home recovering from his wound and quickly requested an appointment under Major General John Bankhead Magruder, commander of the Texas District, so he could serve the remainder of the war in the Lone Star State. Once assigned to a Texas unit, Affleck wrote home, "I am ready to give my life in defence of Texas, and our home if it is required." After the fall of Vicksburg,

Littlefield, Affleck, and other Rangers desired to get back to Texas to defend their state, homes, and loved ones.[55]

Trans-Mississippians in Robert E. Lee's Army of Northern Virginia, those that demonstrated their strong desire to fight for the Confederacy by agreeing to fight so far from home, had similar sentiments. Having just fought at Gettysburg, the Louisianan Rueben Allen Pierson wrote home about his experiences from the battle. Despite the attention the battle gets today, he describes Vicksburg in stronger terms. "The fall of this place [Vicksburg] is quite a sad misfortune to our infant government, and will only tend to prolong this cruel and fractricidal war. Before receiving the news of the sad misfortune I began to imagine that the dawn of peace had already commenced arising but now a dark pall is thrown over the scene and the lowering clouds of new troubles seen to be enveloping the bright rays of a few short weeks ago."[56] Even with Gettysburg ending fifteen days before he wrote his letter, Vicksburg had the greater demoralizing effect.

As time passed and men reflected, their motivation to stay east of the river waned. According to James Henry Hendrick of the 1st Texas Infantry, "Our brigade sent a petition to Governor [Pendleton] Murrah asking him to use his influence to get the brigade across the Mississippi River."[57] The author of the petition was Brigadier General Jerome Bonaparte Robertson, commander of the Texas Brigade, who that winter wanted to get a furlough for the men to return to Texas to rest and recruit. Though unsuccessful in his bid, he eventually returned to Texas, where he commanded the state reserve forces until the conclusion of the war. Another man from the brigade simply wrote, "All I wish is I wish I was in Texas."[58] Other Trans-Mississippi units petitioned for transfer back to their home states, such as the 9th Louisiana Infantry fighting in the Army of Northern Virginia. Sergeant Reuben Allen Pierson wrote home, "There is some talk of our being transferred to the trans-Mississippi department, and the officers of our Brig. sent a petition today to the senators and representatives of our State to use their influence to that effect. I do hope that we may be sent back."[59] Even the most celebrated and proud of the Confederate units in the East succumbed to fears of losing their adopted states.

Once soldiers realized that they would not receive transfers to Trans-Mississippi units, some found other ways to get what they wanted. William H. Lewis provides insight about the effects of the Confederate defeat at Vicksburg on the men in Hood's Texas Brigade. He wrote to his mother in early August 1863,

I am very *tired* of all this and I have written to Uncle Albert to procure me a *substitute* at any *price*. I am fully aware that if I get one, a great howl will be sent up by various people at home and perhaps, it may not accord with your ideas of patriotism but I cant help that, and permit me to say not of yours but others opinion that I care less. . . . When I get there, I shall *repose* for a month or two and then I shall join some *cavalry* Co. Or Regt where I can see an easy time of it the balance of this unhappy struggle.[60]

Some men exposed their extremities, especially their hands, in hopes of getting a minor wound and being sent home on furlough. Joseph B. Polley commented on such an instance during the thick of the Battle of Chickamauga when a comrade, Tom, "stepped behind a tree, and, while protecting his body, extended his arms on each side and waved them frantically to and fro, up and down." When asked what he was doing, Tom replied, "'Just feeling for a furlough' . . . and continued the feeling as if his life depended on it." These feelings proved contagious as the war progressed. During the battle of Knoxville, another friend of Polley was shot in the foot. The man exclaimed enthusiastically, "What will you give me for my furlough boys?" as he limped back behind the lines. Polley and several other Texans "would willingly have changed places with him."[61]

Other men had even less honorable reactions. According to A. B. Hood of the 5th Texas Infantry, "Many from our Brigade are deserting."[62] Similarly, Jeremiah Caddell of the 4th Texas Infantry penned, "There is a good many of the boys in this Brigade will take what they call a French furlough and come home."[63] Lieutenant James R. Loughridge of the 4th Texas Infantry found an ingenious way of getting back to Texas by becoming "a member of the State Legislature for the County of Navarro, Texas." He quickly resigned his commission and was back in Texas "in time for the meeting of the Legislature."[64]

None of the Confederate soldiers were unaffected by the event, even those who had the strongest attachments to land east of the Mississippi. Richard Montgomery Gano of the 7th Kentucky Cavalry, Charles Trueheart of the Rockbridge Artillery (Virginia), and Adam Rankin Johnson, who formed the 10th Kentucky Cavalry, exemplify Trans-Mississippians wanting to fight to defend their childhood homes and extended families. All three men decided to leave the Cis-Mississippi, but only one returned to his home state during the war.

Far from his immediate family and demoralized from the lack of success in recapturing Kentucky, Gano served in John Hunt Morgan's Cavalry Division, commanding the 7th Kentucky Regiment and later a brigade, which contained two companies of Texans that he brought with him from the Lone Star State. Despite his strong conviction to defend his birth state, with the threat to Vicksburg, he now contemplated leaving his regiment to protect his parents, who had relocated behind Confederate lines at Brandon, Mississippi, and travelling back to Texas to assess the conditions of his wife and children. Not wanting to resign his commission and eager to save face among his men and fellow Kentuckians, Gano sought a medical leave. In June 1863, while Union soldiers besieged Vicksburg, fellow doctor B. Marshall, surgeon of Gano's Kentucky brigade, diagnosed the Texan with hypertrophy and valvicular disease of the heart; an enlarged heart which could be potentially life threatening. After receiving his diagnosis, Gano requested a leave of absence to Brandon, because his parents had moved there, and began planning a trip to Texas. Evidence suggests Gano authored or requested the false diagnosis from the surgeon so he could visit his family. During that era people with an enlarged heart normally lived short lives, but Gano lived a vigorous life into his eighties.[65]

That month he paid a quick visit to his parents in Brandon before venturing back to Texas to check on his young family. While visiting his wife and children, Gano had his fears of an exposed family confirmed when news of the fall of Vicksburg arrived, and when he reported to General "Prince" John Magruder, commander of the District of Texas, that "the Indian depredations upon our frontier had created such intense excitement in the minds of those from Parker and Johnson Counties that it was almost impossible to retain them [militia] in camp long enough to organize, their families being in immediate danger."[66] Compounding the already desperate situation, the now isolated Trans-Mississippi began preparations for a simultaneous invasion from Louisiana, Arkansas, and the Indian Territory. Now that the Union army threatened his and his fellow Texans' immediate homes, his original desire to protect his parents in Kentucky was replaced with the need to defend his home, wife, and children back in North Texas. He managed to get a transfer to Texas commanding the State Troops. However, before he could take command he had to return East to report from his leave of absence and to gather his remaining Texans to return to defend their home. Unfortunately, for Gano, his absence corresponded with Morgan's disastrous raid into Ohio, leaving fewer than 300 men to command; the rest were either captured, killed, or missing. When he returned to the East, he found Morgan's brigade severely diminished, demoralized, and leaderless all on the eve of the Battle of Chickamauga. Gano, now being the highest-ranking officer remaining, received orders to take authority of the survivors and serve as escorts for Nathan Bedford Forrest. The men fired the first and last shots of the Confederate victory. Despite this uplifting triumph, Gano and his fellow Texans still left the Western Theater for Texas immediately after the battle.[67]

Once in Texas, Gano did not receive command of the State Troops but that of the 5th Texas Cavalry Brigade on October 24, 1863. He spent the remainder of the war fighting in Arkansas and the Indian Territory alongside General Stand Waite and his Confederate Indians. Other men from Gano's original squadron also left the ranks of the 7th Kentucky. Late in the war, ten men from Company A transferred to the 9th Texas Cavalry, and twenty-five went to the Douglas Texas Battery. Also, nineteen men from Company B transferred to the 6th Texas Cavalry, including Gano's original co-commander of the Grapevine Volunteers, John Huffman. The remaining men served as the general's personal escort, known as Gano's Guards. The men viewed Kentucky as a lost cause and wanted to defend the only home left untouched by their enemy.[68]

Charles Trueheart, a college student in his former state of Virginia that enlisted in the Rockbridge [Va.] Artillery, succumbed to the same demoralization of other Texans along with a strong desire to return home during the latter part of the war. In early August 1864, Trueheart wrote to his brother Henry "I am going to get a transfer to the [Hood's] Texas Brigade. . . . By being in our Texas [Brigade], there are sundry advantages that I shall enjoy in addition to those now mine. Everybody from our state visiting this section, communicates either in person or by letter with the Brigade; so with persons going to Texas, furloughed, detailed or discharged men, and others. The Brigade being very small and all efforts to recruit it, or even to bring back those gone home on furlough." Trueheart continued, "It is not at all improbable that it will be sent to the Trans-Mississippi this winter. Or should the war come to a close during my life time and yours, I would thus stand a better chance than in any other command, to go back to the Lone Star State at an early period." Although Charles wanted to return to Texas, he remained in Virginia until the end of the war.[69]

Similarly, Texan Adam Rankin Johnson, who formed numerous Kentucky units, at least one behind enemy lines, to free his hometown of Henderson, Kentucky, wanted to leave for Texas, but a strong emotional appeal from the men in his regiment kept him fighting for the Bluegrass State. "Colonel [Robert M.] Martin [another Texan] and I," wrote Johnson, "began making preparations to go to the Trans-Mississippi department." "Martin and I were occupying at that time an old deserted cabin, and consumed the rest of the night in making arrangements to cross the Mississippi river, and discussing what we would do after our arrival in Texas." Johnson and Martin never left the cabin for Texas. They remained east of the river because the men in their regiment approached them with pleas for them to stay. Both Texans, moved by this gesture and the emotions of their men, decided to fight for Kentucky for the balance of the war.

The remainder of Johnson's time in Kentucky proved to be some of the most adventurous in the war. When Gano initially left for Texas, Johnson replaced him as brigade commander and participated in the great raid in Ohio and Indiana. When Union troops surrounded the command at Buffington Island and captured Morgan, Johnson, leading a few hundred men, made a daring escape and took command of the remainder of the force until Morgan's escape. Johnson's service to the Confederacy ended abruptly on August 21, 1864, when one of his men accidentally shot him through both his eyes during an attack on a Union camp in Caldwell County, Kentucky, northeast of Henderson. The shot blinded Johnson, rendering him unable to continue the war. Within three weeks of his wounding, President Jefferson Davis promoted him to brigadier general. Johnson spent the rest of his life, fifty-seven years, in Texas, where he founded the town of Marble Falls. When his life ended in Burnet, Texas, he was one of the last remaining Confederate generals.[70]

Demoralization over the loss of Vicksburg affected not only soldiers serving east of the Mississippi River but also many in the Trans-Mississippi. Men of the 28th Texas Cavalry, serving in Louisiana, became dispirited from the combination of the fall of Vicksburg and homesickness. Nor were they alone. Other Texans in Louisiana experienced the same demoralization. Dr. John Claver Brightman of the 18th Texas Cavalry explained the importance of Vicksburg and the control of the Mississippi River to his brother just after the major Confederate defeats at Vicksburg and Port Hudson: "One thing is certain: It is going to have the most demoralizing effect of anything that has occurred during the war. You can hear the expression every day by our men that we have 'gone up the spout.'" In a subsequent letter, Brightman wrote about the prospects that they would return to Texas: "There is a rumor that our regiment will be called back to Texas, and if it is so, the order will be soon issued. Our colonel is now in Texas on leave, and wants to go back very much. If an order can be secured, he will have it issued."[71] Similarly, Thomas Rounsaville in Monroe, Louisiana, wrote that the fall of Vicksburg "caused deep gloom among our officers and arms on this side. Cut off from all communication for the Feds can soon take Port Hudson, then Richmond and we are gone up I fear. Very near that now."[72] Even though the Texans were in nearby Louisiana, they still wanted to return to Texas to protect the localities where their families lived.

The effect of the loss of Vicksburg intensified during subsequent months. A series of letters from Alexander C. Crain of the 16th Texas Cavalry to his wife demonstrates the increased effects on the men from Texas. Initially the men, stationed in Louisiana, responded to the news with some reserved optimism. Crain explained that "Port Hudson and Vicksburg have fallen this is a big slam on us." After a few days, the magnitude of the events made "it all the officers can Do to keep the souldiers from going home." The following day, "We had a big bust up in our camps last evening there were some thirty of our Boys started to Texas but were overtaken and Brout back." The men of the 16th appeared dissatisfied with the war, but according to Crain the problem was growing: "It looks like our army will all bust up Since the fall of Vixburg & fort Hudson." Demoralization even infiltrated the leadership of the regiment, with officers essentially deserting through the privileges bestowed on them with their commissions. The desertion of significant numbers of soldiers was also affecting other regiments camped nearby: "They have got about Sixty of Stones regment now under garde for trying to Dissert." The progression of demoralization and desertion did not affect just the 16th Texas Cavalry; it showed up in many Trans-Mississippi units across the South.[73]

Others in Louisiana, such as Elijah P. Petty, felt the same demoralization created by the loss of the Mississippi River. By August 1863 he was writing, "They seem ready to give up. Our army is not in the best condition. Dissatisfaction and mutinous feelings exist to a considerable extent." More than a week later, Texans acted on their feelings. "There is great dissatisfaction in the army here," Petty wrote. "Men are insubordinate and between us I would not be surprised if this army was comparatively broken up. Men say that they will go home and let the Confederacy & war go to hell etc." Noticing the increased number of desertions in the regiment, Petty began to worry about the security of Texas. "After they [Yankees] get into Texas their steps will all be bloody for we must & will contest every inch of ground, if we are true to ourselves to our country and to our families."[74]

Similarly, Alex E. Spence of the 1st Arkansas Infantry wrote home from Tennessee, weeks after the surrender, that "times do certainly look dark and gloomy. Our army is deserting everyday, but thank God no Arkansians are among them."[75] It appeared that he spoke too soon because the following month he wrote, "A good many [Arkansians] are deserting."[76] Compounding the situation for Arkansians was General Theophilus Holmes's failed attempt to attack a Union outpost at Helena, Arkansas, on the same day Vicksburg capitulated. Morale was high among the Arkansas and Missouri troops under Holmes's command. They hoped to strike a blow against a Union garrison that received orders to support Grant's siege at Vicksburg, thinning their ranks. Unfortunately for the Confederates, the Union forces prepared a defensive line ahead of the assault and received support from gunboats. Rebel forces suffered 1,636 casualties, many captured, compared to the Union's 239 killed and wounded. Fontaine Richard Earle of the 34th Arkansas Infantry wrote home a few weeks after the battle,

> Our own defeat could have been more cheerfully borne had it not been so closely followed by the news that Vicksburg had fallen. "Oh, what a fall was there!" This Department is now fully cut off from the Eastern portion of the government, and we must stand or fall alone. No helping hand can be extended across the Mississippi to aid us. I shall spend but little time lamenting this sad affair. I will count it as a part of the mighty past and look forward hoping ere long to see some beam of light break forth from the heavens bearing to us the smiles of our God.[77]

God never revealed Earle's "beam of light," because just three months later he only saw darkness when he wrote home, "[I]f it had not been for a number of cowardly desertions we would not have been worsted."[78]

The combined losses of Helena and Vicksburg compounded the earlier loss of Arkansas Post, making Little Rock vulnerable and the defense of Arkansas more precarious. Compounding Arkansas's troubles further was the Confederate defeat at Honey Springs, Indian Territory, on July 17, 1863. Though the loss forced Confederate Indians and their families to retreat from their homes to the Texas border, Arkansas troops felt the sting of demoralization. With the loss of the northern half of the Indian Territory, Northern Arkansas was surrounded by Union troops. Arkansians in William L. Cabell's brigade shortly thereafter began to desert; on some nights the number of deserters reached as high as 200 men.[79] James Mitchell expressed the Arkansian mood two months after all these losses in a letter to his wife.

> I do not expect to see you now till the close of the war—but from present appearances that will not last long on this side of the Missippi River. Our men have deserted dreadfully since we left L. Rock—Ham and Dave Moore—John Moore, John King, McCurdy, Jim Wheeler and others 11 in all, and some of them the best soldiers we had—it is so in the whole army—they will not go South—I shall stick to them till the army "goes up." That may not be long—but then I shall run no great risk in going home.[80]

Demoralization continued throughout the following months. David M. Ray of the 19th Texas Infantry commented in September 1863 while encamped in northeast Louisiana, that demoralization "pervades the army to a considerable extent so much so that for the last week or ten days there has been more or less desertions every day. . . . [I]n some regiments they make very bold in talking about it, a few nights ago a crowd of them came by our regt and hallooed for all men who wanted to go to Texas to fall in."[81] And Sam Love of the 6th Texas Infantry wrote from Brandon, Mississippi, "There is one thing that causes everything to look more gloomy than the mere success of the enemy it is the desertion from our army. A very large number of our men have diserted in the last two months . . . there has been several disertions from our Regt. and Whitfields Briagde [also known as the Ross Brigade] in the last six weeks."[82] No matter where Trans-Mississippians served, the fall of Vicksburg affected their morale. This demoralization continued until the end of the war.

Many aspects and events of the war influenced the motivation of Trans-Mississippians. Though demoralized, they continued to fight despite the number of men that deserted. Desertion, though it occurred throughout the war, became a major problem in Trans-Mississippian units with the Union victory at Vicksburg. Vicksburg not only cut off Trans-Mississippians from communicating with their families back home but also dissolved the psychological barrier of the Mississippi River. Once the Federals controlled the river, Trans-Mississippians feared that their state would be vulnerable to invasion. Since their homes and families were now exposed to the Federals, the motivation of Trans-Mississippians to defend their extended families and previous hometowns, far from their current homes, became less important than defending their immediate families and current homes. In response, they deserted their units so they could return to their home states and defend its borders, protecting their families from the depredations other Southerners had had to endure. Jeff Morgan of the 35th Texas Cavalry (Liken's) summed it up in a letter to his wife: "For when the soldear heres there families are a sufferen thay will come home."[83]

Notes

The quotation in the chapter title is from Marr to Sister, Wartrace, TN, June 17, 1863, 10th Texas Infantry File, Erasmus E. Marr, Texas Heritage Museum, Hill College, Hillsboro, TX (hereafter cited as THM).

1. Bell I. Wiley, "Trials of Soul," in Michael Barton and Larry M. Logue, eds., *The Civil War Soldier: A Historical Reader* (New York: New York University Press, 2002), 294. Soldiers from Missouri and Indian Territory will be excluded from this study. Union forces occupied Missouri since the Battle of Wilson Creek in early August 1861 and Confederate Indians from the Indian Territory remained there for the bulk of the war, only leaving to help other Southern forces on their terms. Louise Mayo and Charles D. Grear, *The House Divided: America in the Era of Civil War and Reconstruction* (Wheaton, IL: Abigail Press, 2011), 184–86.

2. John Baynes, *Morale: A Study of Men and Courage; The Second Scottish Rifles at the Battle of Neuve Chapelle, 1915* (New York: Frederick A. Praeger, 1967), 92–93.

3. *Houston Tri-Weekly Telegraph*, July 16, 1862.

4. "The Civil War Diary of Judge William Kuykendall of Tilden, Texas," William Kuykendall, First Texas Cavalry Regiment File, THM.

5. James M. McPherson, *For Cause and Comrades: Why Men Fought in the Civil War* (New York: Oxford University Press, 1997), 35, 44–45, 168–69; Gerald F. Linderman, *Embattled Courage: The Experience of Combat in the American Civil War* (New York: Free Press, 1987), 156.

6. William L. Shea and Earl J. Hess, *Pea Ridge: Civil War Campaign in the West* (Chapel Hill: University of North Carolina Press, 1992), 306; Scott Dennis Parker, "'The Best Stuff Which the State Affords': A Portrait of the Fourteenth Texas Infantry in the Civil War, 1862–1865" (master's thesis, North Texas University, 1998), 24–25; Larry J. Daniel, *Shiloh: The Battle That Changed the Civil War* (New York: Simon and Schuster, 1997), 313–14; Stephen A. Dupree, *Planting the Union Flag in Texas: The Campaigns of Major General Nathaniel P. Banks in the West* (College Station: Texas A&M University Press, 2008), 16; Goodman to brother, May 7, 1862, Goodman (Samuel A. Jr.) Papers, 1854–1970, Pearce Civil War Collection, Navarro College, Corsicana, TX. Pea Ridge had an even greater impact on Arkansas men, especially those whose families were now in Union-held territory. William G. Young of the 15th Texas Cavalry noted the increase of desertions by men from that state in the months after the battle: "I saw five men blindfolded and brought up before the public gaze of ten thousand men and compelled to fall on their knees and be shot. . . . They were all charged with desertion and mutiny. This is a scene that often occurs in this part. They were all natives of the state." Young to Nan, August 12, 1862, William G. Young, Fifteenth Texas Cavalry File, THM.

7. John Q. Anderson, ed., *Campaigning with Parsons' Texas Cavalry Brigade, CSA: The War Journals and Letters of the Four Orr Brothers, Twelfth Texas Cavalry Regiment* (Hillsboro, TX: Hill Junior College Press, 1967), 52.

8. Darr to mother, May 8, 1862, William Thomas Darr, Tenth Texas Infantry File, THM.

9. Street to Ninnie, March 10, 1862, J. K. Street Letters, http://antiquemll.hypermart.net/streetpapers.htm (accessed December 14, 2003).

10. Donald S. Frazier, *Cottonclads! The Battle of Galveston and the Defense of the Texas Coast* (Abilene, TX: McWhiney Foundation Press, 1998), 28, 30; Stephen A. Townsend, *The Yankee Invasion of Texas* (College Station: Texas A&M University Press, 2006), 10–11; Dupree, *Planting the Union Flag in Texas*, 25–35; Norman D. Brown, ed., *Journey to Pleasant Hill: The Civil War Letters of Captain Elijah P. Petty, Walker's Texas Division, CSA* (San Antonio: University of Texas Institute of Texan Cultures, 1982), 108.

11. Thomas W. Cutrer, ed., "'We Are Stern and Resolved': The Civil War Letters of John Wesley Rabb, Terry's Texas Rangers," *Southwestern Historical Quarterly* 91 (1987): 206–7.

12. Ibid., 210–11.

13. Cook to wife, February 17, 1863, Gustave Cook, Gilder Lehrman Institute of American History, New York, http://www.gilderlehrman.org/sites/default/files/transcript_pdfs/Tr.02570.39.pdf (accessed on November 7, 2016).

14. S. W. Bishop, "The Battle of Arkansas Post," *Confederate Veteran*, 5, no. 4 (April 1897): 153; Mark K. Christ, *Civil War Arkansas 1863* (Norman: University of Oklahoma, 2010), 39, 85.

15. Christ, *Civil War Arkansas 1863*, 98.

16. Davis D. Porter, *Incidents and Anecdotes of the Civil War* (New York: D. Appleton, 1886), 95–96.

17. Terrence J. Winschel, *Vicksburg: Fall of the Confederate Gibraltar* (Abilene, TX: McWhiney Foundation Press, 1999), 13, 14, 16, 17; Leonard Fullenkamp, Stephen Bowman, and Jay Luvaas, eds., *Guide to the Vicksburg Campaign* (Lawrence: University of Kansas Press, 1998), 11; James R. Arnold, *Grant Wins the War: Decision at Vicksburg* (New York: John Wiley and Sons, 1997), 1–2.

18. Barcroft to father and family, May 18, 1862, William H. Barcroft, Third Texas Cavalry File, THM.

19. Connally to wife, December 6, 1862, Drury Connally, Alf Johnson Spy Company File, THM.

20. Brown, *Journey to Pleasant Hill*, 108.

21. James to wife, June 30, 1863, Civil War Times Illustrated Collection, James Black, I/First Texas Heavy Artillery Regiment Correspondence, January 1860–March 1865, United States Army Heritage and Education Center, Carlisle, PA.

22. Anne J. Bailey, *Between the Enemy and Texas: Parsons' Texas Cavalry in the Civil War* (Fort Worth: Texas Christian University Press, 1989), 3; W. H. Getzendaner, *A Brief and Condensed History of Parsons' Texas Cavalry Brigade Composed of Twelfth, Nineteenth, Twenty-First, Morgan's Battalion, and Pratt's Battery of Artillery of the Confederate States, Together with the Roster of the Several Commands as far as Obtainable—Some Historical Sketches—General Orders and a Memoranda of Parsons' Brigade Association* (Waxahachie, TX: J. M. Flemister Printer, 1892), 21.

23. "Who Is to Blame," *Little Rock (AR) Patriot*, January 8, 1863.

24. Kassia Waggoner and Adam Nemmers, eds., *Yours in Filial Regard: The Civil War Letters of a Texas Family* (Fort Worth: Texas Christian University, 2015), 119.

25. Marr to sister, June 17, 1863, Erasmus E. Marr, Tenth Texas Infantry File, THM.

26. Rainey to wife, August 8, 1861, A. T. Rainey, First Texas Infantry File, THM.

27. Williams to wife, September 25, 1862, T. A. Williams, Third Texas Cavalry File, THM.

28. Edwin C. Bearss, ed., *A Louisiana Confederate: The Diary of Felix Pierre Poché* (Natchitoches: Louisiana Studies Institute, Northwestern State University, 1972), 8.

29. Daniel E. Sutherland, *Reminiscences of a Private: William E. Bevens of the First Arkansas Infantry, C.S.A.* (Fayetteville: University of Arkansas Press, 1992), 124.

30. Van Zandt to wife, April 7, 1863, Khleber Miller Van Zandt, Seventh Texas Infantry File, THM.

31. Van Zandt to wife, April 26, 1863, Khleber Miller Van Zandt, Seventh Texas Infantry File, THM.

32. Van Zandt to wife, May 10, 1863, Khleber Miller Van Zandt, Seventh Texas Infantry File, THM.

33. Thomas Cutrer and T. Michael Parrish, eds., *Brothers in Gray: The Civil War Letters of the Pierson Family* (Baton Rouge: Louisiana State University Press, 1997), 166–67.

34. Caddell to sister, July 22, 1863, Jeremiah Caddell, Fourth Texas Infantry File, THM.

35. Walter H. Mays, ed., "The Vicksburg Diary of M. K. Simmons, 1863," *Texas Military History* 5 (1965): 27.

36. McNemar to Neicy, August 12, 1863, John Gardner McNemar, Waul's Texas Legion File, THM. After the Union army gained control of the Mississippi, Confederates like Andrew J. Fogle found other ways to get correspondence to Texas: "I dont think hard of you as their is no mail a gain a crose the river and the only way that I can send them by Privet conveyence." Fogle to Miss Louisa, September 2, 1863, Andrew J. Fogle, Ninth Texas Cavalry File, THM. Sam Love of the 6th Texas Infantry stated something similar to his parents during the siege, "[T]here is no chance for us to send a letter home unless we send it by hand." Waggoner and Nemmers, *Yours in Filial Regard*, 200.

37. Mark K. Christ, ed., *Getting Used to Being Shot At: The Spence Family Civil War Letters* (Fayetteville: University of Arkansas Press, 2002), 69–70.

38. Cutrer and Parrish, *Brothers in Gray*, 207, 209.

39. National Archives Microfilm Publications, *Compiled Service Records*, microcopy no. 109, roll 121; National Archives Microfilm Publications, Letters Received by Commission Branch, 1863–70, microcopy no. 1064, roll 114.

40. Van Zandt to wife, June 16, 1863, Khleber Miller Van Zandt, Seventh Texas Cavalry File, THM.

41. Van Zandt to wife, November 22, 1863, Khleber Miller Van Zandt, Seventh Texas Cavalry File, THM.

42. Burke to father and mother, July 31, 1863, Benjamin F. Burke, Eighth Texas Cavalry File, THM.

43. Ella Lonn, *Desertion during the Civil War* (Lincoln: University of Nebraska Press, 1966), 18; Chuck Carlock and V. M. Owens, *History of the Tenth Texas Cavalry (Dismounted) Regiment* (North Richland Hills, TX: Smithfield Press, 2001), 243–44; Donald S. Frazier, *Blood on the Bayou: Vicksburg, Port Hudson, and the Trans-Mississippi* (Buffalo Gap, TX: State House Press, 2015), 380.

44. If something has gone "up the spout," it has gone wrong or been ruined. Ware to mother, July 16, 1863, Theophilus V. Ware, Twenty-seventh Texas Cavalry File, THM.

45. Brightman to family, June 21, 1863, Dr. John Claver Brightman Collection, Center for American History, University of Texas–Austin. Hereafter cited as CAH.

46. Civil War Diary of Christian Wilhelm Hander, July 5, 1863, CAH.

47. Richard Lowe, ed., *A Texas Cavalry Officer's Civil War: The Diary and Letters of James C. Bates* (Baton Rouge: Louisiana State University Press, 1999), xii, 263, 264, 265, 271, 272.

48. Mays, "Vicksburg Diary of M. K. Simmons," 38.

49. "Reminisces," J. H. Cravey, Second Texas Infantry File, THM.

50. Fogle to Miss Louisa, September 2, 1863, Andrew J. Fogle, Ninth Texas Infantry File, THM.

51. Fogle to Miss Louisa, October 18, 1863, Andrew J. Fogle, Ninth Texas Infantry File, THM. Four men are listed in the regiment with the last name Bush and only two in his company, named L. C. and William I. Bush. It is uncertain which of these

men deserted, but it may be L. C. since he entered the war as a sergeant and when discharged was demoted to private.

52. Bates to wife, November 16, 1863, Jesse P. Bates, Ninth Texas Infantry File, THM.

53. Douglas Hale, *The Third Texas Cavalry in the Civil War* (Norman: University of Oklahoma Press, 1993), 193; James to Dearest Patience, August 22, 1863, Civil War Times Illustrated Collection, James Black, I/First Texas Heavy Artillery Regiment Correspondence, January 1860–March 1865, United States Army Heritage and Education Center, Carlisle, PA.

54. David B. Gracy II, "With Danger and Honor," *Texana* 2 (1963): 133.

55. Robert W. Williams and Ralph A. Wooster, eds., "A Texas War Clerk: Civil War Letters of Issac Dunbar Affleck," *Texas Military History* 7 (1962): 279, 283.

56. Cutrer and Parrish, *Brothers in Gray*, 204.

57. Hendrick to mother, November 8, 1863, James Henry Hendrick, First Texas Infantry File, THM; Perry Wayne Shelton, comp., *Personal Civil War Letters of General Lawrence Sullivan Ross: With Other Letters* (Austin: Shelly and Richard Morrison, 1994), xi.

58. Wilson to Dear Niece, March 20, 1864, Robert Wilson, Fourth Texas Infantry File, THM; Alexander Mendoza, *Confederate Struggle for Command: General James Longstreet and the First Corps in the West* (College Station: Texas A&M University Press, 2008), 152, 175. Robertson's commander, General James Longstreet, removed him from command because of a personal conflict between the two of them. Longstreet used Robertson's request to court-martial the general, since the Texan avoided the chain of command and sent the petition to the Tennessean's superior, John Bell Hood. In the end Robertson got exactly what he wanted, removal to the Trans-Mississippi.

59. Cutrer and Parrish, *Brothers in Gray*, 217–218.

60. Eddy R. Parker, ed., *Touched by Fire: Letters from Company D Fifth Texas Infantry Hood's Brigade Army of Northern Virginia, 1862–1865* (Hillsboro, TX: Hill College Press, 2000), 69.

61. J. B. Polley, *A Soldier's Letters to Charming Nellie* (New York: Neale Publishing, 1908), 165, 179.

62. Hood to Cousin Jennie, February 14, 1864, A. B. Hood, Fifth Texas Infantry File, THM.

63. Caddell to mother and father, March 3, 1864, Jeremiah Caddell, Fourth Texas Infantry File, THM. A "French Furlough" was another term for desertion.

64. Loughridge to George W. Brent, October 22, 1863, J. R. Loughridge Papers, Pearce Civil War Collection, Navarro College, Corsicana, TX.

65. John Gano, comp., "Records and Correspondence Pertaining to the Military Activities of Brigadier-General Richard M. Gano, C.S.A." vol. 1, Brown Special Collections Library, Abilene Christian University, Abilene, 1–3; Col. R. M. Gano to Col. G. W. Brent A.A.F. and Chief of Staff of the Army of Tennessee, B. Marshall, Chief Surgeon Second Brigade Morgan's Division, and D. W. Mandell, Surgeon Hardee's Corps Civil War, *Service Records of Confederate General and Staff Officers* (Washington, DC: National Archives and Records Service General Services Administration, 1960), M331–101; Ralph Wooster, *Lone Star Generals in Gray* (Austin: Eakin Press,

2000), 124; Jack D. Welsh, *Medical Histories of Confederate Generals* (Kent, OH: Kent State University Press, 1995), 75.

66. Gano and Terry to Magruder, August 12, 1863, U.S. War Department, *The War of the Rebellion: A Compilation of the Official Records of the Union and Confederate Armies* (Washington, DC: Government Printing Office, 1880–1901), series 1, vol. 26, pt. 2: 159. Hereafter cited as *OR*. All references are to series 1 unless otherwise indicated.

67. Carrington to Pyron, September 1, 1863, *OR*, vol. 26, pt. 2, 198; General Orders No. 149, Headquarters District of Texas, September 1, 1863, *OR*, vol. 26, pt. 2,: 198; Special Orders No. 236, Headquarters District of Texas, September 1, 1863, *OR*, vol. 26, pt. 2, 198–99; Glenn Tucker, *Chickamauga: Bloody Battle in the West* (Dayton: Morningside Press, 1976), 112.

68. Wooster, *Lone Star Generals*, 124; Cunningham to Magruder, October 21, 1863, *OR*, vol. 26, pt. 2, 342; National Archives Microfilm Publications, *Compiled Service Records*, Microcopy no. 319, rolls 39 and 41. It is interesting to note that Gano is the great-grandfather of Howard Hughes, the wealthy businessman, aviator, and hypochondriac.

69. Edward B. Williams, ed., *Rebel Brothers: The Civil War Letters of the True-hearts* (College Station: Texas A&M University Press, 1995), 104.

70. General Order no. 22, June 3, 1863, William Campbell Preston Breckinridge Family Papers, Ninth Regiment Kentucky, Cavalry, Letter Book, December 22, 1862–March 26, 1864, Library of Congress, Washington, DC; William C. Davis and Julie Hoffman, eds., *The Confederate General* (Harrisburg, PA: National Historical Society, 1991), 3:169–70; Adam Rankin Johnson, *The Partisan Rangers of the Confederate States Army* (Louisville, KY: George G. Fetter Company, 1904), 138; West, *Medical Histories of Confederate Generals*, 116.

71. M. Jane Johansson, *Peculiar Honor: A History of the Twenty-eighth Texas Cavalry, 1862–1865* (Fayetteville: University of Arkansas Press, 1998), 75; Brightman to brother, July 18, 1863, Dr. John Claver Brightman Collection, CAH.

72. James Rounsaville to family, July 9, 1863, Thomas and James Rounsaville, Thirteenth Texas Cavalry File, THM.

73. Crain to wife, July 26, July 30, July 31, early August, and August 8, 1863, Alexander C. Crain, Second Texas Partisan Rangers File, THM.

74. Brown, *Journey to Pleasant Hill*, 247–48, 251–52, 253.

75. Christ, *Getting Used to Being Shot At*, 69–70.

76. Christ, *Getting Used to Being Shot At*, 71; Wesley Thurman Leeper, *Rebels Valiant: Second Arkansas Mounted Rifles* (Little Rock: Pioneer Press, 1964), 182.

77. Mark K. Christ and Patrick G. Williams, eds., *I Do Wish This Cruel War Was Over: First-Person Accounts of Civil War Arkansas from the Arkansas Historical Quarterly* (Fayetteville: University of Arkansas Press, 2014), 133–34; Originally appeared in Robert E. Waterman and Thomas Rothrock, eds., "The Earle-Buchanan Letters of 1861–1876," *Arkansas Historical Quarterly* 33 (Summer 1974): 99–174; Christ, *Civil War Arkansas 1863*, 139, 142; Thomas A. DeBlack, "We Must Stand or Fall Alone," Mark K. Christ, ed., *Rugged and Sublime: The Civil War in Arkansas* (Fayetteville: University of Arkansas Press, 1994), 84. David Moore from the same regiment declared, "We were badly whiped" at the Battle of Helena. Christ and Williams, *I Do*

Wish This Cruel War Was Over, 136; Originally appeared in Mark K. Christ, ed., "'We Were Badly Whiped': A Confederate Account of the Battle of Helena, July 4, 1863," *Arkansas Historical Quarterly* 69 (Spring 2010): 44–53.

78. Christ and Williams, *I Do Wish This Cruel War Was Over*, 139.

79. Christ, *Rugged and Sublime*, 85–86; John C. Grady and Bradford K. Felmly, *Suffering to Silence: 29th Texas Cavalry, CSA Regimental History* (Quanah, TX: Nortex Press, 1975), 93–94; Steve Cottrell, *Civil War in the Indian Territory* (Gretna, LA: Pelican Press, 1998), 83.

80. Christ and Williams, *I Do Wish This Cruel War Was Over*, 139.

81. Ray to mother, September 11, 1863, David M. Ray Papers, CAH.

82. Waggoner and Nemmers, *Yours in Filial Regard*, 207.

83. Morgan to wife, January 1, 1864, Jeff Morgan, Thirty-Fifth Texas Cavalry (Liken's) File, THM.

CONTRIBUTORS
INDEX

CONTRIBUTORS

Andrew S. Bledsoe teaches history at Lee University. His work on American Civil War soldiers and officers has appeared in a number of books and journals. He is the author of *Citizen-Officers: The Union and Confederate Volunteer Junior Officer Corps in the American Civil War, 1861–1865* (2015).

John J. Gaines teaches at Calhoun Community College. Social aspects of the Civil War are the primary subjects of his published works, including *An Evening with Venus: Prostitution during the American Civil War* (2014).

Charles D. Grear teaches at Central Texas College. He has written extensively on the involvement of Texas in the Civil War, including *Why Texans Fought in the Civil War* (2010), and has edited several books, among them *The Tennessee Campaign of 1864* (with Steven E. Woodworth, 2015) and *The Vicksburg Assaults, May 19–22, 1863* (with Steven E. Woodworth, 2018).

Martin J. Hershock is the dean of the College of Arts, Sciences, and Letters and a professor of history at the University of Michigan–Dearborn. His publications include *Paradox of Progress: Economic Change, Individual Enterprise, and Political Culture in Michigan, 1837–1878* (2003), *The History of Michigan Law* (coedited with Paul Finkelman, 2006), and *A New England Prison Diary: Slander, Religion, and Markets in Early America* (2012).

Richard H. Holloway works as a park ranger for the Louisiana Department of Culture, Recreation, and Tourism. He has been the president of the Civil War Round Table of Central Louisiana since 2008, a member of the board of directors of the Confederate Memorial Hall Foundation in New Orleans, and an adjunct professor at Louisiana State University and Louisiana State University–Alexandria. He has published biographies of generals Richard Taylor, Hamilton P. Bee, and William Roberts Boggs for *Confederate Generals of the Trans-Mississippi*, volume 3 (2019). He currently writes monthly articles on local history for the newspaper *Cenla Focus*, on Louisiana's culinary history for *Country Roads* magazine, and on Civil War–related subjects for *America's Civil War* magazine.

Justin S. Solonick is the social studies department chair at Lakehill Preparatory School in Dallas and the author of *Engineering Victory: The Union Siege of Vicksburg* (2015), "Saving the Army of Tennessee: The Confederate Rear Guard at Ringgold Gap" (2015), and "Vicksburg: Grant's Masterpiece" (2017). He also worked as a military historian and analyst for Prairie Quest Consulting as part of the Iraq Expeditionary Sustainment

Operations Team, researching and writing a book for the Army Press at the request of Army Material Command. His contributions included segments about Operation Iraqi Freedom and Operation New Dawn.

Scott L. Stabler teaches history at Grand Valley State University, Allendale, Michigan. His publications include "Two Paths to Peace: Oliver Otis Howard, Negotiator to Cochise and Joseph" (2018), "'No More Auction Block for Me': The Fight for Freedom by the United States Colored Troops at the Battle of Nashville" (2015), "Nuanced History: Westward Expansion in the Context of the Civil War and After" (2012), and "Atlantic Slavery: Lost in Trans-lation" (2012). Stabler was a Fulbright Scholar to Ghana in 2011.

Jonathan M. Steplyk authored *Fighting Means Killing* (2018), which examines Civil War soldiers' attitudes toward killing in combat. He has also worked in battlefield interpretation at Harpers Ferry National Historical Park and Cedar Creek and Belle Grove National Historical Park.

Steven E. Woodworth teaches at Texas Christian University and has authored, coauthored, or edited more than thirty books on the Civil War era, among them *Nothing but Victory: The Army of the Tennessee, 1861–1865* (2006) and *Jefferson Davis and His Generals: The Failure of Confederate Command in the West* (1990).

174

INDEX

The Bridge Street
HISTORY CENTER
Granbury, Texas

The Bridge Street History Center is in Granbury, Hood County, Texas. The city and the county were named for Confederate Civil War generals Hiram B. Granbury and John Bell Hood. The mission of the Bridge Street History Center is to collect, preserve, and interpret the life stories of the people of Granbury and Hood County and to examine how they illuminate the history of America. To learn more, visit http://bshc-granbury.org/wp/.

CIVIL WAR CAMPAIGNS IN THE WEST

The area west of the Appalachian Mountains, known in Civil War parlance as "the West," has always stood in the shadow of the more famous events on the other side of the mountains, the eastern theater, where even today hundreds of thousands visit the storied Virginia battlefields. Nevertheless, a growing number of Civil War historians believe that the outcome of the war was actually decided in the region east of the Mississippi River and west of the watershed between the Atlantic and the Gulf of Mexico.

Modern historians began to rediscover the decisive western theater in the 1960s through the work of the late Thomas Lawrence Connelly, particularly his 1969 book *Army of the Heartland*, in which he analyzed the early years of the Confederacy's largest army in the West. Many able scholars have subsequently contributed to a growing historiography of the war in the West. Despite recent attention to the western theater, less is understood about the truly decisive campaigns of the war than is the case with the dramatic but ultimately indecisive clashes on the east coast.

Several years ago, three of Steven E. Woodworth's graduate students pointed out that the western theater possessed no series of detailed multi-author campaign studies comparable to the excellent and highly acclaimed series Gary W. Gallagher has edited on the campaigns of the eastern theater. Charles D. Grear, Jason M. Frawley, and David Slay joined together in suggesting that Woodworth ought to take the lead in filling the gap. The result is this series. Its goals are to shed more light on the western campaigns and to spark new scholarship on the western theater.

CIVIL WAR CAMPAIGNS IN THE WEST SERIES

The Shiloh Campaign

The Chickamauga Campaign

The Chattanooga Campaign

The Vicksburg Campaign, March 29–May 18, 1863

The Tennessee Campaign of 1864

The Vicksburg Assaults, May 19–22, 1863

Vicksburg Besieged

The first five books were published under the series title "Civil War Campaigns in the Heartland."